100
WAYS TO
BOOST
YOUR FIRM'S
PROFIT-ABILITY

HERMAN HOLTZ

BOB ADAMS, INC.
P U B L I S H E R S
Holbrook, Massachusetts

ISBN: 1-55850-022-7

Published by Bob Adams, Inc.
260 Center Street
Holbrook, Massachusetts 02343

Manufactured in the United States of America.

A   B   C   D   E   F   G   H   I   J

This publication is designed to provide accurate and authoritative information with regard to the subject matter covered. It is sold with the understanding that the publisher is not engaged in rendering legal, accounting, or other professional advice. If legal advice or other expert assistance is required, the services of a competent professional person should be sought.

— From a *Declaration of Principles* jointly adopted by a Committee of the American Bar Association and a Committee of Publishers and Associations

Table Of Contents

PART FOUR

PART FIVE

PART SIX

Author's Preface

Maximizing profitability is always an aim of business, especially in the many businesses in which net profit is often on the narrow edge of only one or two percent of sales—dangerously close to red ink. Today, it is a matter of greater importance than usual, as the go-go years of the eighties recede and the economy appears to be tightening up for at least the early nineties.

As this is being written, economists have conceded that we are already in the early stages of a business recession, and some predict that it is likely to be the most serious one since the Great Depression of the thirties. Almost every morning the newspapers carry stories of plan closings, layoffs, cutbacks, shortfalls in government treasuries and budgets, and similarly worrying signs of the times. The fast food industry, for one, is feeling the pinch and reacting to it with price cutting, the introduction of new food items, and (in at least one case) the sale of an entire chain (Roy Rogers) to a competitor (Hardee's). The automobile industry is closing many assembly plants. Governments are letting employees go. Merchants are advertising heavily, and the retail sector is experiencing troubles, as well.

These observations are not meant to sound the tocsin of panic or despair. We have been through hard times before and have not only survived, but emerged with greater vigor than ever. In fact, as you will read, some businesses actually prosper during economic downturns, and most businesses can learn from them many measures to help overcome the worst effects of recession. We are certainly not in desperate straits. But now *is* a time to regard the scene realistically and to react with imagination and courage.

— Herman Holtz
Wheaton, MD

A View Of Business As A Creative Enterprise And Profit As A Tool Necessary To Creativity

Why profit—other than the typical naive view of business that its main objective is profit and its driving force is greed? The most successful businessmen and women refute this notion. In fact, they almost invariably paint their business ventures as creative initiatives. Outstanding industrialists, when interviewed by researchers inquiring into business success, have explained again and again that their major objective in business was never profit per se. The main objective of the most successful businessmen and women, as they report it, is always the achievement of an ideal or the success of an idea, whether that means bringing a new product to the marketplace, or introducing an advanced marketing concept, providing a better or more valuable service, or creating some other new entity in the commercial/industrial/business world. (One idea that has gained some currency in recent times urges the listener to "do what you love," and success will follow.) This does not mean that profit is unnecessary or not worthy of pursuit. Quite the contrary, a business cannot succeed without profits, nor can it flower and achieve primary objectives of the business program, whether "maximizing profits" is a prime objective or not.

A remarkably large number of businesses today do not produce enough profit. Aside from the question of whether profit is the end or the means, it *should* represent a reasonable return on your investment, and it should be large enough to justify the risks you take. But there is even more at stake than return on investment or return on risk: Survival of the business itself is at stake, for the present and long term.

Striving to increase profits in your business is not greed any more than buying the maximum amount of insurance you can afford is greed. Profit is a form of insurance. Your business cannot survive without profit, and the greater your profit the greater your chances for business survival and growth. In fact, ensuring the survival of your business is even more complex than that.

Economists and other experts tell us that a business cannot stand still. It is a living entity, and if it is to endure, they say, it must grow. Swelling, simply becoming larger, is not growth, however: *Growth* is more than increase in size and scope; it also means expansion in the broader sense of keeping up and changing to prevent the obsolescence that threatens and destroys so many businesses in this dynamic era of change. (The relevant conventional wisdom, for which there is ample confirming evidence, is that any business doing and selling exactly what it did and sold five years ago is threatened with obsolescence, and any business doing and selling what it did ten years ago is already obsolescent.) Growing means expanding, adapting to new trends, and strengthening your business base with new ideas, new products, and new services in keeping with the changing world about us. Those who fail to change and grow—e.g., Robert Hall, W. T. Grant, and E. J. Korvette, as recent examples—soon find themselves flogging a dead horse, and are doomed to vanish from the scene.

Growth is funded out of profits, however. And to grow, the business must be more than marginally profitable; it must be substantially profitable—enough to fund the necessary growth. Therefore, even a profitable business is in peril if the profits are not large enough to do the job.

That is not the sole reason that profit is an indispensable requirement for survival. All ventures, even the largest, are captives of the economy and of economic swings. All ventures must have reserves to carry them through the inevitable downturns of the economy, and the accumulation of those reserves (again, an analogy to insurance may be made here) is made possible only through having enjoyed adequate profits during prosperous years.

Unfortunately, most businesses, large and small, are far less profitable than they could be and should be, due to a great many shortcomings in typical business practices. Most businesses waste a great deal of money in activities that add nothing to the business, while they neglect far more important functions—functions that would, if properly attended to, vastly increase the generation of profits. (Those are the functions we shall be most concerned with in these pages.) And all too often the proprietors of long-established businesses permit themselves to become complacent and lazy—"fat, dumb, and happy," in the parlance—and pay no heed to declining sales and profits until it becomes too late to reverse the trend. Note, for example, that where W. T. Grant succumbed to that "fat, dumb, and happy" syndrome, Kresge long ago abandoned the outdated "five- and ten-cent store" concept and created the successful K-Mart stores, as only one example of the importance of growth in the sense that the word is used here.

Profits Must Be Made To Happen.

As a rule, business generally is a never-ending struggle to turn a profit. Profits are certainly not an automatic or inevitable consequence of any business. You buy goods, materials, products, and/or labor at wholesale. You sell services and/or products you bought or manufactured at retail, for some larger amount of money than they cost you, taking a gross profit on each sale. It may even be a large gross profit. That, however, does not guarantee a *net* profit, a profit remaining when all the costs of business have been met, including your own salary or personal draw. (Many beginning entrepreneurs launching small businesses, for example, make the mistake of treating the salaries they pay themselves as profits. It is not so: All salaries paid out, including your own, are business costs. You must treat them as such.) In fact, net profits result only from a carefully managed business, one in which costs are closely controlled and sales are maximized. Both measures—minimizing costs and maximizing sales—are critically important in every business. Minimizing costs includes doing for yourself all those things you can do for yourself at less cost than having them done for you, thus avoiding many expenses for services you really do not need. But even larger in terms of dollars is the matter of buying right, so that your markups are maximized. That alone—the ability to find good sources and negotiate good prices for the goods and materials you buy to resell—is the main key to success for many businesses. However, in many ways losses resulting from waste, inefficiency, inventory shrinkage (e.g., pilfering, spoilage, and breakage), and other leakage of money is even more insidious than losses resulting from ineffective buying: Whereas the costs of goods and materials and the volume of sales are usually highly visible, the leakage of profits through waste and excessive cost tends to be relatively invisible. It can go almost completely undetected if you have not installed measures to monitor and ferret out such leaks.

Multiple Leaks Develop Easily.

There are hundreds of ways in which money can be and is wasted: There are many common deficiencies and weaknesses in administration generally—in accounting, cost control, inventory control, purchasing, and other such areas. Problems of unnecessary costs and inadequate income stem often from passivity. That is, the problem is partially due to passively permitting hemorrhaging leaks to develop and go unchecked. The difficulty is one of failing to seek out and take advantage of many opportunities to cut costs and/or increase markups by energetic and aggressive pursuit of such opportunities. There are many common shortcomings in marketing, resulting in lost sales and missed sales opportunities, in failing to mark up merchandise to keep pace with the market and with inflation, in failing to understand and take full advantage of the tax laws, and of numerous other opportunities to reduce costs and increase revenues. The many ways promised here to improve the profitability of your business is a modest estimate of the curable illnesses one can find in almost any business organization. You may very well find many more ways to cut costs and raise revenues than even those enumerated in these pages . . . once you raise your consciousness of the need, organize efforts to do so, and press forward with them. In other words, when you *make* things happen.

What Awaits You In These Pages.

This is not a philosophical book or academic treatment of sound business practices. Rather, it is a highly practical "cookbook" of specific tips and guidance, primarily in the "do it yourself" genre. For example, there will be presented specific examples and detailed guidance on how to accomplish the steps suggested— e.g., getting discounts on advertising, winning free advertising (read: publicity), doing your own incorporation at minimal cost, registering a "fictitious name," and other such detailed procedural guidance. You will also get, among other things, a directory of sources for various kinds of merchandise, much of it discounted, surplus, or otherwise available at extraordinarily low prices, and a directory of low-cost and no-cost software for personal computers, with descriptions and lists of sources of each, as well as guidance to further sources that will keep you up to date on opportunities you should be alert for and follow up intensively.

Cost Reduction Or Cost Avoidance?

Many organizations, including the U.S. Government, install cost-reduction programs, with suggestion boxes and cash awards for suggestions that are adopted. (I was the lucky recipient of a $10 award from one of these government programs many years ago.) Such programs are invariably referred to as cost-reduction programs. Another similar type of program has been known variously as *value engineering, value analysis,* and *value management.* This program is not known as a cost-reduction system because its avowed purpose is to increase the value of a product or system that is the object of a value study, under the philosophy that increasing value without increasing cost is a benefit equal to and interchangeable with cost reduction. The net effect is thus that of reducing costs.

Much of what you will read in these pages are tips, ideas, and suggestions for reducing costs. However, you can only reduce costs after you have incurred costs that are higher than they ought to be; it is far better to avoid costs than to reduce them. One way to do this is to study these tips, ideas, and suggestions before you make your normal business investments. Find the lowest-cost ways of doing what you want to do—and sometimes you will find no-cost ways of doing it, too—before you do it.

Choose What You Can Use.

Not all the ideas and tips will be suitable for you or be applicable to your own situation, of course. Some of the ideas have universal or near-universal application, while others will be practicable for only certain kinds of businesses. But among the many ideas and tips there will be dozens that will work for you or can be easily adapted to your needs. Study them with this in mind. Use a high-lighter or a pencil to mark the ideas and tips you can use, and keep this book near at hand as a ready reference to remind yourself of the many ways you can increase the profitability of your business. Although various methods and approaches for increasing profitability are discussed separately, and on their own merits, many of the methods and tips are interrelated and even interdependent. For example, the two measures, cutting costs and increasing income, are often linked in a direct relationship: Buying goods for resale at lower prices has the dual effect of reducing costs and increasing income, since it automatically raises your gross profit on each sale. By the same token, what represents too low a markup at a given sales volume might be a perfectly acceptable and profitable markup at a larger sales volume. There are such interrelationships and even interdependencies among many of the ideas presented here, and in many cases you may choose tradeoffs. For example, suppose you can cut the costs of some item you buy for resale by buying a large quantity or otherwise get an unusually good buy. Will you now sell the item at its usual price and earn extra gross profits as a result of the greater markup? Or will you keep the same markup rate and offer the item at a discount, relying on a great increase in sales to produce a greater number of dollars in profit, rather than a greater rate of profit? The choice is yours in this and in many other cases, although guidelines to help you make a choice will be offered. Try to bear this in mind as you read.

To make each point clear and distinct, it was necessary to organize the program presented here into five parts:

   I: Overhead, the Killer
  II: Increasing Markups
 III: Increasing Gross Sales
 IV: Reducing Tax and Insurance Burdens
  V: Coping in Hard Times
 VI: Reducing the High Cost of Labor

The book is further subdivided into chapters, each titled to identify its specific areas of coverage. This organization is designed not only to aid you in following the logic of the presentations, but also to help you use this book to refresh your memory and to use it as a permanent reference as needs arise. Perhaps you should do this in the spirit of the bewildered-looking young soldier who called on his old recruiting sergeant, the one who had so recently encouraged him to enlist. He reminded the recruiting sergeant of that occasion, with all the glowing descriptions of a great military career and a bright future that the recruiting sergeant had painted for him.

"Would you mind giving me that great pep talk again, sergeant?" the young soldier pleaded. "I am getting kind of discouraged."

Holtz's Law.

Read this book with a pen and/or highlighter in hand and mark the passages—the cost-reduction and cost-avoidance ideas especially—that are most applicable to your own situation. Come back to read and reread these ideas again and again, as you need to recharge your batteries for the business battle. But above all, remember that net profit, like business success, is not an automatic consequence of business; it is the consequence of unrelenting effort. I offer what I like to think of as Holtz's Law:

> *When everything is running smoothly, with no problems and ample time to get everything done easily, beware: You are probably losing money.*

PART ONE

Overhead, The Killer

Undermined by Overhead.

Many businesses are like poorly built ships, with profits escaping through a thousand leaks in the hull. Even the best-managed, tightest ships in the business world are rarely completely free of such profit-draining leaks, especially in their overhead accounts.

Overhead is a necessary evil. It is an inescapable necessity of business life and yet, at best, it contributes only indirectly to the welfare of your business. Often it does not do even that, but is only a parasitic drain on your business. It tends to grow like the weed in good times, when the business earns profits with relative ease and many chief executives grow permissive about adding unnecessary frills and small luxuries. But like taxes and bureaucracy, once overhead items are installed they are like some unwelcome house guests: They become quite difficult to get rid of it, even when times are not so good and it is clear that changes are in order. Overhead items almost always fight desperately to survive all cost-cutting efforts. It is far better to head them off before they can settle in.

Retailers, working on limited markups and with the necessity for virtually perpetual sales, are especially sensitive to operating expenses. The Sears chain struggles to keep operating expenses—principally overhead—below 30 percent of revenue. Wal-Mart manages to operate at about one-half that portion of its revenues, running an even tighter ship in that regard than does the great K Mart retailing chain, which is second to Wal-Mart.

If the sensible thing is not to have incurred unnecessary overhead expense in the first place, it is even wiser and more helpful to beware of that overhead that represents permanent, on-going expense (such as office rent), rather than one-time purchases or occasional investments (such as the purchase of fixtures and equipment).

Despite that general rule, avoiding the on-going overhead expense is not always possible or desirable; there are occasional exceptions. You will see one example of ongoing cost versus one-time investment costs shortly, when we discuss how some businesses—supermarkets, for example—usually analyze the alternatives of renting versus buying the stores they operate. That illustrates an important fact: There are no absolute rules; you must use judgment to evaluate and reach decision in each and every case.

What is unnecessary in one case may be necessary in another, depending on what you are trying to accomplish. Robert Hall was successful for a large number of years selling suits and coats displayed on plain pipe racks. It went with their low-cost/discount image, much as it does for Burlington Coat Factory stores today. Neiman Marcus and Bloomingdales could not manage with pipe-rack fixtures, however: They cater to a different clientele and require a different image to command the prices they ask. "Necessary" and "unnecessary" thus have completely different meanings here, depending on the situation.

CHAPTER 1

Setting Up Your World Headquarters

Every Business Needs a Place to Call Home.

The most difficult choice of a business location is the choice of your first one, the location where your business is to start. For one thing, your success may depend on the location; in some kinds of business location is everything, a principal determinant of success or failure. For another thing, you will probably be at that first location for a long time, perhaps even permanently. (And perhaps, in time, your business will become so large that it will indeed be your "world headquarters," all jesting aside!)

The Relocation Problem.

On the other hand, you may have reached that time when you must consider relocating your business, for whatever reason. That is a little easier because you now have some intimate knowledge of your needs. Still, it can be frightening, especially if yours is the kind of business where location is a critical element— e.g., a restaurant or retail store. Relocating has been fatal to many businesses that relocated after doing well in their original locations. You may find it wiser to open an additional location.

The Additional Location Problem.

You may also be in that situation where you are operating a highly successful retail or service business and want to expand, but cannot expand in your present location for lack of space or for some other reason. You thus have the options of moving to a larger location or opening an additional location. The hazard is the same as that one you encountered in opening your original establishment: The new location may or may not work out. Again and again an additional or new location fails to thrive. It is wise, then, to open at an additional location without giving up your original establishment and see how well that works out. More than one entrepreneur clinging stubbornly to an original location while opening at a new one later had cause to be grateful to whatever spirit inspired him or her to exercise that wise caution.

1.

BUY OR RENT THE BRICKS?

Why Buy a Cow?

Many business organizations own the buildings that house them, but not everyone finds it the best thing to do. Many businesses find it more profitable to rent. Supermarkets, for example, often build their own stores and offices so that the facilities are precisely what they want, but then they sell them to investors and lease them back. They prefer to put their money into their own business—the stock on the shelves, what they sell and earn income from—than into bricks. They believe that arrangement to be a more profitable investment of capital.

And this is a typical tradeoff. Cost reduction for its own sake is not the goal; amplification of profits is the goal. And so every decision must be studied in those terms: the impact on the bottom line—profit. Save dollars when you can, yes, but only when it also increases profits.

Thus many businesses, at least those that are dependent on large and varied inventories (otherwise known as capital-intensive businesses), are housed in leased facilities. It makes the most sense economically as an investment in *your* business rather than an investment in bricks. It also offers you many options and alternatives that you give up when you buy the real estate you use to house your business.

2.
_____

DO YOU REALLY NEED A TAJ MAHAL?

The Customer Doesn't Care How Much Rent You Pay.

Maybe Donald Trump can afford the Taj Mahal—maybe not, as recent events suggest. But the urge to install your business in a fancy establishment is an ego trip at best, and a death wish at worst. (After all, the original Taj Mahal *is* a mausoleum!)

The cost of space for your business is a most basic and necessary overhead expense, probably the largest one for most businesses. It ought to have your attention. Think hard about it: What kind of space do you really need? How much space do you really need? How much should it cost you? Do you really need to be in an expensive downtown or shopping mall location? Do you need to be in the most expensive office building in town? Don't answer yet.

Many merchants succeed with discount operations run in warehouse stores in low-rent industrial locations, even remote locations, where the chief attractions are low prices generally, wide selection of merchandise, and ultra-special sales run continuously. They thus induce customers to go out of their way, miles out of their way, to bring their patronage. The Price® and

Pace® warehouse store chains do this successfully, as do many others.

There is the example of Wal-Mart, rapidly becoming the most successful chain store operation of its kind in the United States. It recently passed K-Mart to become the number two retailer, and is likely to pass Sears to become number one. Its annual net income is expected to exceed $1 billion in the near future. (Growth history: 330 stores and $55 million net in 1981, 1,402 stores and expected $1 billion plus net in 1990.) Yet this immense operation is headquartered unpretentiously in a linoleum tiled building in Bentonville, Arkansas, with a simple sign that says "Home Office" out front. All three of the largest retail chains minimize overhead, but Wal-Mart manages to cut overhead far more than do the others.

But it's not only retail sellers of merchandise who use remote, low-rent locations successfully; many restaurants also do this. Restaurants must have something special to attract customers— low prices, exotic and/or unusually good food, ambiance, or other special drawing power—and they must have convenient parking. (Some who lack convenient parking arrange valet parking, which amounts to almost the same thing—convenience—as far as patrons are concerned.)

Commercial and industrial space is generally priced by the square foot on an annual basis. Suppose you are going into a newly constructed office building at a rental of $30 per square foot. A 3,000-foot space will cost you $90,000 annually, or $7,500 each and every month. But you probably don't really need 3,000 square feet. Initial estimates almost always turn out to be too high. With careful planning you can probably manage in 1,500 square feet. You will save $3,750 on rent every month, ample compensation for a bit of crowding.

What? You'll be crowded and uncomfortable? Maybe. But that will be easier on your nerves than finding yourself in a struggle to pay the rent each month. The comfort that really counts is being able to pay your bills and take a bit of profit. That is the tradeoff: convenience for profits, perhaps even for success. (Go back to the Introduction and review "Holtz's Law." Comfort and profit are all too often inversely proportional, even mutually exclusive!) Most businesses start with an overly optimistic estimate of the space needed and then struggle with excessive and unnecessary overhead. Better to be crowded in space that is a bit too small than be burdened with rent that is more than a bit too large!

Many successful entrepreneurs function happily for years in tiny, crowded shops, offices, and restaurants. (This crowded environment often has a salutary effect on sales, impressing customers with your great success and convincing them that they have come to the right place. People to tend to herd, following the crowd.)

Some retailers compensate for shortage of display space by renting nearby inexpensive storage and moving merchandise frequently from storage to the retail location. Some clever retailers even rent nearby warehouse or garage space for storage and then open it as an additional special discount center to which they conduct customers for special bargains. Restaurants, when they get overcrowded, often utilize a porch, patio, or even part of a wide sidewalk in front to seat the overflow in pleasant weather. Again, a constantly crowded restaurant appeals to a certain type of customer, who accepts all the bustle as proof of excellence or assurance that they have come to a place that is "in." (One newly opened restaurant in my area urged its employees to invite people in for free meals during their first few weeks to create a crowded environment as evidence of their appeal!)

3.

SPACE AND LOCATION ARE NOT THE BUSINESS

McDonald's Started as a Hamburger Stand.

When Ray Kroc discovered McDonald's in San Bernardino, it was a single hamburger stand, albeit an unusually successful one. Volt Information Sciences, a firm now headquartered on New York's Park Avenue and with annual sales in the hundreds of millions of dollars, began life at the kitchen table of Volt founder William Shaw's home. (In fact, it was his mother's kitchen table.) The Penn Fruit supermarkets of Philadelphia started in Depression days as a roadside fruit stand. One business in the Silver Spring, Maryland area, now happily selling linens and related merchandise in a reconditioned supermarket, started in an old house on a street that had recently been widened and re-zoned for commercial enterprises. It was crowded and uncomfortable, but the customers eased proprietor Sam Kugler's pain with their orders, and finally Sam was able to move to the big store in the busy neighborhood of its new location.

An auctioneer appears to be in great pain when he gets an unrealistically small opening bid, but he shrugs and accepts it resignedly. He thinks, "It ain't where you start, but where you finish that counts." These are examples illustrating that point precisely.

There are businesses where location is of great importance, of course. More than one highly successful restaurant operator finds that an identical restaurant does not work in another location, for example. Nor is that phenomenon peculiar to the restaurant business. Every chain-store operation finds it necessary to close some stores that didn't work in certain locations. But there are many businesses where location is not important—usually businesses that do not depend on being visited by customers. It is important to make that discrimination when you are seeking a location.

Original Locations Are Often Improvised Ones.

Many businesses start as roadside stands or in old houses in neighborhoods re-zoned from residential to commercial or industrial. These are usually houses showing their age, often small ones without all the modern amenities. But they are available for industrial or commercial use without restrictions and almost always at far lower rentals than a modern commercial building would cost. Some are slated to be razed a year or two hence, in fact, but still offer excellent start-up facilities in the meanwhile. I know of one such house on a wide boulevard opposite a modern shopping mall that houses a small print shop, another that serves as a chiropractor's office, and still another that boasts a popular local restaurant. (The restaurant has been highly successful, and the owner has managed to buy the property outright and do some conversion and modernization to make a permanent establishment of it.)

All kinds of businesses lend themselves to such humble beginnings as a start in one's own home, with benefits in the form of tax reductions—writeoffs—as well as reduced venture capital requirements. Many realtors, insurance brokers, accountants, manufacturer's reps, consultants, writers, artists, and others begin with offices at home. Some remain there permanently, while others grow up and out. But for a beginning, always consider your own home—an unused room, a basement, a garage, a porch, or even your kitchen and dining room—as a potential low-cost location to get started and eliminate unnecessary expense. I moved my own offices from an expensive downtown suite in a large office building to my own home over a decade ago, when I realized that I could do everything in an office at home that I was doing in an office in the middle of the city. Even the Dun & Bradstreet vice president with whom I had been doing business congratulated me on a smart move that cut my overhead, and my home office has never interfered with my doing business with D&B or other major companies—International Telephone & Telegraph, for example.

4.

TOGETHERNESS MAY SAVE
YOU MONEY

Coexistence Works in Business Too.

Jim Fitzgerald operates a small consulting business in downtown Washington, DC. He used to have five people on staff in a suite of three offices. But recent business has been down, and his sales and workload were off so much that he was forced to let two people go. Fortunately, Jim had the foresight to negotiate a lease that anticipated this possibility, so he was able to move his remaining staff into his own office, the largest of the three, and sublet the other two offices to other small businesses.

The sharing of offices is an increasing trend. This idea matches the need for more and more experience with the need for downsizing and retrenchment. Among the great advantages of the method Fitzgerald and others have used to cut costs is this one: They reduce expenses without changing mailing addressees, telephone numbers, or fax numbers. Thus clients need not become aware of their straitened circumstances, and their company images are not affected.

Resourcefulness Counts.

The name of the game is to get what you need by whatever means—make your own rules. Suppose that you have an opportunity to rent a space much larger than you need, but at an unusually attractive rate. How can you take advantage of that? One way is to line up another business—or even two or three—to share the space, subletting from you. Or suppose you have not been suitably conservative in your original estimate; you find yourself with far more space than you need. Subletting is again a way out: Sublet the part of your space you don't need, maybe even put up partitions to create separate offices or even start a mini-mall. (Make sure when you sign a lease that you have the right to sublet so that you can handle such contingencies.)

Your Own Space Can be Free or Nearly So.

If you are disposed to doing it, it is possible to get your own space free or nearly so by deliberately renting a large space, several times larger than you need, with the intention of subletting all except the space you wish to reserve for yourself. You must expend the energy to find the location, make the deal, sign the master lease, assume the risk, find the sublessees, and sell them each space at a rate that lets you come out with your own space free or nearly so—perhaps even with a bit of profit. This is a lot of work, and it involves some risk, but most of the effort is up front. Once you have signed tenants up, it is relatively easy to keep it all going, month after month.

It works both ways. Do you really need a separate space, a place all your own? How about *you* becoming a sublessee? It's easy enough to arrange. The Egghead® chain of computer software stores has at least one of their stores as a separate entity in sublet space of one of the local Staples® office supplies stores. A drug store sublet space to an dentist, and another sublet to an optometrist. Such arrangements have the spinoff benefit of mutual support because each business generates traffic, so all benefit. This is especially appropriate and beneficial to all when the various businesses have some related interests while not being directly competitive, as in the case of the drug store and the dentist. (Print shops can sublet space to printing brokers, typesetters, and graphic arts specialists; drug stores to opticians and dental surgeons; dry cleaning shops to tailors and seamstresses; and so on.)

Another Way to Skin a Cat.

As an alternative method for sharing space and reducing costs, consider organizing a syndicate with other business owners, and renting a large enough space to house all of you in a mini-mall arrangement or suite of offices. Instead of being landlord and tenants or lessee and sublessees, you will be equal lessees of an organization in which you all have equal shares. You will thus not have to do all the difficult work of organizing because the others will have to share in the initial effort.

The advantages of this arrangement is that none of you earns profits at the others' expense. Your mutually owned syndicate either leases space to each partner at the actual cost of the space or you share equally in any profits the syndicate earns. With the right accountant, you can probably find a few tax benefits in the arrangement, as well.

5.

TOGETHERNESS WORKS IN OFFICES TOO

It's Easy to Have Any Office Address You Want.

If you need office space but do not have to receive clients in your office—for instance, if you usually visit your clients or conduct most of your business by telephone and mail—location is of little significance to you except as regards personal convenience and cost. Even where a prestige office address has some importance for you, there are ways to satisfy that requirement without sacrificing the major benefits of low-cost space. Read on.

Your office, as we have seen, can be in your home in many cases for minimum cost and maximum benefits. But if it must be outside your home, you still have several cost-saving options. When location is not especially important, one potential advantage is the option of moving to a low-rent neighborhood. Another cost-saving option is sharing a suite or an oversize office with associates. Still another is renting desk space in one of the many establishments that offer such an arrangement. You can find one of these located in a "good" business location, which satisfies the need for a prestigious business address.

These services afford you desk space in a "bull pen" kind of office, where you may receive mail, keep your files, and get telephone-answering services at a modest monthly rental, usually on the order of $100/month. Most of these establishments also offer secretarial services, and have copiers, fax machines, and conference rooms available.

6.

YOU DON'T HAVE TO DO IT
ALL YOURSELF

Use a "Business Convenience Store."

One reason you don't need a large office is the modern neighborhood "business center." This is a fairly new kind of business that exists to serve the individual and small business with a variety of necessary services that can be troublesome to provide for yourself. The store functions almost like a part-time staff.

These businesses are usually set up in a store front. You can have a box there for receipt of your mail; other services include weighing and supplying the right postage for your outgoing mail, wrapping packages, shipping your parcels and express packages by the major shipping services, copying, fax, and similar conveniences. You thus avoid the need to have such equipment, facilities, and help of your own, with the resulting savings of both your time and money.

Branch Out.

Some people expand their office space without adding overhead costs by having a second office at home, enabling them to work evenings conveniently. (In some circumstances you can even win a legitimate tax deduction for the home office expense.) A Redwood, California lawyer, Richard Enkelis, uses a personal computer (PC) on his desk, but has another PC at home. He leaves his office PC turned on when he leaves to go home at the end of the day. His office machine has access to a printer and all his files and records, and it is equipped with a modem and special software (*Co-Session*, by Triton Technologies, in this case) to enable it to act as the host computer, accepting commands from his computer at home. (In other words, he operates his PC at home as a remote terminal of his office computer, via his modem connections and special software.) He thus does his work on his office computer just as though he were there in his office at night.

---

CHAPTER 2

Cutting Costs On
Capital Items

Overhead is subdivided into numerous classes, such as fixed costs and variable costs. Rent, mortgage payments, insurance, and yellow pages advertising, for example, are generally regarded as fixed costs because they change only once in a while; normally, they are the same costs, month after month. Costs for furniture, supplies, and many other items are variable costs because you buy them infrequently and, aside from the initial furnishing of your premises, only when you opt to do so. One significant difference is that variable costs are usually more controllable than fixed costs; you can usually defer buying new furniture or new stationery, and choose the most propitious time for such purchases, but fixed costs are commitments that you cannot escape easily. That makes then more serious overhead burdens, to be considered even more carefully than you consider major outlays for capital items. Together, they constitute "the nut" on the business, the minimum number of dollars required to keep the doors open on a regular basis. The nut is always a serious matter. However, the line between fixed and variable costs is not absolute; capital items can become fixed costs too, in at least two ways. Here is how.

If you buy something that you will pay for in installments over many months, usually several years, those installments are fixed costs for that period of time. You are committed to them and cannot ordinarily escape them. They become part of the nut for as long as it takes to make all the payments.

Buying major capital items for cash, rather than paying for them in installments, is a bit different. In a sense, the investment becomes a fixed cost because you normally put such investment on a depreciation schedule and carry the cost as an overhead item, requiring several years to recover the cost. Your overhead accounts will reflect that as a fixed cost, although you don't have to write a check every month for the item. You have, however, tied up capital that you may find need for, and that may not be a wise idea. Like the supermarket owner who wants to maximize his investment in inventory to sell, rather than "in bricks," you should weigh the advantages of investing more of your capital in what you sell.

Thus, making even one-time purchases can have a continuing impact on your overhead for a long time, representing a drain on your cash flow. Bear the long-term consequences in mind, as well as the immediate ones, when you contemplate capital purchases.

7.

AVOID TAJ-MAHALITIS ON FURNITURE AND FIXTURES, TOO

Do You Really Need "The Best?"

Admittedly there are businesses for which an impressive "front" is a necessity to success. An upscale store selling to moneyed customers needs furniture, fixtures, and other furnishings of an appearance and quality in keeping with the market to which it aspires. The owners of such emporiums ordinarily seek furnishings of the highest (i.e., most expensive) quality. Lawyers, accountants, investment counselors, consultants, and others in situations where clients visit their offices, require the client's complete confidence and are in a similar position; they are understandably concerned with appearing to be successful. The image of prosperity is a necessity for most such professions. (Physicians and even dentists appear to be exceptions; many highly successful ones have rather drab outer offices, although they usually have gleaming, modern examining rooms.)

Even here there are limits, however. It is possible to buy a serviceable desk (what is often called an "engineering desk") for less than $200, and a handsome one for a few hundred dollars more. Of course, it is also possible to spend several thousand dollars for a desk, and many more thousands for carpeting, drapes, and other appurtenances. It is quite easy to go to extremes. (One prominent company catering to the Air Force as its major client has a conference room fitted so luxuriously that it is referred to by all in the company as the Taj Mahal.)

"The best" is not an absolute. It is whatever you think is "the best." As one guiding principle in deciding what it means to you, remember this: There is a large difference between ordinary quality and excellent quality, but a relatively small difference between excellent and superb or whatever we call the ultimate in quality. Once you move above what would be called "good" quality, you begin to get less return on your dollars, and once you move above "excellent" quality, the return on dollars becomes almost negligible —that is, you get little improvement in quality despite paying the highest prices. (Nor are quality and price firmly linked—paying the highest price does not ensure that you get the highest quality.) You must be the judge of the quality you need, but you should examine that need analytically and objectively. Remember two things: One, excess—paying for more than you need—is sheer waste in pure business terms. Two, "good" quality, in most things, is the greatest value.

8.

FIGHT IMPULSES AND TRY TO
BE OBJECTIVE

Buy Only What You Need.

Normally, when you rent or buy, you rent or buy empty space within a structure; the space, whether you own it or rent it, must be furnished, and facilities have to be equipped. Offices need desks, chairs, filing cabinets, and other furniture. Stores need counters, display cases, shelves, and racks. Warehouses need shelves and worktables. Work shops need fixtures and equipment.

All cost money—a great deal of money. Specifically, all cost you *overhead* dollars. It can cost many thousands of dollars to equip even a small office or store with the bare necessities. But you can cut this cost by at least one-half, and very likely by even more. There are several ways to do this. The first way is by not buying at all—not buying, that is, what you really do not need. Sometimes that takes a great deal of self-discipline. It always takes a large measure of good judgment, that quality we call "common sense."

Want versus Need.

Deciding whether you really need something you have decided you want is not easy. You can always rationalize the want—find a large number of reasons for "needing" what you want. You have to help yourself make objective judgments. One way is to sit down and write out, in cold text, your rationale. Let us say that you want to buy one of the latest model computers for about $4,000. Why do you need it? What will it do for you that is worth $4,000, $4,000 that will be charged to overhead? (Never forget that we are talking about overhead here!)

Start writing. Do some solitary brainstorming! The new computer will speed up your work. You will get more done each day. You can satisfy customers better. You can turn out nicer brochures. You can get back perhaps a $1,000 by selling your present computer. (Or, if you are going to keep your present computer, you really need to have two computers.) Write out all the ideas.

Now edit them. Throw out the obviously inappropriate ones that you know in your heart you wrote to convince yourself. Set up an objective scale, say 1 to 10, on which to value each item that has survived your edit. The scale is an indicator of the validity of your reason, from an admittedly very weak reason (1) to a strong reason (10). Only you know any of this, so you can afford to be honest here.

One final suggestion on this score: Write out also what else you can/will do with the $4,000 if you *don't* buy a new computer. Think especially of how you might invest that $4,000 to improve income and profits of your business. That can be a powerful persuader to postpone buying a new computer if you are not truly convinced of the need.

You may be sure that a great many of your wants will die or be stillborn as a result of these processes. If so, it is the fate they deserve.

When to Buy.

Later, we will talk about when to buy with regard to tax advantages, but there is also the matter of cash flow: When is it most and least advantageous to spend or commit the money? In my own case, there are two times of the year when I usually make purchases of capital items—or decide not to make the purchases. It is when we (my little corporation and I, that is) get royalty statements and know how much cash we will or will not have to spend for other than absolute bare necessities. Consider when the times are that you are in the best position to judge what your business can or cannot afford in new overhead investment. When are you most likely to need all your cash for other purposes? That process alone will dampen desires to buy anything that is not truly a necessity.

Fixtures and Furnishings Can be Rented.

There are situations where renting makes more sense than buying. Renting is best when you know that your need is short term or there is some special consideration. Some companies operating on government contracts, for example, have to rent extra space on a temporary basis—for the length of the contract, that is—and find it much more practicable to rent than to buy. That is one of the exceptional cases. In most cases it makes much more sense to own your furniture and furnishings. At the same time, that does not mean that you must or should pay $300 for an office chair and $800 for a desk. There are ways to furnish your space at far lower costs. Here are a few ideas.

Buying at the Right Prices.

Make it a rule, in advance, that you will never pay the list price for your office furniture. You need to have that mindset: the conviction that you can save at least one-third and probably one-half the normal price of the items. (You almost always can do so.)

There is always the "special" sale that department stores and other dealers hold regularly. But be skeptical. Many such sales do not represent more than minor savings. If you do not know the line you must go out and get an education. Do comparison shopping and learn all about prices and values in furniture and furnishings (or whatever it is you need to buy).

Department stores and chain stores often offer furniture and furnishings at extraordinary bargain prices in what they call "warehouse sales," sometimes even actually held at their warehouses. In fact, they sometimes call in professional auctioneers to help dispose of stocks of slow-moving new merchandise that the owner wants to get rid of to clear inventory and make room for new merchandise. If you are truly unfamiliar with auctions and auction technique, attend a few and observe without attempting to buy anything; the education and subsequent savings will be worth the time and effort.

The IRS will allow you eight years to depreciate furniture, but that is a bookkeeping convenience; most furniture and furnishings of good quality are serviceable for many more years than that, and there is always an abundance of used office furniture available. There are dealers who handle only used office furniture and who almost always have a large stock from which to select what you want. In many cases, dealers in new office furniture also have a stock of used items for sale, but you may have to ask for them; they may prefer to sell the new items. And there are renters of furniture and fixtures who often have such items for sale in used condition and at appropriate prices, after they have been rented out a few times. Again, beware. Don't accept a vendor's assurance that you are getting a good deal. Be prepared to bargain, and don't be ashamed to offer one-half or less of what the vendor is asking. (He is probably not ashamed to ask twice what it is worth!) Again, if all of this—bargaining, that is—is new to you, you can learn to do it by visiting the Middle East, where bargaining is a way of life . . . or you can visit enough sales and learn to be stubborn enough to master the experts.

9.

DON'T PAY LIST PRICES FOR EQUIPMENT EITHER

The Equipment You Need Today.

You aren't finished when you buy all the furniture and furnishings you need to get started. Even the most nontechnical businesses today need some modern high-tech appurtenances: typewriters, computers, fax machines, copiers, cash registers, scanners, shredders, answering machines, and sundry other equipment. Maybe you can get by without owning all of these yourself, at least in the beginning. You can rent most of these kinds of items, as you can furniture, but as in the case of furniture it usually makes better sense to buy eventually.

The rules are essentially the same as in buying furniture or other items, but the conditions are much different in several ways: One, there are a large number of standard or "name" brands and specific model numbers and list prices in most equipment items. As far as computers, fax machines, cash registers, and other high-tech items are concerned, for instance, you can compare prices among brand names and model numbers. However, there are many "off brands," the products of small, little-known manufacturers, with a quite enormous diversity of prices, making it difficult for the lay person to judge. Then, to further complicate this, there is the difficulty that prices fall rapidly in the high-tech field. A year ago, for example, I paid $600 for what was then reported to be the best fax machine at the "low end" of the market for fax machines. Today, the same manufacturer produces a more sophisticated fax machine with more features that is available for about $450. The computer for which I paid nearly $3,000 a year ago is about $500 cheaper now. Not long ago, I paid $600 for my first modem, but less than $200 for my current one, which is superior to the original, and is itself available even cheaper now that I've purchased it!

You can't do anything about that problem unless you want to wait until the market stabilizes on the newest high-tech equipment. But you can take the time to learn a bit about features and characteristics, comparison shop, and buy bargains (new or used) wherever you can find them. More and more dealers in used computers, fax machines, copiers, cash registers, and other such items are springing up. Be alert also for those "warehouse sales" that are occasionally held by the big stores, although high-tech items are not sold that way very often. (That will change, of course, as more and more people trade up to larger, later models and a surplus of used computers begins to accumulate.)

Individuals and business owners often offer such items for sale themselves, instead of selling them through a broker or auctioneer. However, when a large business is liquidated (a not uncommon occurrence today) auctioneers are usually involved, selling off great stocks of items from businesses that have become bankrupt, or whose owners have died and left the business to heirs who wish to dispose of everything. There is also the U.S. Government, holding thousands of surplus sales, sometimes by open auction, sometimes by sealed bids. (See the appendix for information.)

You can easily locate many of these kinds of sources in the yellow pages and in the classified advertising of the newspapers. You can also call the listed auctioneers and ask them to put you on their mailing lists for notices of sales.

Note, finally, that rent is not the only cost you reduce when you share space with others. Together, you can share the cost and use of a copier, a computer, a fax machine, a receptionist, a conference room, the common-use furniture (such as that in the conference room), and other necessities. If you must be out of the office a good bit, you have the advantage of a live person to take messages, a distinct improvement on the answering machine.

However, you can also benefit from the reverse of this, as in the case of renting too much space, if you have bought all the equipment but find that you do not keep it busy full time. Many small businesses with copiers, fax machines, and other equipment they don't use often enough to keep the machines busy make them available to others for fees. A gasoline service station near my home, for example, has a copier that customers may use at a per-copy charge. A local hardware store has a fax machine that is available to the public at a suitable charge for each transmittal. And many well-equipped offices make their machines available to others in the building for suitable charges.

It is not always necessary to buy this equipment new. Much of the modern high-tech equipment is beginning to appear as second-hand or reconditioned equipment. When I bought my present computer, for example, I sold the one I had been using. I had bought it new for some $1,500 and added over $1,000 worth of features to it. I sold it for a fraction of my cost to a dealer, who reconditioned it and sold it for about one-half of its original price.

Many of these equipment items require accessories, which can be quite costly, but which also offer economies to those who are alert to them. These will be discussed later, with discussions of the costs of supplies.

10.

SOURCES

Wholesalers Sometimes Make Special Offers.

Every industry has its wholesalers, and wholesalers often unexpectedly become sources for items they do not normally handle. This may happen because a wholesaler comes across a good buy on some capital items the wholesaler's dealers have use for. In that manner, a grocery wholesaler may temporarily become a good source for cash registers or store fixtures, although this is more likely to be a one-time offer than a regular availability of such items. In these cases the wholesaler is often motivated as much by the benefit of serving the dealers as by the extra profits of handling extraordinary items, and so you often find the prices most attractive.

Other Special Discounters.

Warehouse Clubs, such as the Price and Pace chains, are heavily oriented to food items, but carry many other items for businesses, as well as for individual consumers. They have, more or less regularly, office chairs, desks, copiers, fax machines, filing cabinets, and sundry other capital items, usually at highly competitive prices. These discounters have no regular lines, as they will advise you, but buy up large stocks of items when they can get them at what they regard as the right prices—prices that enable them to offer some rather startling bargains. Therefore you cannot be sure that what you saw there in Tuesday will be available on Friday or will ever be available there again. You must visit these places personally and act promptly when you see something you want. (This is one case where the seller's exhortation to "act now" is good advice.) Their ability to move a great deal of merchandise is almost awesome. An entire skid of VCRs, for example, may move out in a few days.

Mail Order Is an Increasingly Attractive Source.

More and more firms are specializing or expanding their marketing into mail order, and that includes vendors of many capital items. A great many computers, desks, fax machines, telephone equipment, and many other items are available via mail order today. The prices are almost always discounted, partly because the overhead tends to be somewhat lower in mail order and partly because there is a presumption that customers buy by mail only if they can save money in doing so. As a general rule, you must pay shipping charges on the items you order, but in most cases you do not pay sales tax, so you will save money there. If you order from an out-of-state supplier and the supplier does not have a business address or existence (a *nexus*, in legal terminology) in your state, your state cannot force him to collect sales taxes from you.

CHAPTER 3

Buying "Right" In Supplies And Services

All Business Requires Buying and Selling.

At least one-half the art of being successful in business is marketing effectively; most of the rest is buying well, a most important function in any business. It is important to buy well when you buy what you are going to market (resell); in fact, the two, buying and selling, are directly related to each other: Your success in marketing depends heavily on how well you bought in the first place. But it is also essential to your business to buy supplies and services that constitute the day-to-day overhead expenses. The overall cost of these varies in magnitude, according to the nature of your business; they can constitute a large cost or a small one, but no cost is ever unimportant. It is part of your overhead, a critical factor in all businesses, but especially so in those businesses where the markups are generally modest to begin with (e.g., in food products) so that only a few percentage points difference can spell the difference between profit and loss. Reducing overhead costs by even a point or two increases profits proportionately. (It is significant that retail giant Wal-Mart is noted for its frugality in an industry where frugality is a common practice, which is why the Wal-Mart chain can be exceptionally competitive and fund exceptional growth.)

Opportunities to save money in buying supplies and other consumables charged to your overhead are almost surely more numerous than you know. But it does require going to a bit of trouble to enjoy maximum savings. Somehow, even the individual who will be at great pains to seek out good buys of merchandise for resale tends often to be careless when it comes to buying office supplies and related items. Or he or she tends to simply order some known brand name, assuming that to be the easiest and safest course.

Unfortunately, most people are unfamiliar with the all-too-common practices of manufacturers and wholesalers in buying and selling all kinds of merchandise—soft goods, hard goods, food items, raw materials, and even major manufactured items. Understanding these markets, how they work and why prices range so widely, is a useful education for anyone buying supplies regularly and trying to hold costs down. In this chapter you will learn of some of these practices.

11.

A GENERAL PRINCIPLE IN BUYING

The Common Mistake.

Many of us tend to treat the purchase of everyday supplies rather casually, and we therefore tend also to settle on a single supplier, possibly a discounter, for all or most of our supplies. Probably we assume that if the supplier offers generally good prices, he or she offers the best prices on everything. Alas, that is not true. It is rare that any single source offers the best prices on everything. If you want to save money in your buying by getting all your supplies and related necessities at the best prices, you must not rely on any single source.

You must be a shopper and search out the best deals in these areas, as you search out the best deals for any products you resell or materials you buy to create the items you sell. Even if you have a main supplier for most of your needs, apply the test of comparison shopping for every item you buy regularly or in quantity. I have for years been buying more or less regularly from a well-known major supplier of items for office, factory, and warehouse, but my buying there has become less and less regular as I continue to find other and better sources for many items. This, I find, is especially the case whenever I buy some new equipment item for which I must also buy supplies of some kind—e.g., a fax machine that needs special paper and a copier and a laser printer that use paper and toner cartridges. When I bought a laser printer I wanted to increase its capacity by adding two megabytes of memory. I was shocked to find that the upgrade, consisting of one small circuit board full of chips, would cost me nearly one-half the original price of the printer. I therefore went in active search of a better deal and soon found one for $176, which I bought. Subsequently, and not long after, I discovered that I didn't search long enough or hard enough, for even closer to home there was a source offering the item for $136. There are many examples such as this, typical ones, not only for office supplies, but for all supplies for offices, plants, warehouses, stores, restaurants, and other establishments.

12.

COSTS OF CONSUMABLE
OFFICE SUPPLIES

Copying Costs.

A copier is as useful—and almost as necessary—as a telephone in most offices today. Good copiers are now available cheaply enough for even the smallest business to own one. My own copying needs are modest, especially since I invested in a laser printer and fax machine. Still, I do have some copying requirements, and going out to find a local copy shop, as I once did, is wasteful of my time when I can own a copier for so small an investment. I therefore keep a small, tabletop copier, a Ricoh model LR-1, in my office. It uses a cartridge, as do many late-model copiers and computer printers of the laser type. (Laser printers use copier technology—xerography—for printing.) The copier cost me only $400, but the cartridges cost $79.95 each. I bought an extra one with the machine, so that I would have a spare ready when needed. The two cartridges represented 40 percent of the cost of the entire machine, and I was not entirely happy about that. (It is reminiscent of the saga of the safety razor, in which inventor King Gillette found himself forced to first give the razors away to create a market for the special razor blades he had invented and which he now manufactured.)

Despite what I consider a modest copying requirement, I was quite surprised at how fast I went through 1,500 sheets of paper and acetates for transparencies with my little Ricoh copier, exhausting the cartridge and its toner. Almost before I knew it, I had to use the spare cartridge. I then went to the local Montgomery Ward store most reluctantly, expecting to pay the list price, $79.95, for a new cartridge. (I had called my office-supplies wholesaler and found no better a price than this offered. Montgomery Ward's store was closer to me, and so I went there to buy another spare cartridge.) To my pleasure and surprise, I encountered an unannounced sale: The store was selling the cartridges for $49.95. I hastened to buy four, rather than one. I now check frequently with the store to find out whether the cartridges are on sale. (It appears always to be an unannounced sale, or perhaps it is a perpetual sale price; I have never found the sale listed in the store's normal sales advertisements.) Whenever the department manager says, yes, the cartridges are on sale, which appears to be whenever I check, I buy enough to restore my inventory to four spare cartridges. I have never paid $79.95 for a cartridge since I bought the original ones. This was a strange case, where the retailer offered a better price than the wholesaler does, but it is not unprecedented serendipity to stumble across such situations: There are frequent cases where retailers have made deals and can sell items below the normal wholesale price.

Laser Printer Expenses.

Laser printers use dry ink—toner—in cartridges that are quite similar to those used in copiers, although they use a different kind of toner. These cartridges are also quite expensive, and in my case I will replace printer cartridges more often than I will replace copier cartridges. (My printer is in use almost continuously, although my copying needs are intermittent.) The cartridge for my laser printer is listed at $95, but my main supplier (who supplies me via mail and other shipping services) sells the cartridge at under $68 single and under $64 in lots of three each.

You Can do Even Better.

Cartridges of this type are rechargeable—i.e., toner can be added—but it takes special knowledge and skill to do it. There are an increasing number of shops specializing in recharging copier and laser printer cartridges with new toner, and some shops even disassemble the spent cartridge and replace internal parts that are worn, "remanufacturing" the cartridge. This is done at about one-half the cost of a new cartridge. Even for the copier cartridges that I buy at such a great reduction this represents a substantial saving.

Printers and Copiers Use Paper.

If you have a dot matrix or daisy wheel printer, you almost surely use tractor paper. That is paper that has sprocket holes along both vertical edges, is fanfolded in a continuous strip for automatic feeding through the printer, and is laser-perforated so that the pages can be easily separated and the sprocket-holed strips removed, leaving clean-edged sheets of normal size. If you use a laser printer, however, you use individual cut sheets that the machine feeds automatically, as a copier does. (You can, in fact, use standard-size single sheets for both machines, and you can also use letterheads or other special paper.)

A case of tractor paper is most often 2500 or 2600 sheets, although smaller and larger case sizes are available. The case size for cut sheets is invariably 5,000 sheets, ream-wrapped: the case contains 10 reams of paper, each ream (500 sheets) wrapped in an individual package. It is usually possible to buy both kinds of paper at wholesale prices by the case, although some suppliers might offer a slight additional reduction for a larger lot.

I have always bought my paper by the case. Originally, I bought tractor paper in cases as large as 3200 sheets, and initially I bought it from my regular mail-order supplier at what I then thought was a good price. However, I later found a local wholesale source offering a better price than the mail-order supplier, saving me almost 40 percent. Subsequently, I found an even better supplier, a warehouse club where I save an additional 22 percent. (Warehouse clubs cater to the individual and the small business, selling merchandise in cases and large sizes for the most part.) Eventually, I was paying less than one-half the price I originally paid for tractor paper. All this by constantly searching for better sources, never assuming that I had already found the best source. Since I retired my old dot matrix printer in favor of a laser printer, I buy only cut paper, which I can use in both copier and printer, and get that at nearly one-third less than the cost of tractor paper, an additional saving.

Printer Ribbons.

The situation with regard to ribbons for dot matrix and daisywheel printers is somewhat analogous to that of toner cartridges and paper. These types of computer printers, which are in quite common use everywhere, use ribbons that are similar to the ribbons used in typewriters. The daisy wheel printers and a few of the dot matrix printers can use the one-time carbon film ribbons, but most use nylon fabric ribbons impregnated with ink. These cost as much as $15-$18 each, purchased from the OEM (original equipment manufacturer). However, there are many sources for ribbons of equivalent quality and dimensions for most popular printers, and it is usually possible to buy these for as little as $3.75 each. As in the case of toner cartridges, there are shops who will re-ink these ribbons for about $2 each. (A similar situation exists for carbon film ribbons, which come in cassettes and cost $5-8 new, but can be refilled for about one-half the price.) It is also possible to buy an inexpensive machine ($40 to $75) to re-ink your own ribbons, at a cost of about five cents each. Most ribbons can be re-inked many times before they must be discarded.

Other Computer Supplies.

Desktop computers use 5.25-inch floppy disks and smaller disks of 3.5-inch size, and both are, for today's computers, available in DSDD (double sided, double density) and DSHD (double sided, high density) formats. The costs of disks have followed the pattern of computers and related equipment generally; they started high and came down steadily with volume. But some are still relatively expensive within their markets and savings are possible.

Saving Money by Buying Generic Brands.

Few people are conscious of the major manufacturers of paper, rubber bands, file folders, sealing tape, or business cards. As far as they know and believe, all brands are equivalent in all but price, so why not seek out the supplies available at the lowest costs? On the other hand, most consumers are highly conscious of the names of manufacturers of equipment who also sell supplies needed for the operation of their equipment, such as computer disks. Thus "brand names," the common term for well advertised brands, almost always cost more than a similar product with a label few people recognize as a familiar brand. The payoff of advertising is, for a great many products, greater faith in the product whose name is recognized and a corresponding willingness to pay more for the product. However, there is almost always an alternative to the name brand, a "generic" or "private" label that is purportedly equivalent to the name brand in utility and quality, while costing much less.

There is controversy over brand names and quality in all merchandise where consumers have become brand name conscious. Printer ribbons were one case cited. The market in computer disks is another typical case. There are users who will buy only the most prominent brands, packaged neatly in cardboard containers, usually in units of 10 disks each, at prices that are relatively modest when compared with early prices. But they are high when compared with the price of generic disks bought in bulk, usually in minimum quantities of 25, for the 3.5-inch disks, and more for the larger floppy disk. The cost differential is quite great, as much as 3:1. The quality differential is moot. My own experience and opinion are that there is no substantial difference, not even when one buys the alleged "premium" brands. If there is a greater risk of disk failure with the generic brands, it is too slight to be justify the much higher prices of the widely advertised brands.

But my attitude stems largely from my personal experience in which I became well aware of the practices of manufacturers in doing business with each other. For one thing, they sell to each other in bulk, and they will also label part of their product with "private" labels or other manufacturer's labels. For example, name brand disk manufacturer X finds himself short of 3.5-inch DSHD disks because of a surge in orders, which he is unable to fill. He therefore orders 25,000 disks from name brand manufacturer Y, having them labeled with his own X-brand labels. Too, there are sellers of disks who do not manufacture them at all, but buy from manufacturers who supply many others with all their disks, labeling them as requested by the buyers. (These are common practices in virtually all industries.) So it is difficult, if not impossible, for you to know who actually manufactured the disk or, for that matter, any other product you buy. The imprinted brand name thus may or may not have significance as to its source. And, finally, there is the surplus problem of the manufacturer who has been unable to sell all of the latest production at the regular price and is unwilling to compromise future sales by cutting his price. To unload the surplus, the manufacturer will sell them at a greatly reduced price, unlabeled, as a generic product. And so that unlabeled item may very well be the same item that normally bears a prestigious label and is sold at the top price.

13.

CUTTING COSTS IN CREATING PRINTED MATERIALS

This, Too, Is Increasingly a Do-It-Yourself Activity.

All businesses use a great deal of printed material. We all use marketing materials, for example— brochures, transparencies, sales letters, business cards, models, samples, and dozens of other items to help find customers and close sales. Most of these are consumable—e.g., printed materials—and so are items we purchase regularly and in quantity. Controlling waste in marketing and minimizing the expense is discussed later (Chapter 5) and saving money on printing costs per se is also discussed later (Chapter 6). But there are a few related overhead items that should be discussed here. One of them is the cost of generating marketing material for the printer—i.e., the creative processes of writing, illustrating, composing, and preparing the copy for the printer. This is a cost that may rival the cost of production processes, the costs of going from copy to brochures, catalogs, specification sheets, and all the other materials normally used in marketing and sales. Only a few years ago we still contracted with professionals for all of this, and anything we did in-house was cheap and dirty—a simple sales letter or improvised brochure, run up quickly by typewriter and printed in small quantity. If it had to be formally typeset, we sent it out to a professional typesetter or we had the printer attend to typesetting. (He might have in-house typesetting, or he might send it out to a typesetter.)

That has all changed in just the past few years. Today you can create highly professional marketing materials in your own offices, at least to the point of providing camera-ready copy to your printer. There is scarcely an office today that does not have at least one computer and some modern word processor software or even special desktop publishing (DTP) software. However, most modern word processors can do most of what DTP software can do, at least well enough for most needs. The more upscale word processors—WordPerfect, Word, WordStar—also include such refinements as spelling checkers and thesauruses, and often are packaged with still other programs or subprograms that aid the writer with grammar and maximizing readability. There are also programs of ready-made (model) letters, contracts, and other documents that may be easily adapted to your own needs.

If you have a laser printer (and there are an increasing number of models available today for well under $1,000), you can yourself create camera-ready copy of typeset quality for your printing contractor. If you do not have a laser printer of your own, you can still create the copy on a floppy disk and take it to a vendor letter shop or graphic arts shop and have the camera-ready copy produced there quite inexpensively. (Prices start as low as $1 per page.)

Laser Printers are Printers, not Typewriters.

If you happen to own a laser printer and you need a short run of a simple document—if you need 200 copies of a two-page sales letter or 50 copies of an inventory control form, for example—it is probably more efficient and less costly (certainly much faster, in most cases) to make the run on your own laser printer than to send it out to a print shop.

You don't have to confine this kind of do-it-yourself efficiency to marketing materials. It all works equally well for forms of all kinds, for reports, manuals, catalogs, catalog sheets, specification sheets, proposals, memoranda, bulletins, news releases, user instructions, bids, quotations, newsletters, and almost any other kind of printed paper you are likely to need. In fact, it works well when and if you need a special letterhead or other one-of-a-kind piece of paper.

Ready Made Forms.

Today you can get computer software that offers you a wide variety of ready-made forms, spanning the entire spectrum of forms used most commonly in businesses—call reports, expense vouchers, accounting worksheets, catalog sheets, inventory records, purchase orders, receipts, bid and quotation forms, letterheads, newsletter mastheads, and many others. Usually, there are several versions of each, affording you the opportunity to select the one you prefer. In addition, most of these programs include provisions to modify the forms to suit your own needs and to insert your own names, titles, and other customization.

Make Your Own Transparencies.

If you lecture or make presentations, whether for marketing or for other purposes, you probably make use of an overhead projector and transparencies or "viewgraphs," those 8 x 10-inch plastic sheets with words, charts, and other illustrations that you project onto a large screen for everyone to see. In fact, they are simply copies of your material printed on acetates or other clear plastic sheets. You can make them yourself on a good office copier or even print them directly with a laser printer, but you need larger and bolder text than your typewriter can produce for an effective transparency. You can buy these or have them made up for you in a graphic arts shop, but a laser printer and a good word processor will enable you to create transparencies of adequate quality in your own office. If you want illustrations—drawings, graphs, charts, and the like—for your transparencies or printed materials, there are many computer programs you can buy that will generate such illustrations at a quality level that is quite acceptable for most purposes.

Ready-Made Illustrations.

As in the case of documents and forms, you can get computer software that provides a wide variety of ready-made illustrations, usually referred to as "clip art." (This is also available in printed form.) The DTP programs generally include an assortment of such clip art, but additional assortments are readily available.

The assortment, overall, is extremely wide. It includes seasonal material, material oriented to religious themes, short forms, symbols, common headlines (e.g., "SALE," "FREE," "MANAGER'S SPECIAL," etc.

Figure 3-1 presents a few samples of computer clip art, and Figure 3-2 offers samples of printed clip art that may be pasted up for use in posters, signs, forms, catalogs, newsletters, manuals, or other uses you wish to make of them. To conserve space, these illustrations are shown in a small size, but they are usually available in a variety of sizes. Note that some of the illustrations provide space in which to present textual information.

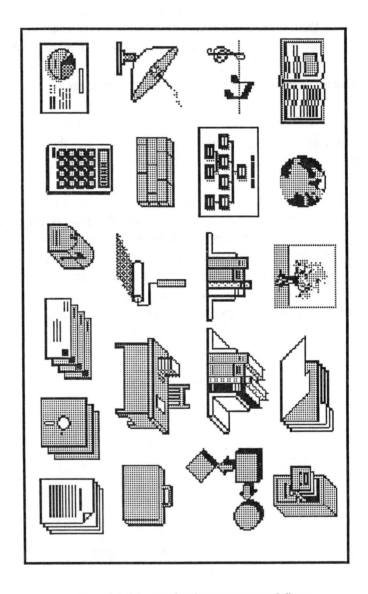

Figure 3-1. A few samples of computer-generated clip art

©COPYRIGHT ART·PAK 1979

FOLIO NO. 290

Figure 3-2. A few samples of printed clip art.

CHAPTER 4

Advertising Costs Can Be Cut

All businesses advertise in one form or another. They must; advertising is as necessary to business generally as are essentials like insurance and telephone service. The forms and media are varied, however, and they change. Once, advertising included as its most prominent methods and media, roadside billboards; signs wherever one could post a sign, including the sides of barns along country roads; newspaper and magazine print ads; catalogs; and circulars. The roadside signs and billboards of local businesses are largely gone today. Most such "signs" and "billboards" that survive are found in the thick volumes of telephone company yellow pages, spawned by the universality of the telephone, but the original roadside signs and billboards have fallen victim to the superhighway system. Radio and TV advertising have more than filled any vacancy created by the changes, and direct marketing methods, dominated by direct mail, have grown quite enormously; in addition, print advertising in periodicals and catalogs has continued and grown over the years. In any case, advertising has grown and is today more essential to business than ever before. It is a rare business of even minor consequence that does no advertising at all.

But everyone has business problems, even those people who sell space and time for advertising use. Their problems are your opportunities, as a buyer of advertising space and time with your *own* set of business problems. When two people with problems put their heads together, it is possible to solve the problems of both, to the benefit of both. A real bargain is always struck only when each party gets what he or she wants and is satisfied. In such truths lie the opportunities to make your advertising dollar work harder.

In this chapter we are going to explore a number of ways to cut advertising costs when using the conventional media for conventional advertising. Later, we will discuss other advertising and promotional methods, such as direct mail and publicity—just two of the many truly low-cost ways of advertising.

14.

GETTING THE BEST BUYS IN TIME AND SPACE

Basis for Rates.

The high cost of advertising discourages many small business owners from doing as much advertising as they would like to—and probably should do—for the sake of their business success. The costs, however, are much less for the cognoscenti than for the uninitiated. There are many ways to slash your advertising costs dramatically, and it is possible to get such bargains often enough to constitute getting them on a more or less regular basis. Bargains in advertising are not merely occasional strokes of good fortune.

The major advertising media today are the periodicals—newspapers and magazines—and the broadcasters—radio and, especially, television. Their rates—which we should really call their *asking* rates, for reasons that will soon become apparent—are based on such factors as circulation (number of readers/-viewers/listeners), size and position of the advertising, amount of advertising space/time bought, and a number of other considerations.

Rate Cards and Discounts.

Publishers and broadcasters have rate cards, on which they present their list or asking prices. More than a few of the small and occasional advertisers no doubt pay the card rates unquestioningly. They do not even suspect that they can almost certainly negotiate much better deals. (Make a vow now that *you* will never pay the card rate again!) Experienced and knowledgeable advertisers practically never pay the card rate; they know you can almost always negotiate a discount of at least 20 percent, and often as much as 50 percent. Like middle-eastern traders, the publishers and broadcasters do not really expect to get those rates, and they are incredulous at their good fortune when they encounter naive buyers who pay those rates and ask for no reduction.

Once in a while you may run into the relatively rare situation where there is a stubborn publisher or broadcaster who offers no discount at all, and insists that no discount deal will be entertained. Don't get discouraged even in that situation. Negotiating a discount is only one of many possible options for saving advertising dollars. Some publishers and broadcasters have the notion that they must never offer a discount from card rates, that it is harmful to their business posture generally. Still, they realize that many advertisers are not going to pay their listed rates, and that they must offer *something* if they are to sell space and time. They therefore invent other kinds of concessions and inducements, and create euphemisms for the discounts they provide that are disguised as other kinds of *quid pro quo* deals. No matter; the trick is to get what you want: advertising space and time at rates you can afford. And there are many ways to do so other than straight discounts from card rates.

Buying Remainder or Remnant Space.

You may have noticed that the thickness of any periodical, newspaper or magazine, varies widely from one issue to another. Today's *Washington Post* was rather slender, for example; I could lift it with one hand. Yesterday's edition required me to use both hands. I nearly threw a new issue of a magazine to which I subscribe into the trash this morning: It was so thin, I thought it was an advertising brochure!

As a general rule, the size of a periodical reflects how much advertising has been sold for the issue. There is some minimum size, however, especially in a magazine, which is printed in "signatures"—a packet of several pages printed together on a single sheet that is later folded, cut, and assembled into individual pages. This makes it rather awkward to have only enough copy for part of a signature; blank pages have to be filled somehow. A book may have a few blank pages at the back when the final signature cannot be filled, but magazine and newspaper publishing tradition forbids that practice in the case of these publishers. (They may use small fillers, such "news" items as "The blue whale is the largest mammal on earth," to fill tiny chinks of white space, but it is impractical to do this for large areas of unused space.) When they must "put the issue to bed," and get ready to go to press, they must do something with that space. They could fill it with standby editorial filler material of appropriate length, such as an article the editor has been saving for emergencies, but it is far better to sell the leftover space for whatever they can get for it. It does not do the bottom line much good to surrender commercial (income-producing) space and use it for editorial material (overhead-consuming space). So if you are a shrewd advertising space buyer who understands the publisher's dilemma, you can negotiate a much-discounted rate to buy some of that leftover space for your advertising.

Understandably, publishers and broadcasters sternly resist admitting that they enter into the kinds of deals mentioned here; they certainly will never advertise the availability or acceptance of such deals. Don't pay attention to their denials when you inquire. Just ignore the protestations, let them know that you know about these deals, and ask them to let you know when they have leftover space. In other words, let them know that they have a dependable resource in you when they are stuck with unsold space. (In that respect, you do them a great favor as an emergency solution to a frequent problem.)

This kind of placement is also referred to by some as "standby" advertising because the advertiser "stands by," as in the airport at a fully-booked flight, hoping for a last-minute cancellation. The difference here is that the advertiser saves a good bit of money by standing by because the space is then treated as a remnant (like those odd-sized pieces of fabric left at the end of a bolt). What's more, the standby is not dismayed if he or she misses this "flight;" he/she is still standing by for all subsequent flights!

Consultant/direct-response marketing expert Gary C. Halbert reports in his newsletter, as reprinted in his book *How to Make Maximum Money in Minimum Time,* that a former employee of his managed to place newspaper advertising consistently at discounts approaching 50 percent of the card rates through this method. He touts her as the best space buyer he knows, based on this. But what she does so successfully you can do also, now that you know the secret.

15.

WANT FREE ADVERTISING?
(THERE IS A SMALL CATCH.)

Entering into Partnerships with Publishers.

What is the best possible advertising deal you can get? How about getting advertising at zero cost? That this is possible is a fairly well kept secret. Nevertheless, you can arrange this as another way to help publishers and broadcasters solve the problem of having leftover space and commercial time, while you help yourself. It can be a profitable let's-make-a-deal time for both of you. (Actually, there is more than one way to arrange this marvelous kind of an advertising deal.)

One of the ways in which publishers (and broadcasters) can put unsold space or air time to good (i.e., profitable) use is by agreeing to a "P.I." or "P.O." deal with an advertiser. The letters stand for Per Inquiry or Per Order. That is an arrangement whereby your advertising gives the publisher's address as the address to which to send orders and payment. You pay nothing for the advertising space or time. You provide the copy, and the other party, publisher or broadcaster, provides the space or time to run the advertising, working on a commission in a kind of partnership deal. He or she collects for each order, keeps a commission, and sends you the rest of the money. You fill the order.

The publisher has not increased his or her risk, and has usually earned income instead of taking a loss; you have made sales at perhaps a lower markup than you might usually get (the commission in these deals is usually greater than the discount offered dealers), but without the costs of investment in advertising—and without risk of any kind.

Publishers and broadcasters prefer that this not become well known for the same reason we saw earlier. If it becomes common knowledge that they often have remnant space and time and will sell space and time at bargain prices, it will injure their sales of space and time at regular rates. So they tend to deny this practice quite firmly when asked. Hubert K. Simon, today a Yonkers, New York businessman, was at one time an independent advertising man struggling mightily to earn a living, as he relates in his little book, *Out of the Rat Race and Into the Chips*. He explains how he turned his personal fortunes around and started himself on the road to prosperity by discovering a number of radio stations that would accept such P.I./P.O. deals, despite fervent denials. That launched him into a project of gathering the names of more stations who would accept such arrangements, and he found a profitable venture in selling the list to many advertising agencies who could put that information to good use.

That it is a good deal for advertisers is undeniable. One enterprising business acquaintance and sometime associate of mine, Hubert Bermont, wrote and published a book about his early adventures as a consultant, and made P.O. deals with several periodical publishers to advertise and sell his book. The book was listed at $25. The periodical publisher kept his share or commission of each order received and sent the rest to Bermont, who filled the order. He managed to sell 65,000 copies of his book in this manner, a quite handsome total for this type of book. (The split varies; usually a minimum of 40 percent goes to the periodical publisher or broadcaster who does the advertising and collects the orders, and in some cases it goes as high as 65 percent to the publisher or broadcaster, but 50 percent is probably the average. Accordingly, the items must be profitable enough to stand up to this arrangement.)

Inquiries Are Leads and Worth Money Too.

Some people use the term P.I. as a synonym for P.O. However, it is really a different term. It is possible to make arrangements with someone who will run your advertisement and receive inquiries—sales leads—rather than orders. You then pay some fixed sum for each lead—perhaps $2 or more. You thus acquire a list of prospects or sales leads to follow up—or additions to your mailing lists, if you prefer to regard the responses as such—and the publisher fills up his pages and earns some money collecting the leads for you. One publication that does this regularly—i.e., once a year—is the Parade magazine section included as a Sunday supplement in many newspapers. Appearing in this publication's annual P.I. listing can produce leads numbering in the thousands.

You can work out these kinds of deals with radio and TV broadcasters, as well. Stay up and listen to or watch some of the late night shows, especially on the small, independent stations. Listen and watch carefully as they sell records, compact disks, potato slicers, automobile wax, and other items. Many of these are P.O. deals, on the same basis as those run with periodical publishers. (Broadcasters are allowed by FCC regulations to use up to one-third of their air time for commercials, and they calculate that they are losing money when they devote much less time than this to income-producing material—i.e., advertising or commercials.) You do have to provide an audio tape or video tape of the commercial, normally, which you can have made outside or by the station. But don't make it yourself; have it made properly by someone well qualified to do a professional job of it. This is one place not recommended for the do-it-yourself approach. Don't be misled by the success of Lee Iaccoca, Frank Perdue, and others as spokesmen for their companies; they were managed in the role by experts. If you want to do it yourself—be your own spokesman or spokeswoman—do it only with the help of qualified experts.

Having it Both Ways.

You do give up some of your profits when you make a P.O. deal with a publisher or broadcaster, because the commissions take a large percentage of the income. Some shrewd advertisers have used P.O. deals only to test their products and advertising material at minimal risk. When they find an advertisement successful, they switch from P.O. deals to regular, full-paid advertisements and keep the entire sale for themselves. This is a brilliant method of testing your advertising without risking your own capital.

16.

HELP IF NEEDED AND GUARANTEES

Help If Needed.

When you can't negotiate a deal for either remnant space or P.I./P.O. deals, you can often manage to negotiate an H.I.N. or Help If Needed deal. In this arrangement, you pay for the space or time you order, but if your advertisement or commercial does not pull enough orders to make the campaign worthwhile, the publisher or broadcaster will run your copy again without charge. Obviously, the publisher or broadcaster will make this deal only with someone they believe they can trust; they have no way of knowing whether you made or lost money on the advertisement other than by your declaration. If the advertisement paid off, however, you will want to continue running it. This can cause a problem for you if you have not been honest in your H.I.N. contract: You would hardly want to continue your advertising if it had not paid off in the first place, so a lie would be revealed. It is in all respects very much against your interest to be dishonest with trusting publishers and broadcasters who agree to these guarantee deals. You need them as much as they need you, and once you establish a good relationship with publishers and broadcasters they become valuable business assets. It is foolish to lose this asset. Aside from morality, it makes good business sense to be honest with these people.

The Guaranteed Advertising Result.

The H.I.N. has a variant, a guarantee of advertising effectiveness. The publisher or broadcaster who won't go for one of the other deals may be willing to give you a guarantee of pulling some minimum number of orders. Under this kind of agreement, if your advertisement or commercial does not pull the number of orders agreed on, your copy will be run repeatedly without further cost until you get the agreed upon number of sales. Again, this depends on mutual trust between you and the publisher or broadcaster. The same caveats apply as in the case of the H.I.N. deals.

17.

THE BULK-BUYING PLAN

Buying Space or Time from Bulk Buyers.

There are some individuals who buy advertising space or time in bulk—that is, they contract for some minimum amount of space or time (usually because they can get special rates or extra-large discounts with guarantees of amounts of space or time) and they then sell portions of that space or time to others, usually those who can afford only small amounts of space and want to spend very little advertising money. Dottie Walters of Glendora, California—today a sought-after speaker, publisher, and entrepreneur—explains how she started in business years ago in just this manner. She bought space in a local newspaper for a shoppers column and then sold little blocks of the column to local business owners, taking a profit on each such sale. Instinctively, unknowingly, and by native wisdom she was doing what some rather large operators thought was a brilliant idea of their own. Perhaps she unwittingly invented the concept!

Must You Wait Until You Can Find a Bulk Buyer?
You may or may not find it easy to seek out a bulk buyer with excess space/time to sell. (The sales office of the publisher or broad-

caster may or may not be able to suggest someone, for example.) That suggests a need for another approach to buying advertising space/time, analogous to ideas we discussed with regard to renting office or plant space. Why wait until you can find a bulk buyer with whom you can deal? Why not be the bulk buyer yourself or set up a syndicate to buy in bulk?

Both are entirely viable ideas. If you want to get the advantages of free or nearly free advertising and full markup on what you sell, it is possible to do so. You will have to contract for a fairly large block of space or time, large enough to get the absolute rock bottom rates, and you will also have to find enough buyers for portions of your space so that you can sell all that you do not need or want for yourself, doing so at rates that ensure your own space/time will be free! Yes, it is possible to do this if you are willing to invest the time and effort. The work is required to set the deal up initially. After that it requires little energy to keep it going week after week or month after month.

CHAPTER 5

Controlling The High Cost Of Marketing

Marketing is critical to the success of any enterprise, even to that of non-profit organizations, for even they market—for members, for votes, for contributions, for whatever support is needed to carry out the main missions of the organization and ensure its survival. But marketing is always especially critical for profit-seeking organizations. It is the chief reason for their existence and the chief tool for their survival.

Marketing is costly, usually the most costly of all business operations. It entails advertising, direct-mail, trade shows, public relations, conventions, literature development and distribution, sales activities of all kinds, and even other functions and elements necessary to produce sales and generate income.

The fact that marketing is absolutely necessary—an indispensable activity of business—does not mean that it must not or cannot be as carefully cost controlled as other business activities. Even in marketing one cannot afford to waste money except at peril to profits. Yet, in most organizations, whether large or small, too much of the marketing dollar is wasted. In this chapter we'll have a look at some ways to control marketing costs and minimize waste in making sales.

18.

FIND OUT WHAT YOUR ADVERTISING DOLLAR IS BUYING

Don't Shoot Yourself in the Foot.

Marketing—making sales and, especially, making customers—is the heart of all businesses, the prime objective: Without it, the business is doomed. That doesn't mean that marketing costs should not be controlled and cut when there is waste, but it does mean that you must be sure you cut waste and not productivity. To do this, you need some means for discovering which part of your advertising dollar is wasted and which produces sales, customers, and profits. You cannot afford to be like that legendary (and anonymous) executive who said he knew that one-half of his advertising dollar was wasted, but he didn't know which half. You must identify the wasted one-half and eliminate it from your advertising budget.

Measuring and Validating Results.

You can guess all you want, but you can't know how well your advertising works without validating it, without measuring results that are directly attributable to specific marketing effort. How you do this, matching your marketing effort with sales resulting directly from the effort, varies with the nature of the business and the means of sales promotion.

Recognize first of all the relationship of kinds of business with kinds of sales promotions. Wholesalers do not advertise in daily newspapers, corner groceries do not market by mail, and automobile dealers don't hand out samples on street corners. Obvious? Perhaps these few examples are, but there are many cases where the mismatch of type of business with type of marketing is less obvious and thus overlooked. Validation is therefore inevitably and unavoidably different in different cases, and more of a problem in some businesses than in others.

Mail order and direct-mail promotions are relatively easy to validate: you can code or key promotions so that you can tie each sale to the tactic or program that produced the sale. Retail store sales are much more difficult to validate, and big-ticket sales even more so. However, with a bit of imagination and resourcefulness, it is usually possible to do at least some validation of even these to reduce the waste and eliminate advertising and promotions that do not produce good results. If you can't find a way to validate marketing results of some promotion, consider the practical alternative of assuming that the promotion ought to be dropped—guilty until proven innocent. Harsh but necessary; this is the nature of business.

The most basic methods for validating a marketing promotion are keying and testing. That is, you key or code your advertising in such a way that it is possible to identify each sale that results from that advertising. It can be used to measure the effectiveness of the offer, the copy, and the medium. (You need to know all three.)

Testing Mail Order Advertising.

Experienced mail order firms test their advertisements by varying their offers and/or copy, keying each version to see which version brings the best results—and note that I said *best*, not *greatest*. Suppose one advertisement brings in 1,000 orders at $10 each with a gross profit of $2,000, and another brings in 800 orders at $12 each, with a gross profit of $3,200. Obviously it is better to sell 800 items at a $4 gross profit on each than 1,000 at a $2 gross profit on each. The problem, however, is determining what factor made the difference. If the copy was identical in each case, it is possible that the $12 price had more appeal than the $10 price. But if the advertisements were in different newspapers or magazines, it is possible that the medium made the difference. Testing is necessary to determine which is the cause. And testing is done by first keying each advertisement so that it is possible to identify the advertisement to which the customer responded.

There are many ways to key an advertisement. One popular one is to add a "department number" to the address—e.g., "Dept LHJ1." Every order coming in so addressed resulted from your first advertisement in the *Ladies Home Journal*. Thus you identify the advertisement and the medium.

Using Split Runs.
You can test the $10 price against the $12 price by using a "split run." That option is available to you in many newspapers and other periodicals. It consists of placing two versions of your advertisement, each suitably keyed for identification, and each run in one half the number of the same edition or issue of the periodical. That comes as close as you can to keeping all conditions and influences equal except price, and offers an objective and probably reliable measure of the relative appeal of each price.

You can do that with parallel tests in other media, keying your copy each time to see whether you get similar results with other periodicals. You can also test the pulling power of each periodical in this way.

Measuring Advertising Results.
Figure 4-1 illustrates one method for tracking advertisements placed in periodicals, comparing results from one periodical to another.

Key	Periodical	Issue	Cost ($)	No. Orders	Sales ($)
Dept A	People's Journal	1/90	950	164	3,435
Dept B	Income Enhancement	2/90	1,457	91	1,650
Dept C	Popular Hobbies	2/90	3,750	365	4,872
Dept D	Money Making Monthly	3/90	2,055	266	3,967
Dept E	Star MO Journal	3/90	857	91	1,999
Dept F	Farm Journal	4/90	654	87	1,505

Figure 4-1. Record tracking advertising-media effectiveness

Testing Direct Mail Promotions.

Direct mail is similar to mail order except that the solicitation is made by mailing sales literature and/or catalogs to a list of names and addresses.

In direct mail, many assume immediately that if your mailing is not successful, the cause is the mailing list. Don't be too quick to leap to that assumption. Test. You can divide a given mailing list into halves to make the equivalent of a split-run advertisement by mailing two different offers—e.g., two prices—to the two halves. Test price, test copy, test mailing lists. But in all testing, be sure that you vary *only one item at a time*, from one test to another, or you will never be sure what change made a difference. Again, measure total result, not rate of response or number of orders. Some direct mail mavens (self-styled mavens, too often) will assure you that you must get a 3-5 percent response to a mailing to make it pay. Some renters of mailing lists will assure you that their lists produce 10-12 percent response (almost surely a false claim). But the rate of response is not the significant factor; total profit—return on investment or return on equity (to use a more recently popular measure)—is. I personally did very well with a one to one and one-half percent response in one campaign, and barely recovered costs in one that produced a return of nearly 6 percent in number of orders.

Figure 4-2 illustrates how a form may be prepared to compare mailing lists with each other, for they have many different characteristics, and these must be taken into account in evaluating them.

	LIST NAME, TYPE, OR OTHER ID			
SPECIFICATION ITEM	LIST A	LIST B	LIST C	LIST D
Size of list				
Cost per 1,000				
Buyers or inquirers?				
MO buyers?				
Type of items bought				
If buyers, size of sale				
Recency of sales/inquiries				

Figure 4-2. Form for evaluation of mailing lists

Testing Retail Store Advertising.

It is more difficult to test your advertising for specific results if you operate a walk-in retail establishment—a store. Obviously, a great deal of the business you do every day in any retail store would occur whether you advertised or not, simply as result of established customers, passerby happening in, attracted to your store, or other imponderables. However, consider just what you are trying to accomplish with your advertising. On the one hand, you are trying to bring people in to buy certain, specific items or lines of items (e.g., cosmetics, glassware, appliances) that you wish to feature for one reason or another. However, much store advertising, especially of loss leaders, is done to create traffic—bring people into the store—knowing that once in the store, many will buy other items. It is possible to key even these advertisements in a way that enables you to link them with the sales made of the items advertised. That is, you can determine what brought the buyers of your special advertising into the store even if you cannot validate other purchases made by these patrons.

One way to do this is to print a coupon with your advertising that enables the buyer of an advertised item to a special discount or free gift of some sort. Only those responding to the advertisement will have and present the coupons. If you are advertising via radio or TV, you can issue a "secret" word that the buyer can utter to get the special discount or gift.

If you are offering a loss leader, make the special sale price or gift item conditional on some such key or control device so that you can be sure that it was that item that brought the customer into the store. Of course, you can test various media, as in mail order and direct mail, to find the offers and media that produce the best results for you.

Testing Telephone Responses.

If you are running a marketing promotion based on having customers call in their orders, you will want to be able to discriminate between the telephone orders resulting from your special promotion and those that would have come in anyway, during the normal course of doing business. One way of keying this kind of promotion is to instruct the respondent to ask for some specific individual or department—"Mrs. Parker" or the "Special Sales Department."

19.

DATABASE MARKETING

The ubiquitous computer and its accompanying technology have had an enormous impact on direct marketing. The mailing list has long been a chief tool of the huge direct marketing industry. Success for direct mail campaigns depended on the right mailing lists, carefully chosen and lovingly nurtured. Now the mailing list, even with detailed demographic indicators and classifications, is becoming a dinosaur, rapidly losing ground to the database. A mailing list contains only name and address information about individuals, although general information—e.g., demographic data—about all on the list is known. A database is a file with individual information about those listed, beyond names and addresses, describing data useful for marketing purposes. In this age of computers and sophisticated software, marketing to large groups defined by mailing lists and demographics—by income, interests, profession, residence, and other group factors—is rapidly becoming passe.

It is still easy to select a list of home owners, engineers, bank presidents, individuals who earned over $70,000 a year, people who had bought books by mail or spent at least $100 by mail in the past year, or people categorized in any number of similar ways. But that has become a primitive approach to marketing. We now use *databases* to target customers and to drive marketing strategies and techniques. With these tools we can communicate with and market to *individuals*, to their known needs, wants, and characteristics, targeting markets with precise rifle shots instead of barrages of scattergun shots. The new way is called *database marketing*.

What is the difference between mailing lists and databases? It is in the much greater information about each individual on the list and in the ability to utilize the list in ways never before possible. Mailing lists have long been classified by certain data, but databases can classify individuals by buying habits and preferences. Armed with this kind of detailed information and with the physical preparation and distribution of direct marketing literature in the "hands" of computers, it is no longer necessary to target everyone on the list with the same packet of sales literature. The computer and database make it possible to break the database down into multiple lists and multiple variations of the basic packet of sales data, each geared to the smaller list. It all but approaches customizing the sales literature to the individual (and perhaps will one day do so).

The split run of newspapers and other periodicals is likewise beginning to be extrapolated into multiple runs. Today, some publishers are beginning to accept advertising that will be included in some but not all copies of their publication that go out to subscribers. An advertisement of a product intended for and useful only to retirees, for example, will be inserted into only those copies going to subscribers who are retired. The computers will search the database and select those subscribers. Some are also using this technology to print the subscriber's name and address on the cover. (Actually, that appears to be a necessity to make the system work more efficiently.)

Of course, this greatly increases advertising efficiency. It will save you money, since you target your audience and pay for the space in only those copies going out to the subscribers of the characteristics you prescribe.

20.

YELLOW PAGES ADVERTISING

Directory Adverting Works for Some—but Not for All.

It is not easy to validate Yellow Pages advertising because testing is impractical. (When you advertise in those pages, you are committed for the full year.) However, you can do some analysis and exercise some judgment before making the commitment. Aside from the question of validating your advertising, however, is the wisdom of using this medium for your business in the first place. The telephone company's yellow pages and similar directories are an excellent, low-cost advertising medium for many businesses, but a total misuse of the advertising budget for others.

A great deal of money is wasted every year in Yellow Pages advertising because advertisers have a great misconception about who reads and acts on such advertising as well as when and why they do so. Here, to illustrate that point, are citations of several advertisers selected at random from a Yellow Pages directory:

    a) 24 hour emergency service (plumbing)
    b) Portable chemical toilets
    c) Camper supplies
    d) Welding service

e) Consulting services
f) House siding
g) Wholesale food distributor (for restaurants, clubs, etc)
h) Mechanical contractors
i) Memorials

Advertisements a) and c) have a good chance of paying out. It is likely that people will turn to the Yellow Pages when they need such supplies or services. Items b), d), and h) have only a fair chance of paying out because these items and services are not often used by individuals, and because industrial users—building contractors, for example—do not often turn to the Yellow Pages to find suppliers and subcontractors. Likewise, restaurants, clubs, and similar institutions rarely seek out their suppliers in the Yellow Pages. People usually buy siding from a well-known department store such as Sears or Ward, or from salespeople who make personal calls on them; they rarely turn to the Yellow Pages for this. Similarly, they usually find someone to make memorials and grave markers through their religious institutions and other organizations, not through Yellow Pages advertising. And experience reveals clearly that few consulting or other professional services other than medical and legal services are sought out via the Yellow Pages.

Yellow Pages advertising is valuable for those businesses that lend themselves to it. It is useful for those who sell primarily to the individual consumer who is making a small-ticket purchase and looking for a local source. It is a resource people consult when looking for many small services, such as lawn mowing, hair dressing, dry cleaning, copying, printing wedding invitations, or other services for which they have only an occasional or unanticipated need. It is a much-used reference by those encountering emergencies in which they need rescuers, such as plumbers or electricians. For many other businesses—those selling to the large organizations and those doing most of their business under contracts won competitively—this kind of advertising is only "institutional." It may contribute to the general image and visibility of the organization, but does little in generating sales directly. Consider carefully whether such advertising is for you before you commit yourself to a fixed monthly expense for it.

There are other directories published that you may use for advertising, although they are far less prominent and less frequently used by the general public. The same principles apply to these: Such advertising can be useful, but only if it is right for your circumstances. Otherwise it is total waste.

21.

PHYSICAL DISTRIBUTION OF SALES LITERATURE

The ancient practice of distributing handbills and circulars by placing them under doors and windshield wipers and handing them out on street corners is not yet dead. It is still widely practiced, and still an effective and inexpensive way to get your sales message across to prospects. It is also quite easy to validate, using the methods described earlier. Physical distribution is normally an inexpensive marketing method, and it can be used as a normal marketing method or as a special way to test your approaches, your offers, your prices, and your sales messages—if you can reach representative prospects this way. You can even classify and stratify your target population to a large extent by choosing the neighborhoods and the methods. Slipping the circulars under doors is distributing by neighborhood, for example; you can choose the types of neighborhoods you want. As another example, you can choose supermarket shoppers by placing the circulars or cards under windshield wipers on supermarket parking lots, or by handing the circulars out to customers leaving the supermarket. You can address the renters of the offices in given office buildings by distributing handbills to the offices on all the floors of the building.

Some advertisers distribute sales literature to the general public via direct mail, using the postal carrier as the delivery man or woman. You can arrange to have the Postal Service deliver your literature to each patron on its routes or on any routes you wish to cover. Consult with your local postmaster to get the details of how to arrange this. An alternative is to mail to each address. Most mailing-list brokers and local mailers can furnish a list of "residents," usually divided by zip codes.

You can monitor and test these distributions as you do direct-mail campaigns: Key the copy in some manner that enables you to identify business resulting from it, and you will have some basis for deciding which mode of distribution is most profitable.

22.

OTHER MARKETING METHODS

The Nature of Your Business Dictates Your Marketing Methods.

Despite the restrictions of some of the built-in mandates of your business, you have choices of methods for bringing your goods or services to the marketplace. For many, there is the problem of resisting the tendency to do what others are doing or what "they" all say is the right way to do things—the traditional methods. It takes courage to defy conventional wisdom and try new ideas. The first marketer to offer customers an unconditional money-back guarantee was denounced by his competitors, who predicted early bankruptcy for him. Before long, however, they all found themselves compelled to offer that same money-back guarantee conceived and pioneered by Montgomery Ward. There are many roads to the marketplace, and new ones are being blazed constantly.

Sales Personnel versus Sales Representatives/Dealers/Agents.

If your business is such that you decide that you must have sales personnel—true, professional salespeople calling on customers—you must decide which of several options you should choose to get such sales representation—i.e., which will give you the best result per dollar invested. There are probably more options than you suspect, at least the following:

a) Salaried employees, with or without commissions or "overrides."
b) Independent sales representatives or agents, on commission or discount.
c) Independent dealers, on discount or wholesale prices.
d) Brokers, also on discount or on wholesale prices.
e) Specialists, such as "finders."

In most cases, if you opt for employees, they must be salaried, even if the salary is small (dictated by minimum-wage laws, in most cases), with the main compensation a commission of some sort. Moreover, you must provide a few benefits for employees, including some paid time off, insurance, and probably a few other marginal or fringe benefits. In addition, you undertake tax liabilities for every individual on your payroll. On the upside, you do have more control over direct employees than over salespeople utilized under other plans.

Independent sales representatives (you may hear them referred to more familiarly as "sales reps") generally work on commissions. They usually work "out of their hats"—in other words, they have no need for a place of business because they spend the entire business day calling on customers, and they carry no inventory, simply placing orders for you to ship. While some may represent a single supplier, many represent several suppliers of related but noncompetitive items.

A dealer generally has a place of business where he or she displays merchandise, yours and others', and sells at retail. Dealers usually carry a bit of stock—an inventory—to fill orders directly. (However, there are also catalog stores, dealers who carry little or no inventory.)

A broker is probably closer to a rep than to a dealer. The broker is a special kind of "middleman," acting as the marketing agent or marketing department for a supplier—for you, perhaps. Most mailing lists offered for rent to those in direct mail are customer lists generated by publishers, mail order houses, and others, but are marketed by brokers who prepare them for renting and rent them at a 20-percent commission. Printing brokers, on the other hand, work differently and probably more independently, bidding on printing jobs and then finding printers who will give them a large enough discount to earn a decent profit.

The wise move here, if you are undecided, is to try each method that is applicable to your own business and see for yourself which one produces the best results for each dollar invested. Perhaps it is traditional in your industry to sell to customers through door-to-door salespeople. But maybe you can do as well by wholesaling to dealers. Or maybe your merchandise will sell just as well by mail order or direct mail. Perhaps yours should be converted to a catalog sales business. Or maybe you ought to consider a warehouse/discount sales operation and do away with the expense of salespeople and expensive locations. Which is best? Why not try a number of steps and compare results overall to find out which is best?

23.

SPECIAL MARKETING METHODS AND PROMOTIONS

Piggyback Marketing.

There are many special ways to market whatever you sell "on the back" of other, larger promotions.

You can set up a booth and exhibit at trade fairs that are relevant to what you sell. You can participate in conventions held by associations in your industry. (These usually have exhibit halls that are actually miniature trade fairs, but many entrepreneurs rent special rooms in the convention hall or hotel as "hospitality suites" at which they entertain prospects and collect leads for future sales.) You can participate in special sales—e.g., flea markets—on weekends in shopping malls.

Wagon Jobbing and Flea Markets.

Many small businesses are operated from a vehicle, a small truck fitted out as a mobile store and either calling on prospects—for example, the seller of tools calling on garage mechanics—or parking the vehicle at flea markets, farmers markets, and similar locations, doing business from the truck. This is a diverse and relatively new field.

As a closely related alternative, you can rent a booth or table space at these events, which are held in open fields, but are also held both indoors in malls and outside on the grounds (parking lots) of malls and shopping centers. There are many small businesses that operate only on weekends and always at these kinds of events, moving about on a circuit similar to those of the early days of vaudeville. They deal in merchandise that they can pack into a van or truck, of course, and travel constantly.

24.

PARTY SALES

The Private Home as a Place of Business.

Many items are marketed effectively by party sales: sales held in private homes and apartments. Clothing, appliances, diet plans, and many other items have been sold in this manner. Sale of "club aluminum" pots and pans was one of the earliest manifestations of this marketing method, and is still widely practiced. Among the many who have employed this idea for small-investment and relatively risk-free marketing have been the well known Tupperware firm and numerous prominent sellers of cosmetics and lingerie. (The approach generally has more appeal to women than to men.)

You can hire people who are experienced in selling this way, and who know how to arrange to recruit hosts and hostesses for such parties. These are pure commission arrangements; financial risk is therefore minimal. The hostess in whose home the "party" is held is rewarded with a share of the profits, and can earn extra rewards by helping the seller find hostesses for additional parties. Finding such hostesses and arranging for additional parties is one of the main goals of the presenter.

25.

SEMINAR SALES

The free seminar is an effective marketing vehicle for many situations. In a sense, it is a modern version of the more ancient "pitch," often depicted humorously as the rather obvious flack peddling snake oil from a horse-drawn cart in the rough-hewn towns of pioneer days. It is also the descendant of that generation of direct marketers represented so well by the youthful Ed McMahon selling potato peelers on the Atlantic City boardwalk, as he describes it in *Ed McMahon's Superselling* (Prentice-Hall, 1989).

The methodology is simple: You rent a hall, usually a meeting room in a local hotel, and advertise your free seminar in the local newspapers. You get the visitors' names and addresses in one way or another; you can require them to call and register in advance, ask them to sign in on a log, or hand out a form and ask them to fill it out. You then deliver your sales presentation. The Evelyn Wood organization gave attendees a free introductory lesson in speed reading and signed up as many for their regular speed-reading course as possible. The Albert Lowry organization ran free seminars at which an excellent presenter revealed enough about the lure of easy riches in real estate to induce the attendee to sign up for a full weekend training seminar on the subject.

The idea is to offer something that makes attendance at the seminar worth the hour or two, and whets the attendees' appetite for whatever you are selling. You may sign some up on the spot, and can also gather other names and addresses to use as sales leads and/or a mailing list to follow up.

This method may be and is used successfully to sell a variety of physical products—books, cassette sets, cosmetics, and other items as "back of the room sales," following a lecture, which includes a sales presentation. It is a relatively low-cost, low-risk marketing method. It requires a good speaker and sales presenter, of course.

CHAPTER 6

Administrative Overhead: The Enemy Of Profit

The cost of supplies and minor equipment—e.g., staplers and tape dispensers—is a significant category of overhead costs, one we discussed earlier. An even larger portion of overhead cost for many organizations is the cost of administration. This is mostly the routine, everyday services performed by staff and purchased from vendors. It includes such items as accounting, inventory management, telephone service, shipping, delivery, purchasing, recruiting and personnel services, mail handling, and many other functions and duties necessary to administer a business organization. As a business grows, so does its administrative machinery, but often out of proportion and often with a steadily decreasing efficiency. The result: administrative systems begins to become a bureaucracy.

Most administrative costs are for necessary services and functions, of course, and that is why waste often goes unnoticed and unchecked. No one is taking the time to discriminate between the necessary expenditures and the wasteful ones. The following examples will illustrate this.

26.

GETTING DIRECT

Don't Support Overhead.

In the free-wheeling days when the Cold War was at its height (in the mid-fifties, and thereafter for more than a decade), the Department of Defense was frantically paying out billions of dollars on its many notorious "cost plus" contracts. The economics were upside down then: Overhead and all other costs were reimbursed by the government, with little control and even less accountability. Contractors in that topsy-turvy business climate often treated overhead as though it were profit, and in a sense it was: It shielded the organization from loss, a convenient end-of-the-rainbow pot of gold where rescue from mishaps and mismanagement could always be found. Thus managers were urged to "support the overhead"—i.e., keep the overhead as high as possible, because creative accounting made it the most profitable item being billed to the government. Alice in Wonderland rules prevailed.

Such practices are much less common in government now, and are certainly not typical of the more traditional world of business, where overhead is cost, undisguised and unchallenged, and letting it run free is done only at the expense of profit. One cost-conscious vice president of U.S. Industries, Inc. constantly exhorted all of us in executive and managerial positions there to

"Get direct!" That plea, not unheard elsewhere today, means doing work that can be charged directly to—i.e., paid for by—clients and their projects and not charged to nor paid for by your own overhead. That drive to minimize overhead is what makes employers today dole out pencils one by one, insist that employees travel coach or tourist class on business trips, and set up stays in Holiday Inns or bread-and-board hostelries: rather than the luxury hotels. It's also what makes (or should make) your company's comptroller an expert at snapping "No!" as a reflex response to every request for authorizing an overhead expenditure before hearing the argument for it. (Try requesting it as a direct charge to a project and see the difference that makes!)

Make it an inflexible rule: Never charge to overhead anything that can be fairly charged as a direct expense. We have come back from Wonderland, and all is right side up again. Lean overhead is the order of the day. It contributes both directly and indirectly to profits. It makes you more competitive, for one thing. It is not by coincidence that the three biggest retailers, Sears, Wal-Mart, and K Mart, have the three lowest overhead rates in their industry.

27.

CONTROLLING TELEPHONE
COSTS

The Most Common Overhead Escapees.

The days of the nickel telephone call ended a long time ago. But
that isn't the only reason telephone usage is a major business expense today. Another reason is that it is one of the overhead items
that most commonly manages to escape careful control and esca-
late rapidly. There is more than one cause for this, and the entire
situation is more complex than it might appear at first.

Employees Making Personal Toll Calls.

Telephone costs seem to rise as the square of the number of
employees when no limits or restrictions are placed on the use of
the telephones. To reduce this leakage of overhead dollars, either
personal toll calls made by employees must be paid for by the
employee, or the use of the telephone for personal calls must be
restricted. This can be done by fiat or by having the telephone
company install measures to block toll calls from all but selected
offices and telephones. (The telephone company may be able to
suggest other measures and will be glad to discuss them with
you.)

In many companies most of the work is performed under contracts with specific clients. If all toll calls made on such projects are charged to the contract and client the charges will not appear in overhead accounts, but will be direct charges to those projects, as they should be. To do this it is necessary to establish controls, such as a telephone log. Each toll call must then be recorded in the log to ensure that the calls are properly charged. All toll calls that should be charged directly to contracts and clients can then be identified easily and charged properly. It is absolutely necessary, however, to instruct the staff *directly* to do this as a matter of inflexible policy, for they will otherwise tend to the more convenient expedient of not charging the call. It will then wind up in overhead by default.

Eliminating Unnecessary Ongoing Charges.

If the telephone company supplies your telephones, the telephone company probably owns them and rents them to you. In that case, your monthly telephone bills include charges for the use of these. You may find it less costly to buy and own your telephones, as most people do today.

There are many extra services available today and new ones being added frequently, including call waiting, identifying the number of the caller, and others. You may be unknowingly paying for services you neither want nor have use for. Have the telephone company send over a sales representative to go over these things—the WATS line, the 800 number, the modern version of a PBX (private branch exchange), and all other alternatives to "plain vanilla" telephone service—and to advise you on the most efficient system and configuration for your business by giving you the cost figures for each option. Then make your own cost analysis, based on that advice and the facts provided. There is an excellent possibility that you will reduce your basic telephone costs immediately.

28.

OTHER USES OF TELEPHONE LINES

Using Fax Machines.

Almost everything that has been said for voice telephone usage applies equally to fax machine usage. Fax machines use commercial, dial-up telephone lines for their transmissions, as telephones do, and the relevant charges ought likewise be recorded and charged properly on the log. (Most fax machines keep records of transmissions and will print them out on command to help you maintain a record. These should become part of the record overall.)

The Fax Alternative.

Use of fax in place of voice calls should be encouraged wherever fax is a viable option. Fax is almost always more economical in terms of time spent on the line than voice-to-voice calling, and so is more economical in dollars. With fax transmission, for example, there is no time wasted in social greetings, small talk, and waiting for the specific individual being called. The average fax transmission is usually completed within the minimum time charged by the telephone company and long-lines service.

Moreover, a fax transmission often accomplishes its purpose even when the other party is not available, thus avoiding leaving messages, wasting time in discussion, and making follow-up calls. (I much prefer getting and leaving messages on fax machines to getting and leaving them on answering machines. When I leave a message by fax, I know that there is a written record of my call and I have left a complete and detailed message. I need not depend on someone seeing to it that a message is written and delivered to an addressee.)

Computers and Modems.

It's a rare office these days that does not have a personal computer on at least one desk. As a consequence, a quite enormous flow of computer-to-computer traffic has sprung up, conveyed over telephone lines via a device called a *mode*m at each end of each line.

The fax machine is a most efficient way to send brief messages, drawings, and non-verbal information. But when it comes to lengthy transmissions, such as a file of 50 or 100 pages, fax transmission is less efficient than computer transmission.

The fax machine has a modem that converts a printed image to signals carried over a telephone line, and the modem of another fax machine reconverts the signals to a printed image at the other end of the line. The modems used with computers do the same thing with the computer signals, transferring information of many kinds for many uses and purposes. (Many modem transmissions simply could not be done by fax machine or would be impractical by fax.) Lawyers can use their computers and modems to do law library searches conducted by another computer system designed for the purpose, and physicians can ring up the National Library of Medicine in Bethesda, Maryland to search for medical information stored in that computer. Individual users may exchange files or messages too lengthy to be transmitted by fax. For this and many other kinds of uses, the computer-to-computer transfer has special applications that no fax machine can match.

Because of this, if your office is sending many lengthy transmissions by fax, you may find it worthwhile to conduct a little study and consider training someone to transmit computer files. This is likely to save you many dollars in line charges, and perhaps additional money in overnight letter services.

29.

REDUCING PRINTING COSTS

Businesses Need Printing.

To run a business you need many printed items, including letter-heads, envelopes, business cards, forms of many kinds, labels, and brochures. You may also need envelopes in several sizes, memo pads, pamphlets, booklets, specification sheets, catalog sheets, and even full catalogs, among many other printed items.

Basic costs of printing depend on two main factors: the quantity ordered and the type of printing plant. Printing has a much greater economy-of-scale factor than do most business needs: The unit cost descends sharply with quantity. Printing one copy of one page may cost $10; one hundred copies would cost perhaps $12, 1,000 copies $25, and 10,000 copies $100. In other words, there is a definite minimum preparation charge that is relatively high, compared with the cost of paper and running the printing press—"cost per impression" (usually calculated and billed as cost per 1,000 impressions). However, even that varies widely, depending on the type of printing plant.

There are several different types of printers and printing plants, each designed to satisfy certain kinds of needs. To keep printing costs to a minimum, you need to make the right choice when it comes to printers and print shops.

The Local Small Print Shop.

Local copy shops and other small printers use small presses (capable of handling 11 x 17-inch size sheets at most) designed for short-run work—small printing jobs. "Small," in this case, means printing runs of a few hundred to a few thousand copies of ordinary items such as catalog sheets, sales letters, circulars, flyers, and simple brochures or pamphlets. This kind of printing is labor-intensive, using relatively inexpensive small presses and other equipment for making plates, folding, binding, cutting, and otherwise processing print jobs with little automation. That makes it the least costly and most practical method for small, short-run printing and the most costly method for large, long-run printing.

The Big Press Printing Plant.

The big printer, operating the long-run shop, will turn away your small print jobs (or at least recommend against using them) with an explanation that they cannot possibly handle such a job at a competitive price. It is never economical to send small jobs to a large printing plant. That is the shop that normally runs many thousands or hundreds of thousands of copies on big presses, which often include the folding and binding operations in one continuous process. Such shops cannot compete with the small print shop for small jobs. The equipment alone imposes a minimum cost that makes short-run work prohibitively expensive. On the other hand, this *is* the right shop for long run printing.

The Specialty Printer.

There are many kinds of printing that require special equipment—printing multi-part, snap-out forms with carbon-paper interleaving, for example. Such work is usually done by a specialty printer, one whose equipment is designed to do such work. That equipment is costly, and specialty printers are usually quite large operations. Thus, unless you require a large quantity of forms, it does not pay to have them made up especially for you. You do, however, have a viable alternative: You can turn to one of the many large printers who turn out various forms in representative styles and designs as standard items available to all. You can have the printer "surprint" a quantity for you. That means you can buy a few hundred or a few thousand copies of a form imprinted with your own name and address at a reasonable cost, whereas it would have been prohibitively expensive to have had the forms made up especially for you. This is usually done by what is called "crash printing." Surprinting your name and address on standardized forms is also a practical and preferred method for getting quality labels, business cards, and high-quality stationery printed for you economically and in short runs. Most of these kinds of printers and their dealers will furnish a catalog of styles from which you may choose your preferred style and format. (Your office-supplies dealer—or even your local copy shop—may be an authorized dealer for one of these kinds of large printing plants and may be able to handle your order also.)

Few local printers print business cards; that is really specialty printing also. They will accept your order, but will usually ask you to wait a couple of weeks for delivery because they themselves have the cards done by large printing houses. The nature of my own business is such that I use up business cards quite slowly. A box of 500 cards lasts me a long time. By the time I need more I have gotten another card or circular from The Stationery House, Inc.®, a Hagerstown, Maryland specialty printer who has for years used direct mail to make an introductory offer of 500 business cards in raised ink on white bristol board for $7.95 (only recently raised to $10.95), a true bargain of which I hastened to take advantage. I have ordered my business cards from that firm for years. (The firm often offers other introductory specials also.) Unfortunately for them, I have no need for most of the other things they offer, but that is the typical risk of all special offers.

Finding a Low-Cost Printer.

Some years ago I moved my office from Washington, DC to my home in a Maryland suburb of the capital. Among the many adjustments I had to make as a result was finding a new local printer for my many almost daily short-run printing jobs. I turned to the Yellow Pages and began to call small print shops who had advertised there. I was shocked immediately to learn that having moved out of a high-cost center-city area, where I had become accustomed to paying a relatively high price for my printing, I found little neighborhood shops in suburbia with even higher prices!

The solution lay in calling the small print shops who had tiny advertisements, often not more than a line of boldface type. It seemed almost a pattern: Those with the largest advertisements had the largest prices! I soon found one with a small advertising notice who gave me excellent work, good service, and reasonable prices. It proved to be an approach well worth trying when I was in quest of other services. I recommend this method as worth trying for satisfying other needs as well.

30.

THE COST OF MONEY

Minimizing Interest Charges.

Even money costs lots of money today. Interest is a major item of cost in contemporary business, and an expensive one at that. It is thus a significant item in your general overhead expense pool, and one most of us must suffer, even if we have not borrowed capital for our primary financing. If you accept credit card charges from your customers, for example, the card issuer—a bank, in the case of Visa and MasterCard—is lending you the money represented by the charge, and you are paying the lender interest on that money. For many years most merchants simply absorbed that interest charge, but with today's high interest rates and slender markups (especially for those merchants offering discounts and highly competitive prices), many merchants add a surcharge of about 2½ to 3 percent on credit card orders to recover at least some of the interest charges they must pay. In addition, many insist on minimum purchases of $5 or $10 when using a credit card. Their rationale is that the profit in a small sale is not great enough to absorb the interest charges and the extra paperwork involved in credit card billing.

31.

LEGAL SERVICES

Reducing Legal Expenses.

You will undoubtedly need legal services now and then; many business problems require the services of an experienced lawyer. However, if you wish to save legal costs, you can handle a great many of the minor legal chores yourself quite easily. Incorporation, for example, is no longer a laborious chore requiring highly specialized knowledge; it is now an easy do-it-yourself matter in most cases.

Incorporating Your Business.

In most states today you can incorporate yourself by filing a simple form, available usually from the state's Secretary of State, and paying a marginal fee, usually about $40 to $50. You can get a seal, standard bylaws and other necessary forms from local suppliers for about another $50 or thereabouts. (Consult the Yellow Pages of the nearest city to find suppliers of corporate seals, bylaws, and other corporate necessities.)

It is not much more complicated to meet the legal requirements for trading under a fictitious or "dba" (doing business as) name than filing for incorporation. Bookstores and libraries offer many volumes of instruction, written by experienced lawyers, on how to do these filings, write contracts, form partnerships, and otherwise meet and satisfy routine legal requirements. Write to the Secretary of State of your own state for information on the State's requirements, but check also with your City Clerk and County Clerk; they may have information on relevant ordinances you should know about.

Other Legal Chores.

Today you can get books of standard legal forms—contracts, leases, collection letters, and other documents—usually written by experienced lawyers. My personal library includes 14 volumes of such guidance written by John Cotton Howell, a retired lawyer, and a well-publicized book on incorporation by Ted Nicholas. In these volumes, the authors offer explanations, how-to instructions, and forms for a wide variety of legal chores.

32.

ACCOUNTING NEEDS

Reducing Accounting Expenses.

It is difficult enough to make up and file your personal tax return these days; many people today turn to specialists to do this for them. But even the hardy individuals who tackle this task for themselves are usually daunted by the task of filing tax returns for their businesses.

It is certainly understandable to want to turn to accountants for this formidable task. However, that need for an accountant to file tax returns for your business does not mean that you must have your accountant handle the rest of your accounting work. It is easy enough to keep books for a small business even with a manual system, and easier still to do so with a small computer. If you have a computer, as most businesses do today, you can quite easily install an inexpensive and relatively simple accounting program that will require you to do no more than to post income and payouts to the right account numbers. The program will do the rest. However, it is not absolutely necessary to use a computer for the task, either. For the small business, a pen and paper system is often quite adequate and quite easy to operate.

The Dome® system is one that I have used, for example. Dome offers more than one system, but the one I have used is a single book that contains all the elements needed for a simple, single-entry system. A page that represents the day journal (called a "log" or "diary" by some accountants) appears opposite a ledger page, and you can post by the month or by the week, as you choose. The book also contains tables and forms for payroll and tax calculations, as well as forms for reports (balance sheets, net worth statements, etc.). There are, of course, other publishers of such systems also, and most well-stocked vendors of office supplies can offer you a choice.

33.

TRAVEL AND RELATED COSTS

Business Travel is Now a Way of Business Life.

Travel and per diem costs are a major item of expense for many businesses today. It is the nature of our world and business systems that constantly we dart about, usually by air. By far the bulk of passenger miles during weekdays are flown by men and women traveling on business. And most such trips entail at least one night's stay in a hotel, plus local travel by taxi or by rented automobile.

These costs should always be charged directly to the clients and projects when possible. Often this is not possible because the travel is on behalf of the organization's own business and not that of a client. There are ways to minimize the costs, however.

Travel plans and reservations should be made as far in advance as possible so that you have the opportunity to choose among all the options and select the one that is most economical. Even if your travel is always by coach, airlines have frequent special discount plans that can save you even more money.

Much the same can be said for hotels. With advance reservations, you have a choice. Without them, you must take what is available at whatever price it costs.

Per Diem Versus Actuals.

You should have a policy for travel expenses other than transportation. You can establish a per diem rate your employees will have to manage with, or you can permit them to charge actual costs for reimbursement. If you choose a per diem rate, you are essential saying you don't care what they spend for food and lodging as long as it is below the level established. If you have them apply for reimbursement of actual expenses, you will have to set limits and monitor expense accounts carefully. In either case, you will have to do what the government was finally forced to do and recognize that some areas of the country are much more expensive than others. Your rates must reflect that. One cannot find acceptable food and lodging in New York City as cheaply as in Pittsburgh or Pocatello.

34.

SUPPLIES AND MISCELLANEOUS COSTS

The Cost of Supplies Can be Cut.

I keep an account open at a local office supplies emporium, and once in a while I stop by there to pick up some minor items, paying the full list prices. However, I have two local wholesale sources for most of my general office supplies, and I can cut my cost for office, shipping, and other supplies virtually in half by turning to these sources. I also keep an account open with a large mail-order supplier and buy some of my items from that source. And, in addition to that, I save some of the mail order catalogs that come in the mail and the huge (about 750 10- x 13-inch pages) catalog-disguised-as-a-magazine, *Computer Shopper,* to which I subscribe. I can usually buy what I need at 25 to 50 percent reductions from list prices from such sources, as I related in Chapter 3.

Miscellaneous Other Direct Costs.

You may encounter many costs, one-time costs in many cases, incurred as part of your cost of sales. ("Cost of sales" includes every direct cost connected with each sale.) If you have a report printed or duplicated for a customer, that is a direct cost, just as telephone calls, fax messages, and express shipments are when incurred as part of a contract. Among the many items that you may encounter as belonging to this category are travel and per diem costs, car rentals, postage, cablegrams, courier services, office copying, special supplies, and printing.

Using as many of these cost-cutting measures as can be applied to your case should make a substantial difference in your overhead rate.

CHAPTER 7

Cutting Shipping
And Related Costs

Shipping costs are a major concern to many businesses. The front-page headline in a recent issue of *DM News*, a bible of the direct marketing industry, reads "New UPS Rate Schedules Called A 'Terrible Blow' To Catalogers," a reaction to an increase in rates by the United Parcel Service. (UPS has applied for a greater increase in their residential rate than in their commercial delivery rate, a change from their single, uniform rate of the past.) Catalogers number in the thousands, and the larger of them—for example, Sears, Spiegel, L.L.Bean, and Land—ship large quantities of merchandise every day. Obviously, shipping costs are a large element in the overall operating costs of their businesses. Of course, mailing—postage—costs are also a large expense item for catalogers, the largest of whom may mail catalogs in the millions every year. But despite the steady movement of parcel shipments away from the Postal Service and toward private industry, many in direct marketing still rely on the Postal Service to ship their parcels, so that that outlet still handles a large volume of parcel mail. Based heavily in direct mail as they are, catalogers and the entire direct-marketing industry look forward only with great trepidation to the impending postal rate increases as another inflationary factor that will have negative business consequences.

Coupled with the steadily growing rate of inflation, these two events alone make it necessary for all of us to give more thought to how we choose and use delivery and shipping services. Ignorance of rates charged by the various common carriers and the factors affecting them alone will cost you money, and carelessness in choosing the optimum service for each case will cost you even more.

That is only one side to this coin. As the widely advertised change of the United States from an industrial economy to a service- and information-based economy proceeds, we "ship" software—information—almost as much as we ship hard products. And often the physical product is relatively unimportant; the information content is the important element. New services—e.g., fax machines and overnight express—have responded to these newer needs, and we need to learn how to utilize these most effectively too. They can be costly, as new devices and new services often are, but used wisely they can also save you money and increase your profits.

35.

REDUCING WASTE IN POSTAGE COSTS

Tips on Using the Mails Economically.

We all use the U.S. mails, at least for ordinary correspondence, although many businesses use the mails on a large scale as a main element in doing business generally. Direct mail is a subset of direct marketing, but it is the mainstay of direct marketing and no business or industry in the United States is more affected by and sensitive to changes in United States Postal Service rates. If your own postage expense amounts to more than an occasional roll of stamps, you ought to know a few basic truths that no USPS employee is going to volunteer (and perhaps does not even know of, in many cases). Let's look at these first.

Being "All You Can be" with First-Class Postage.
A first-class stamp entitles you to send one ounce of mail by the most expeditious surface transportation the USPS uses for first-class mail. One ounce allows for the delivery of five sheets of ordinary 20-pound bond in an ordinary business (number 10) envelope. If you are sending someone a letter that requires only one page, so be it. The USPS benefits here by being paid first-class

postage for handling only one fifth of the weight to which you are entitled. But if you are sending out sales literature, invoices, statements, or other routine business literature, you are probably cheating yourself out of money by not utilizing the full capacity of the first-class postage. If you are sending out sales literature first class, for example, and want to get the maximum benefit of your first-class postage stamp, use both sides of five sheets—10 pages—to present your sales offers and arguments. ("The more you tell, the more you sell" is a marketing truism. Ten pages of sales arguments will normally produce far more orders than will two or three pages.) If you are sending out invoices, statements, or other routine notices, enclose a sales brochure or two to use the full allowance and get the extra sales that result. (Those sales are called "bounceback" orders, and they can be an important part of your business if you take full advantage of the opportunities to win them.) In both cases, if the volume of your first-class mail is great enough, you can take advantage of the extra saving of using a 9-digit zip code and sorting the mail to get an additional saving in postage costs of about 16 percent.

The Fallacy of Air Mail.

Most mail destined to travel more than a few miles is airlifted, even if it does not have an air mail stamp. And most first-class mail traveling only a few hundred miles—from New York to Pittsburgh for instance—arrives as rapidly when sent ordinary first-class mail as when sent with the more expensive air mail stamp. Air mail postage is totally wasted here. In fact, for short lifts, such as Philadelphia to New York, an air mail stamp may even slow the delivery down because with that stamp it *must* travel by air, even if that itself causes a delay! Use air mail postage for long flights only—across the country or to foreign countries—and even then only when speed is urgent. With today's postal service, you can never be sure that air mail will truly speed up delivery. (Mail rarely travels directly to the state and city addressed, in any case, but usually goes to a centralized sorting facility first, one reason deliveries have slowed down generally.)

Using Parcel Post.

There are two popular fallacies about parcel post service. One is that it is cheaper than first-class mail. That is occasionally accurate, but the rule must be qualified: In many situations the cost difference is minuscule; it hardly merits being considered a saving. It pays to check and compare. You may be able to get the better first-class service for virtually the same price. The other fallacy is that parcel post takes forever to arrive. The postal clerk may tell you that it will take up to four weeks, but except for unusual periods, such as during the Christmas rush or during summer vacation periods when the postal service may be a bit shorthanded, parcel post rarely takes much longer than first-class mail. I find that it is sometimes even faster. (I have known first-class mail to take two weeks to travel less than a hundred miles, unfortunately.) And so I ship by parcel post only if swift delivery is not urgently required and there is a significant price difference. Otherwise, I use first-class even for small parcels.

Multiple Parcels to Same Address.

If you are shipping several items to the same customer by USPS and you package them individually, you are probably wasting money, because you are paying a minimum charge on each and because the unit cost declines as the weight increases past certain points. That is, it is usually cheaper to package all the units together. They need not be combined in one container, however. They can be individual parcels that are taped or strapped together with one address label to get the rate for the entire assembly as a single package.

Mailing in Quantity.

If you make large mailings there are additional opportunities to reduce postage costs. You can mail first class at a reduced rate (currently 21 cents with a first-class stamp at 25 cents, as this is written) by using the 9-digit postal code and sorting your mail, bundling it by zip codes. The next step up is bulk mail, which cuts your postage bill roughly by nearly one-half. Then there are various other rates, including second-class mail and a special rate for nonprofit organizations. The U.S. Postal Service has literature explaining these various options and alternatives, and will even send one of their marketing representatives out to consult with you and advise you if you wish.

Charging Postage to the Client.

If you do custom work of any kind, can contract to bill direct expenses to the client, and estimate that there will be significant postage expenses as part of the job, add the postage expense to those "other direct cost" items that will be billed to your client. As in the case of telephone services and other such items, postage is often a direct cost item and should be billed to the client for reimbursement, rather than being absorbed as an indirect cost. Bear in mind that this also applies to fax transmissions, computer-to-computer communication, MCI mail, and other electronic mail services. (Many of us used to "absorb" these costs—charge them to overhead—as minor incidental expenses, but that was another time. Today, they are neither incidental nor minor.)

Alternative Forms of Mail.

The meaning of "mail" has changed: Electronic mail exists in various forms today, including fax and computer-to-computer communication as among the latest media. One of the well-known forms of the latter medium is MCI mail. One freelance writer in this area, David Rothman, says, "I'd go berserk without MCI Mail. It's part of my life, a way to file stories to magazines and otherwise streamline my routine." The costs, he reports, are only $1 for every 1,000 words sent to another MCI subscriber and the subscription cost is just $25 per year. Using this electronic mail in researching a book on laptop computers saved him many hundreds of dollars he would have otherwise been forced to spend in telephone calls. Of course, the saving in time is also a factor. Time is itself money, especially for those who sell their services or custom products they create for clients.

Those of us who use modem-equipped computers regularly and converse on electronic bulletin boards (computer-to-computer talk via telephone lines) use a form of electronic mail too, by leaving messages for each other. I correspond with many business associates in this manner, saving myself the expense and time of corresponding by letter mail. The bulletin boards are also a useful resource for shopping, referrals to and from others, and other functions that make them almost a daily town hall meeting.

36.

OPTIONS IN SHIPPING

Shipping and Delivery Costs: Who Pays Them?

Shipping has become increasingly expensive, along with everything else, and is no longer easy to absorb as an overhead item, despite the many options now available. Railroads are still best for certain kinds of shipping, but the United Parcel Service, and parcel post service of the USPS are still widely used, as are the newer express services.

On the downside, trying to choose the most efficient, most economical ways to meet your shipping needs can be confusing. On the upside, you have many ways to reduce those costs by selecting the right option for each case, and charging the costs properly. Add to the methods and means already mentioned trucking companies, airlines, and buses. It appears to be not well known, but bus companies often offer a low-cost method for making deliveries to cities and towns along their routes. Then there are the numerous express and overnight shipping services described earlier, which are sometimes the best answer to a shipping problem. But the best way to save money on shipping is to have the customer pay directly for it.

Charging Shipping to the Customer.

Estimate the probable cost of shipping and delivery costs when you are bidding a job in which you will be entitled to reimbursement of "other direct costs" types of expenses. Don't burden your own business unnecessarily with those costs. You can overcome this as you do other such charges by charging the "S&H" (shipping and handling) to the individual customer, thus ensuring that you are reimbursed for such expenses and need not add the cost to your own overhead pool. This should apply also to express shipping charges. Make it clear to customers that they may have overnight or other express delivery service, if they wish, but at added cost.

Express Shipping Costs.

Express shipping has become a business necessity and a vigorous, growing industry, as the postal service has declined in efficiency and reliability. A most costly method used earlier when speed was absolutely essential and express shipping was not conveniently available was to send one's own employee on an air flight as a special courier. Fortunately, that is no longer necessary although express shipping with guaranteed on-time delivery is relatively expensive. However, services and costs vary widely among the many services available. Most of the organizations offer more than one kind of express service, the most costly being the overnight service, which usually guarantees delivery the following morning. But there is usually an array of several possible services at different rates, such as "priority overnight service," "standard overnight service," "special handling," "second day air," "Saturday delivery," and even others. Many users pay for faster service than needed, opting for the most expensive service, next-morning delivery, when next afternoon or even the second day would be adequate. It's worth noting, too, that the services can vary widely from one region to another. Where I am, for example, in a metropolitan area, I can usually get a Federal Express pick-up as late as 7:00 p.m., but in smaller communities it may be difficult to get a pick-up later than 3:00 p.m. In any case, if you use express shipping services consistently or to any large extent, make a survey of services and costs available to you in your own locality, and choose the service most relevant to your needs, but not in excess of those needs. You will almost surely be able to save money in so doing.

As just noted, express shipping is used routinely and casually today, perhaps excessively so, whereas a faster and less costly medium may be available. For example, fax transmission is faster and for many applications less costly than even the best express shipping service. It would be impractical to fax a package of hundreds of sheets of text and drawings, and it is unquestionably not an acceptable method when the original pages, drawings, or contracts must arrive at a destination overnight. Those needs definitely require express shipping services. On the other hand, when only a few pages are involved and it is the information, not the original documents, that must be transmitted, fax is often a less costly alternative and a far more convenient one than any other. It is necessary, however, to adopt a policy and guide to direct your staff in making such distinctions. (Without a distinct and clear policy to guide them, employees tend to do what they are most familiar with or what is most convenient—easiest—for them, but, too often, most costly to you.)

Fax, however, is not the only alternative as a shipping method, and not always the most convenient or most economical one. For transmission of textual information over long distances, MCI Mail and some other electronic communication systems are far less expensive because they rely on networks that cost users far less than dial-up long-distance lines. (Fax costs for long-distance lines are the same as costs of long-distance lines for telephone usage.) Moreover, in many cases it is more useful or more efficient to receive a computer file than a fax printout. For one thing, the transmission is at a much higher rate of speed. For another, if the recipient wants to enter the received information into his or her own computer, computer-to-computer transmission is by far the only way to do so directly.

Local Deliveries.

For local deliveries, there are other, less costly alternatives to sending one's own employee as a courier. Many communities, especially large, urban ones, have regular courier or messenger services. (For example, I use such a service to send records to my accountant when he needs them to prepare my tax returns. The cost is generally about $7.50, which is probably representative. This method is much less costly than spending my own time making such a delivery.) In smaller communities, where such a service is not regularly available, the local taxicab companies will generally provide a local delivery service for similarly reasonable fees.

CHAPTER 8

Reducing Front-End Financing Costs

What would have once been usurious and illegal rates of interest, levied only by loan sharks with hard-nosed and cauliflower-eared collectors, are now the prime rates charged by large, respectable banking institutions (although the rates have receded somewhat from their peaks). In fact, interest charges are so much an important element of money management today that firms go to special trouble to get receipts deposited on the day they arrive to gain the advantage of that day's interest. (Yes, in commercial accounts, interest is calculated daily.) But even when money was relatively cheap, front-end financing of business start-ups was a problem for many and rarely easy for anyone—whether the approach to financing was debt financing (straightforward borrowing from individuals or institutions), equity financing (selling shares in the business), or other means (which we shall discuss).

Aside from the difficulties in finding financing for business ventures, there are many risks to consider. Putting up your home or other property as security or collateral for a loan means risking the loss of that property if the business is not successful. In some cases, it may also mean risking your personal savings and good name as a sacrifice resulting from a business failure.

All of this does not apply only to the initiation of a completely new enterprise, however; it is equally valid with respect to the front-end financing an established business often needs in expanding or adding to the original venture—e.g., the print shop proprietor who wants to add a typesetting facility or the independent route salesman-dealer who wants to open a wholesale establishment. With a record of success in business, borrowing is a bit easier for such entrepreneurs, but only a bit easier. On the other hand, the risk is perhaps even greater, since an established, successful business is now at stake and could be placed in peril by a new venture that does not succeed. So perhaps caution and risk reduction are more important than ever in the latter case.

Normally, the three major uses of/needs for capital in the start-up are 1) investment in leases, fixtures and furniture, and equipment; 2) starting inventories; and 3) daily operating expenses—payroll, rent, telephone service, and other on-going costs. Those three general capital needs will be addressed here.

37.

"FINANCING" DOES NOT ALWAYS MEAN CASH IN HAND

Sweat Equity and Other Capital.

Jim Straw, entrepreneurial publisher and an international banker today, started his ventures with the U.S. Army mustering out checks amounting to a few hundred dollars. He built from that modest beginning, not without setbacks, and advanced his fortunes—always with little or no cash, trading up and growing. It is not unusual for enterprising individuals to do this. In fact, I once launched a successful small business with only $10 in cash, and I started others with little more than that in hard cash. Many other successful business enterprises have been seeded on equally small bases of cash in hand.

But there is other capital and currency than cash. The $10 in cash I used to start the venture referred to was a down payment on a used panel truck. The rest of my front-end financing was my credit, my relationship with local builders who donated scrap lumber from their projects so I could build the racks I needed on my truck, my own hand tools, my knowledge, my sweat in putting it all together, and my salesmanship in lining up my first accounts. "Sweat equity" is a recognized currency, as are many other substitutes for cash, including negotiating skills and barter.

(I once actually bought a house with sweat equity as my down payment: I negotiated a deal with the builder to paint and do other finish work to the house myself, for which he would credit me the down payment! Another buyer I knew installed the tile in bathrooms and kitchen of the house he bought as his down payment.)

Using Barter and Negotiation for Capital.

The concept of trading things of value other than currency works in many applications. Many freelance copywriters write and self-syndicate monthly small-business-advice columns to periodicals in exchange for advertising space. A lawyer I know exchanges his legal services for hangar space at a small local airport, where he houses his private airplane. When renting a suite of offices in downtown Washington, DC, I learned that my rental included a certain amount of allowed office renovation—moving partitions about and repainting. On the basis of accepting the office space as it was (I would myself make any changes I wanted) I was able to negotiate a much lower rental figure. Always ask whatever a stated figure includes, and then probe to see what is negotiable and can be used to reduce your own commitment. But always consider what goods or services of your own you may be able to barter as a means of reducing the cash requirements of financing a business.

38.

BUSINESS LOCATION ALTERNATIVES

A Place to Work.

You need a place to work, but an office, store, or warehouse is not always an absolute necessity as a starting address for a business. Many highly successful businesses have been launched in the entrepreneur's home. Volt Information Sciences (Chapter 1) was only one example. Jack Miller started the Quill Corporation, now a major mail order vendor of business supplies employing a large number of people, in the basement of his own home. Many kinds of businesses lend themselves to such humble beginnings, with benefits in the form of tax reductions—writeoffs—as well as the benefit of reduced venture capital requirements. Always consider rooms in your own home—an unused room, a basement, a garage, a porch, or even your kitchen and dining room—as potential low-cost places in which to get started.

39.

FURNISHING AND EQUIPPING
A PLACE TO WORK

Furnishings and Fixtures.

Places of business need furniture and fixtures. But if you are able to start your venture in your own home, you can probably make use of whatever furniture and furnishings are available there, at least temporarily. (If a multimillion dollar venture can begin at a kitchen table, obviously a desk is not an absolute necessity—at least not in the beginning.) Even now, after two decades of independent operation and a few years in formal offices in a downtown location before returning to an office at home (where I started) my current office furniture and furnishings include many items that were my personal property at home before I launched an independent venture.

Equipment.

Many entrepreneurs start with equipment they already own as their personal property: perhaps a portable manual typewriter, possibly a minimally configured computer, a set of hand tools, or other equipment needed to operate the business. (They have value, and they are capital too.) On the other hand, the individual is not likely to own a fax and copier, most useful items in today's business world, but it is not essential to own these items. It is possible to use a local copy shop to make copies, and fax services are increasingly available. Or you can rent such equipment, if you can't buy it immediately and need it in your office. If you are in a regular office building, there are usually copying and fax facilities available in the building itself or nearby (since most office buildings are in neighborhoods zoned commercial or industrial).

Tax Implications.

When you convert personal property to use in your business (provided the property is dedicated to the business and thus used solely as a business asset), you are transferring ownership from yourself to your business. Even if you operate a sole proprietorship, the status of that property has changed. Assign it some reasonable value, remembering that it is used and is not worth the price you paid for it originally, and place it on a depreciation schedule—or expense it, if you prefer and if it meets the rules for expensing capital items. Either way, the property becomes a deduction, its cost part of your overhead. However, treating your business as a separate entity (which you should), the business must buy the items from you, and you must treat the price you paid for them as income, to be reporting in your personal returns.

40.

"WALKING-AROUND MONEY" FOR YOUR BUSINESS

Operating Capital.

We have been talking about investment capital, money to buy or rent physical necessities. But there is also a need for operating capital: money to meet daily expenses such as a payroll, rent, heat, and light, while waiting for the business to get off the ground and begin to produce income. There are some answers for that need too.

Getting Customers to Supply the Operating Capital.

There are many ways in which you can manage a business start-up with virtually zero operating capital up front, relying essentially on capital provided by your customers! Some businesses are by their nature essentially cash and carry or cash on delivery. In some ventures you may get paid even further up front, well in advance of delivering the goods or the service. This is not unusual. The post office, for instance, always gets paid in advance of delivering the service, often many months in advance. (Every postage stamp in your possession and every dollar on your postage meter or otherwise on deposit with the USPS is payment in advance.) Subscriptions to periodicals are usually paid in advance, often several years in advance! Most customers ordering by mail pay in advance, including those using credit cards, which are cash for the merchant. (He or she deposits the slips as cash.) If you order custom printing, consulting services, or legal services you will find that you are usually required to make a substantial advance deposit or retainer. If you have something ordered especially for you—when you buy something that is not normally carried in the merchant's stock, even if it is a standard proprietary item—the merchant often requires that you leave a substantial and non-refundable deposit with your order. This is as it should be in any custom business, and you should apply the principle to your own business wherever possible. If you make advance deposits a standard way of doing business when you think the circumstances justify it—i.e., if you make it a firm and clear policy—you will not meet with too much resistance. (You can always make exceptions if you wish to.)

Even businesses that normally bill customers often offer special inducements to pay in advance. Magazines are one common example: Many appeals for subscription offer a clock, calculator, telephone, book, or other special gift if payment accompanies your order. Some offer special cash discounts for advance payments.

I find that whenever I order any kind of special publication that is available only by mail order I must wait four or more weeks for delivery—four or more weeks in which the seller has the interest-free use of capital I have supplied! It is not only publications to which this applies, either; I pay in advance for everything I order by mail or telephone, with only one exception (the sole open account with a mail order supplier), and many of these orders are not filled for a few weeks, during which the merchant has the free use of my money.

This idea can be adapted and applied to many ventures. When I wrote and self-published my first book, customer money paid for the initial printing! I solicited advance orders, promising in exchange priority on delivery and a little bonus (unidentified at the time, because I didn't yet know myself what it would be, but I decided a newsletter was needed and gave a free 3-month subscription to those who paid in advance). I got thousands of dollars in advance payments before I went to press, more than enough to pay for the first printing.

The late Joe Karbo, a talented marketer, sold a reported 600,000 copies of his little $10 paperback book, *The Lazy Man's Way to Riches*, through full-page advertising. He related that he ran test advertisements first, before writing the book; only when he had received enough orders to prove his idea a viable one did he write the book and have it manufactured to begin deliveries. (He said that if the orders had been too sparse, he would simply have returned the money with apologies. Many others have done and recommend doing the same thing, including Joe Cossman, another mail order millionaire.)

Progress Payments.

If you are in a service business that engages in long-term custom projects, write a clause in your standard contract for progress payments, so that you may bill for services at least on a monthly basis, although billing more frequently—for instance, biweekly—is not unusual.

These are just a few of the many ways you can arrange things so that you get paid in advance and otherwise enhance your cash flow. With a bit of imagination the ideas can be adapted and applied to most ventures—by offering, for example, special discount or other bonus for advance orders with payment.

41.

CAPITAL FOR INVENTORY

Stocking the Shelves.

Some businesses depend on having a substantial inventory on hand, which calls for both investment and operating capital. There are ways to get an inventory with little or no capital up front for many kinds of businesses and in many circumstances. One is to get products to sell on consignment. In that mode the owner of the products places them in your hands with an understanding that he or she gets paid only when the items are sold. You settle up with the individual on some regular basis, perhaps once a month. Of course, you do not make as large a gross profit as you can when you own the inventory outright, but you do not have capital tied up, and you take no risks of being stuck with unsalable or very slow moving merchandise.

Another method is to sell via samples and catalogs, as in party sales and catalog stores. In this mode you carry only a few samples or demonstration models and take orders from customers for future delivery—for example, the following week. In many cases, the supplier ships you your first order on credit. You pay for that order when you place a second order, which is after the customers for the first order have paid you. (You should get deposits from them *when taking the orders*.) As your business grows you may begin to build an inventory and fill orders from that.

There is also ordinary trade credit. You must pay for the goods received within 30, 60, or 90 days, depending on the arrangements you have been able to make. If operating capital is in short supply, order conservatively, according to how long a lead time you require to get your orders filled.

PART TWO

Increasing Markups

The most direct and simplest way of increasing profits—net profits, that is—is by increasing gross profits (markups). This is, in theory, the most direct and simplest way of increasing profits; in practice it is somewhat less simple.

Obviously, you are not free to simply raise your prices as you see fit . . . not if you expect to keep your customers and remain in business. Even the most upscale, highest-priced stores have their competition—other upscale, high-priced stores—and so must control their prices.

There are, however, a number of indirect ways to increase your markups which we will examine here.

CHAPTER 9

Higher Markups
Through Better
Buying

Better Buying Means Better Selling.

Purchasing is a function only slightly less important than marketing. In fact, the two—buying and selling—are not unrelated to each other: Better buying means gaining advantages for marketing, because it provides greater flexibility in marking up and pricing. That is true for every business, although more so for some—i.e., in businesses where the chief activity is reselling purchased products or materials, either directly or after some form of additional processing. Distributors, wholesalers, and retailers must buy salable merchandise at the right prices—at prices that enable them to resell the goods with enough gross profit to meet all expenses and have a bit left over to count as net profit.

That seems pretty simple. It is . . . in principle. It is the basis for all businesses, even the most complex ones. You buy and sell, taking a profit as your compensation for the services you render, one of which is distributing the products, making them available to those who want them. Depending on the nature of your own business, you may resell what you bought as you bought it, you may repackage it before you sell it, you may use what you bought to manufacture new products to sell, or you may use it in the furnishing of a service, as in buying cloth to upholster someone's furniture, or parts to repair someone's automobile or TV set.

In practice, buying is rarely simple. To buy right—virtually never paying the asking price, for example—you will have to learn to adapt yourself to many situations. You must learn to wheedle, argue, cajole, threaten, walk away, horse trade, make faces, appear indifferent, and display a poker face, among other acts. Good negotiators can and do use all of these tactics. But you will also have to be a good researcher, always questing for new sources, new items, better items, better terms, exclusives, and anything else that can give you an edge of any kind. And you must also attempt to evaluate new products, trying to judge how the public will receive them. Ask yourself whether you would have accurately estimated public reaction to hula hoops, mood rings, the Rubik's Cube, the Pet Rock, the Wall Walker toy, maxi-skirts and maxi-coats, and the Nehru jacket. Would you have gambled on devices that produce square hard-boiled eggs, scrambled eggs in their shell to produce a hard-boiled scrambled egg, turn lights and TV sets on and off when you clap your hands, or grow grass on a clay figure? (These items sell every Christmas, along with several dozen other clever but uninspiring novelties, then disappear for the rest of the year.)

There is as much competition in buying as there is in selling. In fact, competing successfully in buying means buying better than your competition does—coming up with better deals, better merchandise, and other kinds of "better" to give you an advantage in the marketplace.

That raises another point about buying. Better buying is not only buying at better prices. It is also finding and buying better merchandise than your competitors offer and/or new items your competitors do not even have yet. Better buying often means, therefore, better purchasing research. It means recognizing the enormous potential of the yo-yo, the hula hoop, and the Rubik's Cube when it first appears and is still unheard of, beating your competitors to a big winner. No training, no logic, no cold, rational judgment can help you do this; success in gauging the winners results from some kind of instinct, some unconscious ability to understand and anticipate public reaction.

42.

RESOURCEFULNESS IN
FINDING GOOD BUYS

The Bargain May be a Function of the Buyer.

Necessity is apparently the mother of ingenuity, as well as of invention. It certainly made Morris a resourceful upholsterer.

Morris had his little shop in Philadelphia during the Great Depression of the thirties. It was in a low-rent industrial district, where he did all the work himself and lived with his family in more or less makeshift quarters behind the shop. He had, in fact, a relatively prosperous trade for those hard times, because he turned out good quality work at modest prices. One reason he was able to do this was his ingenuity as an upholsterer, which enabled him to use fabrics he bought right, at a fraction of their normal market price. (He had actually started out as a furniture finisher, but added upholstering to his skills when the economic slump demanded diversification.)

Morris never bought full lengths of fabric from the bolt; the fabric was too expensive. He bought remnants, leftovers that were not large enough for the needs of most upholsterers. These are like carpet remnants: They are short and odd-sized lengths left over at the end of the bolt and closed out for whatever prices they will bring, always a fraction of their list because most upholsterers can't use them and so won't have them at any price. They might be used to make antimacassars and other small goods—perhaps to cover a footstool—but not for general upholstery of chairs and sofas.

Morris was not afraid of a little extra effort, and he was ingenious in finding ways to fit these odd, ill-shaped pieces together and use them for normal reupholstering purposes. That is what made the remnants a bargain to Morris, although of little value to anyone else. (A bargain requires that someone have some use for it to be a bargain.)

Imagination and Resourcefulness.

The late Joe Karbo was a masterful marketer and a highly imaginative writer of sales copy. He once came across a warehouse full of those gadgets one finds installed in the front door of most apartments: a device with a small lens that permits the occupant to see who is at the door without opening it. They were surplus, of little use to the owner of them who was eager to dispose of them at almost any price. Karbo bought the lot at a giveaway price and launched a mail order campaign, taking full-page advertisements in pulp magazines, the advertising copy headlined "See Through Walls." With his gift for writing copy, he had little difficulty in disposing of the entire lot and making a handsome profit in doing so.

A Talent for Serendipity.

The Karbo story is an example of serendipity—finding something you didn't know you were looking for, but are smart enough to recognize as something of value and take advantage of when you happen across it. It's a useful characteristic in purchasing, and not entirely a matter of chance. Bargains, for example, don't fall into your lap every day, but they seem to come along much more frequently when you have arranged to make fortuitous accidents more likely and conditioned yourself to be alert for them. Serendipity may be a fortuitous accident, but it happens only when someone recognizes the fortunate circumstance and does something to take advantage of it. Most people wouldn't have given those "spy int he door" devices a second thought, no matter how cheaply they were offered. Most people would assume that they could have been sold only to a builder. Joe Karbo saw in them an opportunity for another way to sell them. That is serendipity, which happens much more frequently when you condition yourself to watch for it.

Don't Wait for Good Fortune to Find You.

Sales are not always announced, for many reasons, and you will miss many opportunities to make good buys if you wait for someone to tell you about special sales. It is necessary to check for yourself, and to do so constantly, being always alert for opportunities. Develop your own "radar" for sales and special bargain offerings. And when you get an exceptionally good buy, stock up as much as you can. It's a sound investment. As an old adage says, you can't do business from an empty wagon.

Price is Not the Sold Objective in Purchasing.

You should always be seeking the best prices, of course, but a "good buy" is not necessarily buying the merchandise you deal in regularly at lower prices than you or your competitors pay regularly. A good buy is also finding new, different, and better items to sell. One of the services you provide as a business owner is bringing new and better products to the buying public. Always watch for the items that you may deal in profitably, even if they are items that are somewhat out of your regular line. The department stores were rather slow to bring in computers; they hesitated too long and so lost out on a great deal of that market. (Most are still handling only a limited line in computers and virtually nothing in accessories.) Some merchants who sold office supplies and equipment (Quill Corporation, for example) soon perceived the computer as an office necessity, on the other hand, and began to deal in computers, accessories, and other high-tech office equipment, such as fax machines and telephone-answering devices.

Research is Key.

Finding bargains and other opportunities to make good buys is not always a matter of chance, as it was for me and my copier cartridges or Joe Karbo and his "door spies." More often, it can and probably should be the result of deliberate effort—research, if you will, a diligent and continuous search for good buys. You cannot base a business on the chance uncovering of bargains, special sales, and special sources. You need to have some control over finding the things you need at the right prices, an organized method for finding what you need. There are several ways to organize your efforts.

One way is to read the relevant trade journals of your own and adjoining fields. Here you can learn of closeouts, bankruptcies, auctions, surplus sales, new products, and other relevant information. But you need to read widely. If you sell general merchandise, you will want to know what is going on in other industries who make and sell the products in which you deal.

There are some general business journals of interest, including the *Wall Street Journal*, the *New York Times*, and *Business Opportunities Journal*, a tabloid circulated widely by mail.

There are many special publications, such as the *Business Opportunities Digest*, a newsletter that has wanted-to-buy, wanted-to-sell, and other such notices in every issue. (It is a monthly publication.) The trade journal of book publishing, *Publishers Weekly*, will often give you leads to books being remaindered or becoming good candidates for remaindering.

Still another resource is the use of "finders," individuals who can help you find items you are looking for—for a fee (usually a small percentage of the value of any resulting transaction). You will find such individuals posting notices in such journals as *Business Opportunities Digest*.

43

NEGOTIATING YOUR WAY TO GOOD BUYS

Make Your Luck in Buying.

As author Herb Cohen says in his book *You Can Negotiate Anything* (Bantam Books, New York, 1990) almost everything is negotiable. That is especially true in the business world, where trading between businesspeople takes place constantly. You can poke around and hope to stumble over a great buy now and then, or you can *negotiate* good buys, which is a somewhat more reliable proposition.

Negotiation is not difficult to define. It is a bargaining process, the process where two people who want to make a trade, although poles apart on terms initially, make a series of compromises until they reach a point of agreement and make the trade. As a buyer, you will be negotiating with a seller. One difference will be between what you are willing to pay and what the seller wants to be paid. The compromises do not all concern the price, however: Other considerations may be and often are traded in lieu of price.

Classic negotiating tactics are for both of you to begin by professing only passing interest in any transaction involving the goods or service, and no interest at all in negotiation. The seller quotes a price, supposedly fixed and immutable, and you shrug and indicate that the price is too high to merit even recognition, much less serious consideration. (After all, you are not that interested to begin with.) Frequently, both of you change the subject entirely as an indication of disinclination to consider a trade on the terms stated by the other, and the lack of great interest in the trade, in any case. It is traditional among those who are experienced negotiators to conceal your interest behind a facade of indifference, or, at most, only mild interest. That is considered to be a proper beginning position for a negotiation.

One business that involves negotiation on a more or less continuous basis—i.e., for virtually every transaction—is that of supplying technical and professional temporaries (those working for engineers, writers, accountants, and physicians). As in the case of office temporaries, the supplier pays the temporary at some rate (usually hourly) and bills the client at a higher rate, to earn a gross profit and, ultimately, a net profit. Once again, despite the fact that one is buying and selling the services of another person, this is a case of buying at "wholesale" and selling at retail. In some cases the rate charged the client is fixed by some factor, but it is necessary in most cases to negotiate the rate paid the individual. Most individuals hiring themselves out as temporaries the first time accept the terms offered, unaware that the rate is usually negotiable. Most, however, get an education rather swiftly, as they meet other more experienced temporaries on their first assignment. They learn quickly that the rate offered them was only a starting point for negotiation. Most learn to negotiate for the best rate, and never again accept the first offer.

Negotiations are not always that simple, of course, and in most cases the commodity being traded is merchandise or supplies of some kind. But the principles, strategies, and tactics are the same. Cover up your eagerness for the trade, while you probe to try to detect the other's real attitude and related wants. Search for items you can use as leverage in trading. For example, if appropriate, make cash deals: payment promptly on delivery. This can be a powerful inducement to trade in these days of high interest rates and cash-flow difficulties. You can trade things other than money, and even make demands—especially for the purpose of creating bargaining chips you can use later. For example, you might begin by insisting on your need for immediate delivery, but be prepared to yield a bit on that if you can trade that flexibility in delivery date for a further discount. Offer to pick up the merchandise yourself as another inducement, if you can trade it for a price cut. You might offer to increase the size of your order for cost reductions as another persuasive factor. Listen carefully to what the other says, be conscious also of what he or she doesn't say, and try to find some other bargaining chips to trade for dollars. (In the case of the technical and professional temporaries, for example, bargaining chips may include per diem allowances for out-of-town work assignments and fringe benefits.)

The Virtue of Patience in Negotiations.

Impatience indicates a strong desire to make the deal and thus encourages the other party to hold the line on whatever he or she demands. Patience—displaying no apparent urgency to get an agreement—has the opposite effect. It signals the other party that you may drop the entire negotiation if you can't get better terms. That creates an air of uncertainty as far as the other party is concerned, which is in your interest. You have a much better chance of determining whether the other party really wants to make the trade and feels some urgency in doing so.

Perhaps even more important, however, is that patience tends to reduce the emotional content of negotiation. If you make what the other thinks immediately is an unrealistically low offer, he or she may react emotionally at first with a snort and an emphatic, "Forget it. No way will I accept that kind of offer!" If you push at this point, you polarize the negotiation and force the other to end it. But if you allow time—perhaps even several days or a week—for emotions to cool and reason to take over, you have a much better chance of making a deal.

Hence, many negotiations take days to complete. It is not possible to negotiate successfully if you are impatient and feel a need to hurry the final determination. You will either kill the deal entirely or you will pay more than you should have paid. Let patience prevail.

44.

BUY FROM OR NEAR THE PRIME SOURCE

Cut Out the Middlemen.

Many products are distributed at several levels before they reach the wholesaler or retailer—e.g., importers, jobbers, and distributors. Each marks up the goods that pass through his or her hands, of course, so that you may very well be paying as much as twice the original price of the product as it originated with the manufacturer or processor, the prime source.

One objective in seeking good buys is to cut out as many as possible of those middle dealers and their many markups. If you can find and buy directly from the prime source—the manufacturer or importer—you have much more room for negotiating a good deal than if you buy several levels of distribution below the prime source.

Even having found the prime source or the supplier from whom your wholesaler buys, it may be necessary, in some cases, to buy in larger quantities than you usually do, although that is not always true. You may very well be able to negotiate a quantity discount price for small amounts. It is always worth trying for.

When the required minimum purchase is too great for you to handle and you *can't* negotiate the quantity down a bit, consider buying through a group purchase of some kind. Many computer owners who operate small businesses belong to computer clubs, made up of others who own computers. Along with other services, computer clubs make group buys of computers and related items, equipment and supplies. Check with trade associations in your industry. You may be able to find similar cooperative buying opportunities offered to members of associations; there may already be a purchasing cooperative in your industry. Finally, consider forming your own buying group, a syndicate or informal cooperative formed with others who have the same interests you have in buying.

45.

DON'T OVERDO BRAND OR
SUPPLIER LOYALTY

Be Ready to Change Suppliers and/or Brands.

No matter how good you think your sources and prices are, always be alert to the opportunity to do better. Be receptive to all changes that can save you money and contribute to your profitability; be willing to change suppliers and/or brand names when you can buy better by doing so. Even if the new supplier is no closer to the prime source than your current one is, for example, you may be able to save considerable amounts of money by making such a change. Another supplier may be willing to offer you better prices—because he or she manages to have a lower overhead, buys more favorable than your former supplier, is willing to shave profits a bit to win your business, does not advertise heavily, or for any other reason. This may include changing brand names. If you have been carrying Smith's line of costume jewelry, perhaps Jones's line of jewelry is equivalent and costs you less.

In some cases, brand names are important, and customers are influenced by them, even to the point of developing a kind of brand loyalty. This is primarily as a result of extended, heavy advertising campaigns, such as those of laundry products and cosmetics. Therefore, customers often become "sold" on one brand of cosmetics, or laundry detergent and are not easily persuaded to abandon their favored brand and buy another. Be cautious about changing brands you offer to consumers in such cases. Try new and different or unknown brands without abandoning the ones you normally carry *before* you decide to drop any well-known branded product. On the other hand, in many kinds of merchandise, customers do not have a brand-name consciousness, and so do not really care who manufactured the bracelet or milled the flour. In the latter class of products, you can usually save money without losing sales by finding the lowest-cost brands and suppliers, which are more often than not completely equivalent to each other in quality.

In most cases, leading brands of any given product are about equal in all respects, and often the leading brands are no better than new or unknown brands. In fact, the labels may be misleading, and products that appear to be different may actually be identical. It is common practice for sellers to arrange to have manufacturers and processors label a supply of their products with the seller's name (e.g., the "house brands" sold in many supermarket and department store chains), so you cannot always be sure that a brand name means anything as far as the origin of the product is concerned. Example: A small TV on our own kitchen table is labeled "Ward." A cousin has an absolutely identical TV on her kitchen table labeled "GE." The cloning is obvious.

Similar practices are commonplace in every industry. Bottlers of whiskey, for example, buy from and sell to each other, so the Hiram Walker whiskey you buy may very well contain bourbon bought from Schenley or Seagram's warehouse.

Years ago one high-priced brand of rubbing alcohol was sold in a distinctive bottle and labeled "Mifflin" (for Mifflin Street in Philadelphia, where the product was bottled by Publicker Distilleries). But the same plant also turned out the product in more commonplace bottles and sold it at much lower prices than the leading brand commanded. It is not unusual for manufacturers to compete with themselves in this manner so that they can function in competitive markets that are ordinarily mutually exclusive.

Don't be confused about the issue of loyalty, either. Loyalty is a two-way street. You are no more obligated morally to continue buying from any supplier to accommodate him or her than he or she is obligated to meet his or her own competitors' lowest prices to accommodate you. Do not permit friendly relations to interfere with business judgment.

CHAPTER 10

Strategic Packaging
For Higher Markups

Generally speaking, high-priced items are almost always packaged more attractively and more expensively than are their lower-priced competitors, although that (aside from the price) may be the only difference between them. Packaging, however, does not refer only to containers, wrappings, and other external appurtenances; it refers to the total impact any product or service has on the prospective buyer, for even services are or may be packaged. In fact, in some industries—entertainment and personnel placement, to name only two—even people are packaged.

Packaging can and does make a difference. That difference is why retailers such as Nordstrom and Neiman Marcus can get full-list price for a well advertised coffee maker, while the East Side Bargain Basement fights to persuade customers to buy the same coffee maker at a heavily discounted price. Or why Henri the hairdresser charges and gets far more for his services when he works in Bloomingdales than he did when he worked at Irene's

Beauty Shoppe around the corner: Bloomingdales beauty salon is simply a more impressive—and thus more expensive—package than is Irene's beauty salon.

This is not to say that there is no difference between Bloomingdales and Irene's. Far from it, there is a great difference, not in the basic service itself—Henri did as good a job for Irene's patrons as he does for the women at Bloomingdales—but at Bloomingdales there is a certain ambience and perhaps a bit of panache that makes the difference.

What we are talking about here is perception. Perception is a critically important element of marketing, and packaging has the sole purpose of creating the right perception. When the customer perceives the product or service to be of highest quality and the supplier to be solid and dependable, confidence, trust, and acceptance result. Obviously, if the perception is one opposed to all of this, mistrust, rejection, or, at the very least, skepticism. Packaging, then, is surrounding the item with whatever makes for the right presentation.

46.

PHYSICAL PACKAGING FOR
ESTEEM VALUE

The Magic Act.

Smart packaging alone adds value—*perceived* value, that is (but is not all value perceived value?)—as in cosmetics, where the physical packages, the metal lipstick tube and the crystalline decanter, for instance are actually worth more intrinsically than are the contents. This is not uncommon. In fact, manufacturers often pay great sums of money to those specialists—package designers—to create packages that are unique and positively reek of style, luxury, quality, and other negotiable assets (such as Elizabeth Taylor's name) that justify high markups.

Even the *exterior* packaging, the case, carton, and/or packing in which the product is encased, is costly in the case of such items. That is because what one sells in a line of (for example) cosmetics is primarily esteem value: Customers buy the package—what it *says about the product*—as much as they buy its contents.

Packaging here amounts to increasing to many dollars the value of a few cents' worth of aromatic chemicals in a vial so tiny that it can be concealed in milady's delicate palm. Consider, for example, that the most expensive scents are today available as "fakes," imitations and knock-offs that are alternates to and indistinguishable from the "genuine" perfumes, as far as most of us are concerned. And yet they *are* different. Although almost identical objectively to the originals they emulate, these imitations do the far more expensive originals little or no damage in the marketplace. The customer who can afford the far more costly original prefers the original. The difference may be—is, in fact—almost entirely packaging and thus subjective, but it is a real difference, nevertheless, and it makes a concrete appearance in the reality of the dollars and cents that customers will pay for the original.

Not all cosmetics are inherently expensive; there are some that are by nature relatively inexpensive even in the name brands. (The manufacturer of a line of name brand products can afford to have some inexpensive products in the line, but that manufacturer cannot afford to have any cheap-*looking* products in the line.) But even an inexpensive cosmetic product is enhanced in value through packaging. And price itself is an important part of packaging because it creates an aura. When hairspray for women appeared on the scene a number of years ago, most sold for at least $3 per container, a significant price for those days. One manufacturer brought out a hairspray product for $1.79 a can, and found it difficult to sell to the public. He retained a marketing consultant who quickly identified the problem: With competitive products priced at $3, most women did not trust the $1.79 product to be of acceptable quality. Raising the price of the new product increased its market success immediately.

Here is another classic example of what strategic packaging can do: When detergents first appeared on the market some years ago, an innovative entrepreneur bought quantities of one of the most popular kitchen detergents in inexpensive wholesale lots. He added a bit of scent to the laundry detergent, rebottled it suitably, and packaged it as a bubble bath, marked up appropriately as an expensive cosmetic product. (The history of Hollywood movies depicting bubble baths as a luxury of wealthy and glamorous women helped enhance the whole idea too.) As the late Charles Revson, founder of Revlon, put it, "In the factory we make cosmetics. In the stores we sell hope." Revson understood marketing quite well.

Packaging and Repackaging is Not Confined to Cosmetics.

The cosmetics field offers us some outstanding examples of adding value to products through the art of physical packaging, but it is certainly not the only field in which value is added through that art. The diamond merchant showing a customer one of his gems always presents it on black velvet under good lighting to dramatize its sparkle and brilliance, itself an act of packaging. (The drama is itself a salable commodity, enhancing the markup.) Even relatively inexpensive pieces of jewelry are always encased in velvet-lined boxes that add esteem value (and markup). Here in the Washington, DC area we have for years been bombarded, especially as Christmas approaches, by the advertising of "fabulous fakes" by "Lady Wellington," a local vendor of crystals sold as imitation diamonds. Are they zircons? Other crystals commonly used as "paste" diamonds? "Lady Wellington" won't say. But they are not diamonds, of course, and they command much better prices than most zircons and other costume jewelry does. It is the clever packaging that enables "Lady Wellington" to market her products successfully at enhanced prices.

The packaging idea is applied and works with many other consumer items. Radio and TV receivers, for example, are housed in highly polished cabinets that offer value as items of furniture. The Germans have been particularly assiduous in presenting cabinets with extremely highly polished surfaces, as evident in Blaupunkt products and other brands. Some of those handsome cabinets are given to remarkably wide-open spaces in their interiors, occupied by only a relative handful of components. In these days of chips and other miniaturized electronic elements, it is obvious that the very size of the cabinet and what it implies is itself more of a packaging and less of a technical consideration. Refrigerators and other kitchen appliances are no longer white only, as they were traditionally, but are offered now in a variety of designer colors. At least one dishwasher has a reversible front panel so that it can be either black *or* white. More and more utilitarian and undramatic items are being enhanced with embellishments to lift them out of the mundane and elevate them to a more romantic plane—and a higher price tag.

47.

PHYSICAL PACKAGING FOR
UTILITARIAN VALUE

Some Packages are More Useful Than Others.

Sony 3.5-inch computer disks are sold with each disk enclosed in a clear plastic envelope or sleeve. This sends a distinct message, especially to those who have bought other manufacturers' disks and never seen evidence of such tender loving care. Sony is sending a message with this sleeve, of course, and that message cannot help but enhance the value of the product.

But Sony is not finished yet; their packaging has more to say. The disks are presented in a sales-unit package of 10 disks, and those are presented in a hard plastic case with a hinged lid, which may be used for storage purposes. This plastic case is useful as well as attractive. Again, a message is sent with this package. (There is an external pasteboard package too, of course.)

Sony applies the same packaging strategy to its data tapes. Data tapes sold by Sony—cigarette-pack sized items selling for $15-$20 each—are each encased in a reusable hinged case, whereas some others' data tapes are simply wrapped in thin plastic film that must be discarded, as though they were of a value no greater than that of a carrier of onions or a notepad. The message is unlikely to be lost on even on the most naive consumer.

Many expensive mints, chocolates, cookies, and other goodies come packaged in reusable tins, often decorated tastefully enough so that they are not out of place on a vanity or dresser later, when pressed into service to hold other items. Sometimes such items are even packaged in good-quality wooden chests that are quite acceptable as useful and attractive furniture items after they have served their original purposes.

Packing food items in or with containers that make perfectly useful items when the food has been consumed is a common practice. Gifts of fancy fruit are often packed in baskets, meat-and-cheese assortments are packed in a serving tray or on a cutting board, and other items are enclosed in such containers as crystal bowls with lids.

48.

PACKAGING IS MORE THAN WRAPPINGS AND CONTAINERS

Packaging is Image and Presentation.

Most people think of packaging in terms of the physical container in which a product is housed. The term *packaging* is truly more far-reaching in significance than that, however: It refers to how a product or service is *presented* to the customer.

Packaging is a *presentation*. It is communication, a message sent to the customer reflecting what the manufacturer or seller thinks of the product or service and how it ought to be perceived or regarded. Chateaubriand may be only steak with a college education, but its presentation in a fine restaurant is packaging that a lunchroom or diner simply cannot emulate. One can dine reasonably well in most places in the United States for as little as $5 or $10, but many patrons choose, deliberately and consciously, to pay several times that for *ambience, service,* and *atmosphere*. It includes, in the finest establishments, tuxedo-clad waiters, captains, and headwaiter or maitre d' in attendance in a thickly carpeted, hushed atmosphere; even a glass of water is a formal presentation in expensive stemware. (I once witnessed in a fine restaurant the preparation of a dessert, Cherries Jubilee, done so spectacularly that the young couple for whom the dish was prepared ordered a second serving because they wanted to see the performance again!)

These refinements are salable commodities or enhancements to commodities that would otherwise be valued only at far lower prices. They convey to the customer a sense of comfort, privilege, or luxury—and perhaps even an enhancement of self-image in being able to be a patron of a fine establishment and a purchaser of fine things. The customer is glad to pay for this. But fine restaurants and other hostelries are not the only examples of value added via enhancements of this type. Almost any service can be enhanced so as to enable and justify a greater markup. Where I have my automobile serviced the floors of the service area, unlike those of most garages are spotlessly clean. The service manager approaches me respectfully and courteously, explaining exactly what my automobile needs. The mechanic spreads a plastic cover over the seat before sitting in my automobile. When service is completed, the vehicle is delivered to me with a detailed list of services performed and old parts, if any were replaced, stored in a box for my disposal.

The IBM "Uniform."

Until relatively recently, the IBM salesman or executive who failed to wear a white shirt, dark tie, and dark suit was asking for severe difficulties with his superiors. Even today, although the requirements and unwritten rules are relatively relaxed, any attire that is not reasonably conservative and businesslike or "professional" is most definitely frowned upon at IBM, and in a great many other establishments of a similar nature. These kinds of companies deal in "big tag" items, and it is essential that their employees convey the image of sober and conservative professionals.

Real Uniforms.

Most large service organizations provide a uniform for employees who are in routine and frequent contact with the public, and insist that employees wear that uniform. As in other cases, this is a message from management, a message of careful organization and control; it helps to establish the image that justifies service rates higher than those imposed by establishments that appear to be of lesser stature.

A Principle, Not a Practice.

The concept is applied in many places and in many ways. The white-tie-and-tails-clad pianist in the upscale Nordstrom department stores is part of the packaging of the store overall, as is the sonorous and dramatic organ music and the great brass eagle on a pedestal in John Wanamaker's department store in Philadelphia. TV commercials have featured the venerable Strawbridge and Clothier department store of Philadelphia, pointing to the store's existence of well over a century as evidence of its dependability. Bloomingdale's, Neiman Marcus, Lord & Taylor, Gucci, and others each have their own distinctive images that they have created and cultivated most carefully. Those images are packaging too, information about the establishment *per se*—haute couture, dependability, conservatism, quality, or any other factor.

Labeling is Part of Packaging.

When the new book *Five Acres* was not doing well in the marketplace, the publisher consulted the now-legendary mail order copywriter Maxwell Sackheim. Sackheim recommended the simple packaging change of retitling the book *Five Acres and Independence*. With that fresh aura, the book conveyed a new and different message and image, whereupon sales took off and the book began to do quite well.

Selling Hope.

Marking up is relatively easy when you are selling up, and selling up is what we have been talking about: how to raise the value of what you sell. An astonishing number of merchants do not know what they are selling. They make the common mistake of thinking that they sell products or services. When the late Charles Revson, of Revlon, remarked that he was selling hope, as quoted earlier, he knew whereof he spoke. All products and their packaging imply a promise of benefits, even when the advertising does not specifically state the promise, and the customer buys the hope of fulfilling that promise.

Everybody buys hope. The buyer of a training programs buys the hope of a better job and a better career. The buyer of a diet plan buys the hope of being more slender and more attractive. The buyer of life insurance buys the hope of peace of mind, knowing his/her family is provided for. And so on. Packaging promises fulfillment of that hope. That is why it sells.

CHAPTER 11

Adding Higher-Markup Items To Your Line

Increasing your markup does not necessarily mean raising the prices you get for the items you sell, nor does it always mean lowering your costs for purchasing the items. There are several other ways to raise your markups and profitability overall.

To understand this and put it to work we must dispel some of the myths that are circulated in the business world, even the notions that seem to make sense, such as the idea that bigger the sale, the greater the profit. It just isn't necessarily so. It may or may not be the case for any given sale.

Diversifying your line by adding new, higher-markup items usually helps for a number of reasons that will become apparent as we examine various scenarios. But we also have to discuss also what diversifying and adding higher markup items *means*. You may be in for a few surprises before we finish.

49.

BRAND NAMES AND MARKUPS

Which Brands Offer the Highest Markups?

Most retailers are simply resellers of merchandise, as it was manufactured, packaged, and received from the manufacturer or distributors. If any given item is a well-advertised, standardized item that is easily identifiable—e.g., a given model TV, a name brand ketchup, or a heavily advertised laundry detergent—customers may and usually will price shop to compare your prices with others. That, of course, puts you directly into price competition, sometimes even into price wars and controls your markups. It follows that you cannot be significantly higher than your competitors if you want to survive. Or does it?

The proposition stated is especially true for heavily advertised name brands, of course. But how much do those factors—brand names and heavy advertising—really count for in pricing? More to the point, how much does it count for in markup and profit? Must you really cut prices to the bone so as to compete with competitors who do so? The answers are not absolutes. They tend more to the "iffy" than to the cut-and-dried.

Let the Customer Decide.

Some customers are more conscious of brand names than others, and most are more brand-conscious for some kinds of items than they are for others. They don't usually care who grew or packaged the potatoes and onions they buy, but many do care about whose name is on the canned chicken soup and mayonnaise. The extensive, continuous advertising by makers of these products has made the public brand-conscious generally, although not necessarily wedded to the most advertised brands.

There is no certain way to predict how your own customers, individually or collectively, feel about brand names: You can find that out only by experience—trial and error. Beware of "conventional wisdom"—established beliefs. Don't make the mistake of assuming that what appears to be obvious or is commonly accepted is the unshakeable and unvarying truth—e.g., that the carriage trade always buys the widely advertised and most expensive brand names, and the blue collar or bargain basement customers always buy the brand X or cheapest items. The reverse often turns out to be the case. The moneyed class is as eager as anyone to save money, and the factory worker is often entirely willing to pay a high price for what he or she thinks is worth a high price. Smart merchandisers do not presume to know the customer's mind; they invite the customer to decide. (Who is better qualified to decide what customers want than the customers themselves?)

You can find out what those decisions of your customers are only by starting without prejudices, keeping careful records, analyzing them, and letting the facts—and customers—speak for themselves.

Which Brand Produces the Higher Markup?

There is no reliable rule stating whether a given name brand will provide a higher or a lower markup than a given brand X or even whether name brands in general offer higher or lower markups than brands X in general. Each case rests on its own merits, and even trends or generalizations have too many exceptions to be relied upon in something as serious as running a business successfully. Make prejudgments at your own peril.

"Markup" is, to many, the rate at which cost is marked up to determine the selling price. A 40 percent markup would mean charging the customer 1.4 times whatever you paid; what cost you $10, you would sell for $14. As the term is used here, however, it refers to the total gross profit (dollars and cents) on an item, not to the rate at which the price was marked up. ("Rate" does not pay your bills; only dollars and cents do.)

It seems reasonable to assume that there will normally be a markup in proportion to the price of the item—e.g., that there will be a greater gross profit on a $90 pair of shoes than there will be on a $60 pair of shoes. Alas, the logic of this premise—what *appears* to be logic—does not hold for a variety of reasons. The $60 shoes may easily prove to be more profitable and may even be of higher quality. The manufacturer of the $90 shoes may be simply recovering high advertising and distribution costs (not unlikely if the $90 shoes are a widely advertised brand name), and passing none of the higher price on to distributors and retailers.

Within these constraints it pays to make as many trial fits as you can to learn whether switching the line you carry from brand X to some well-known name brand will be more or less profitable in providing markup or, for that matter, whether it pays to carry both. The name brand offers the advantage of being nationally advertised and thus supposedly of greater value (at least greater appeal to customers) justifying a higher price than brand X. But the customer cannot easily price-shop brand X because brand X is often really unbranded (i.e., privately branded and nowhere else to be found with that same label). Even if it sells at a lower price than the name brand, brand X may deliver greater markup to you, either because you can buy it at a remarkably low wholesale price or because you need not mark down its list price at all in selling it. You may, for example, be forced to pay $8 for a name brand item that is listed at $15 but find that you must sell at $11 in a competitive marketplace, whereas you may be able to get its unbranded equal for $5 and be able to sell it for a listed $10. You thus have the double advantage of being able to undersell the name brand, while taking a greater profit. It pays to experiment with name brands, non-name brands, and combinations thereof. Keep records as you experiment so that you can tell with certainty which are the most profitable offerings. In general, however, a diversified line affords you more opportunity to complete sales and meet competition than does a narrow line.

Another way to maximize markup is to sell your own brand, if you can do so without meeting excessive resistance from your customers. There are two ways to do this. One is by having a manufacturer of the product label a quantity for you. You will have to place a large enough order to make it worthwhile for the manufacturer to give you a special price. Not surprisingly, you must generally sell your private brand at considerably lower prices than you sell the advertised brands. Even so, you can usually get a better markup on your own private brand.

There is another way that may be practicable as well as more profitable for you. That is to buy the product in bulk and do your own packaging or repackaging of the product as your own brand. The product is now yours, a unique brand, giving you a great deal of control. This practice discourages price comparisons, making comparison impracticable, if not impossible. The customer simply cannot find an exact duplicate of your product, service, or offer with which to compare your price.

Trading Up Offers Higher Markups.

In many products, especially hard goods (for example, appliances, tools, and furniture), there are multiple levels of quality. There are, for example, TV receivers with various features, according to price. Again, there are no rules to follow in estimating profitability. The most expensive version of any given kind of product does not necessarily offer the highest markups in that line; the cheapest version or even some midrange version may be highest in markup. However, there are many customers who have previously bought a lesser model of something and now want to trade up to a more expensive version. Or the customer may have begun showing interest in only the cheaper version but can, after a bit of "education," be persuaded to develop a greater interest in a more expensive model. Such customers trade up, in effect, even before they buy the first item, usually as a result of being educated by a progressive and persuasive seller.

It is thus always a mistake to prejudge what a customer will decide to buy finally. Add higher-priced versions of whatever products you sell to offer your customers choices over a wide range. Many customers who start with the expectation and intention of buying the lowest-priced item in the line can be persuaded to switch their affections to a more sophisticated model.

Selling the Item with the Greatest Markup.

As we have seen, the highest-priced model in a line is not necessarily the one offering you, as the seller, the greatest benefit. A given kind of item, brand-name or unbranded, may prove most profitable (that is, offer the greatest markup) in the low, high, or middle range of prices and models. Having stocked and offered a wide range of merchandise, it is important that you determine which item in each given line—e.g., TVs, VCRs, CD players, aspirin tablets, men's jackets, or pantyhose—offers you the greatest markup. That is the item you must push and you must instruct your salespeople to push. Fortunately, this often happens to be the best buy for your customers, so you may push it with a clear conscience, knowing that you are helping your customers get the greatest value for their dollar.

50.

MARKUP ON TOTAL SALES
COUNTS TOO

Package Deals Increase Markup.

As a young salesman I had the opportunity to watch a master salesman by the name of Harry increase the markup of each sale he made, if not of each item he sold, by spontaneously improvising package deals. Harry never volunteered a price and never quoted the price of a single item. When the customer asked the price, Harry always quoted a package deal of one kind or another. If it were furniture polish that the customer was interested in, Harry would quote a price for perhaps six bottles. If the customer demurred, Harry would offer to sell the customer only three bottles. He thus practically never sold only a single bottle of furniture polish. But Harry also knew his merchandise so well that he could and did improvise other kinds of packages spontaneously and without hesitation. He could react to a customer's interest in shampoo by instantaneously offering three bottles of shampoo and a quality hair brush for a total price that he calculated without appearing to even think about it.

Aside from increasing the size of the transaction by creating and encouraging tie-in sales, packaging of companion items is an effective counter to the price comparisons that many customers make; the package you thus create is unique. The price quoted is, of course, for the package. The customer cannot therefore conveniently compare your prices with anyone else's, which is itself a great advantage in increasing markups. Start training yourself to think and sell this way. It's easy enough to make up package deals in advance, perhaps even physically combining several items.

Add Companion Items to Your Line.

You must, of course, have the companion items in your line if you are to tie them in to whatever items interest the customer. Harry happened to have a highly varied line of merchandise; the large number and variety of the items in his line gave him great freedom to improvise his package deals spontaneously. To do this successfully, you must add items to your own line that are natural companions to each other so that you, too, can increase the size of each sale. Every line has natural companion items, even the rather specialized ones, such as shoes. The shoe store ought to carry more than shoe laces and shoe polish as companion items, for example, although relatively few do. There are socks, shoe trees, shoe racks, shoe shine kits, shoe horns, home shoe-dying kits (especially appropriate for women's shoes), and even a few other shoe-related items, such as shoe covers for traveling. Even the most specialized businesses can find companion items. The Marriott Hot Shoppes, for example, have long carried large displays of candies, chewing gum, condiments, and other sundries near their cash registers, and even books and magazines are available at their toll road establishments.

Carrying the Largest Sizes Increases Markups.

The Pace and Price Club warehouse stores offer great bargains to their customers, who are not only individual consumers but also small businessmen and women. In fact, they have special memberships for patrons who are themselves owners of small businesses buying items for resale in their own establishments. Many of the prices are even lower than these individuals can get from their own wholesalers! One of the common characteristics of both of these unusual merchandising operations (and perhaps one of the reasons for their ultra-low prices) is that they handle most items in the largest sizes only, often sizes that are not to be found in the normal retail outlets like supermarkets. However, when the item is not an unusually large size but is of the typical size found in the supermarket or neighborhood retail outlet, it is usually offered only as a package of several units or large size— e.g., three bottles of shower detergent or five pounds of sliced baloney. Where my erstwhile mentor, Harry, improvised his "packages" on the spur of the moment, packages in these outlets are physically packaged in advance. It is an entirely viable idea to prepackage "deals" and/or carry larger-than-usual sizes when you can get them, thus increasing markups.

Service Increases Markups Too.

It is, of course, possible to sell package deals by physically packaging items together and putting them on display, or by posting signs explaining the packages. However, in this age of impersonal, find-it-yourself-and-bring-it-to-the-register merchandising, merchants are asking customers to sell to themselves, thereby losing millions of dollars in sales, tie-in and otherwise. Effective merchandising means providing personal service to the customer. Customers are susceptible to suggestion, and tie-in sales will be far more numerous and easier to consummate if you work closely with customers and show direct interest in helping them satisfy their needs. Even in so-called warehouse outlets where patrons wander about in great numbers, making it impossible to wait on each one individually, it increases sales to have a few of your people circulating about, watchful for patrons who obviously need help. Those individuals ought to be employees who have been taught at least the rudiments of customer service and selling techniques.

Competing With Yourself.

Earlier (Chapter 9) you read the story of Mifflin rubbing alcohol, priced higher than competing brands primarily because it was packaged to look more expensive. The merchandising theory here is that there will always be competition at the other end of the price range—i.e., if you make or sell an expensive item, there will be similar items sold more cheaply and competing with you; if you make or sell the cheaper item, you will be competing with the more expensive one. If you make or sell both, you have an excellent chance to appeal to both kinds of customers, the one who favors the high-priced brands and the one who favors the low-priced brands. Your diversified line should carry items that enable you to compete in both arenas, for quality and for price.

CHAPTER 12

A Few Special Measures To Boost Profitability

There are many opportunities to boost your profitability both directly and indirectly through aggressive management. Almost every area of business management—in purchasing, in accounting, and in sales, to name just three—offers opportunities. Some of these opportunities are fairly obvious—getting better buys, for example—but others may come as a bit of a surprise.

51.

PROFITS IN PURCHASING

Cost Reductions in Buying May Mean Even Greater Sales and Profit Percentages.

Fred Klein, a highly successful entrepreneur and founder of several successful companies, quotes another unnamed entrepreneur in his *Handbook on Building a Profitable Business* (Entrepreneurial Workshops Publications, Seattle, 1990). He quotes that other entrepreneur: "I don't make nearly as much money selling as I do in buying and tracking my merchandise." Klein says that a five percent reduction on costs generates the same percentage increase in profits as does a ten percent increase in sales. His figures actually show the five-percent cost decrease to produce slightly more increase in profits than does a ten-percent increase in sales. That is the direct saving, with selling price constant. There is also the possibility for an even greater impact on sales due to the ability to discount a bit more by buying for less. That could result in much greater sales and profit increases.

Middlemen and Multiple Discounts.

The normal channels of distribution in business involve several levels of distribution between the prime source (e.g., the manufacturer, importer, or processor) and the consumer. Traditionally, there is a wholesaler and a retailer (at minimum) in most lines. However, there may be other levels too, and such terms as *jobber*, *distributor*, and even others come into play. Some product lines may have a national distributor, with the chain running down to local or state-wide distributors, wholesalers, and retailers. (Sometimes a distributor or wholesaler is also a retailer of the line, even operating in a storefront location.)

The usual arrangement calls for discounts at each level of distribution. The retailer normally gets the largest discount because retailing is more costly in overhead than wholesaling or distributing is, and because retailers move merchandise item by item, with a much smaller order size. So a retailer may get 20, 30, or even 40 percent discount from the list or suggested price (set by the prime source), while the wholesaler is likely to be getting 45 or 50 percent discount, thus working on a five or ten percent margin. Take, for example, an item for which the prime source suggests $100 as a retail price and sells via a national distributor and a chain of local wholesalers and retailers. The retailer may get about 40 percent discounted from the list, affording a $40 gross profit from which to discount part of profit (remember, it is increasingly difficult to sell anything at its full list price today) and yet have enough left to pay the overhead and earn a bit of net profit.

If distributors and wholesalers are involved in the distribution chain, each has also gotten five or ten percent discount to pay for their role in getting the goods marketed to the retailers. In many cases it is possible for the retailer to get at least a portion of that additional margin of discount. Years ago, when electronic devices still depended on vacuum tubes for their operation, many of us were offered vacuum tubes and other electronic parts at "fifty, ten, and five" or similar arrangements. What this meant was that we were being offered successive discounts (which, presumably, would normally be the wholesalers' and distributors' discounts) as follows:

	PRICE
List:	$10.00
50% ($5) discount:	5.00
10% ($0.50) additional discount:	4.50
5% ($0.225) additional discount:	4.275

Many industries still offer additional discounts (and, of course, the trend to increased discounting is magnified when business conditions tighten), but won't usually volunteer them. The opportunity for increasing your profitability is clear here. Let suppliers know that you are aware of the practice of allowing extra discounts and ask for them.

52.
_____

MANAGING PAYABLES FOR
EXTRA PROFITS

Taking Advantage of Prompt Payment Discounts.

Many suppliers offer extra discounts for prompt payment, usually on the order of one or two percent for payment within 10 days of receiving the invoice. If you find such notations as "2/10, net 30" cryptic, it means that you may take an additional two percent discount for payment within 10 days, or you may take up to 30 days to pay the bill at "net" or without any additional discount. Obviously, you can cut costs considerably if you can take advantage of all prompt-payment discounts.

The way to do this is to manage your payable invoices by "aging" them. That is, establish a policy of taking advantage of all such discounts by organizing and prioritizing all payables in order of their prompt-payment provisions. Those offering no such extra discount must be "aged" for the prescribed 30 days or longer. Those offering two percent discount must be paid first (that is, on the tenth day). Those offering one percent must also be paid then, if cash flow permits, and those offering one-half of one percent are also candidates, but with lowest priority, for payment on the tenth day.

Many companies pay only after 30, 45, or even more days, but take the prompt payment discount anyway. (The federal government was once notorious for doing this, although Congress finally passed a Prompt Payment Act designed to curb the practice.) Suppliers, fearful of confrontations that might cost them customers, often accept this practice, wrong though it is. I mention this here, not to endorse or suggest that you follow an unethical practice, but because you should know of it in your dealings with your own customers.

53.

VOLUME BUYS AND SALES

Buying in Volume.

Getting those extra discounts may require that you buy in greater volume than you have been accustomed to buying. That increases the risk of being stuck with unsold inventory, but with extra discounts you can probably cancel that risk out by holding special sales.

Suppose, for example, that you normally sell 500 of a certain item at a $10 gross profit per item. But now you can buy the item for $3 less by taking 2,000 of them. With the extra discounts, you can afford to offer them at a very special price that will give you a lower $6 gross profit per item, but ought to move the entire lot of 2,000. In the normal sale, that is, you can look to $5,000 gross profit (500 items at $10 each). In the alternative scenario you are considering, you can look at the probability of $12,000 total gross profit (2,000 items at $6 each). Even if you were stuck with half the lot unsold, you would be $1,000 ahead! It's a good gamble. Profit is not mere percentage, nor even markup; it is *total dollars*.

The Super Sale.

Some merchants, having made a quantity buy, hold a great sale, and are left with many unsold items, despite having turned a net profit on the original deal. Now you (assuming that you are the lucky and successful risktaker) have a sizable lot of merchandise that owes you nothing: You have it at virtually no cost, as the residue of an already profitable deal. You can afford to unload this remainder merchandise at a true "loss" figure in a super-sale! Sell it with "scare headlines" at one-half the price of your original sale. Run advertising that laments your buyer's folly in buying this item. Weep all over the morning newspaper, but give the item away at one-third its listed retail price, thereby reaping additional profits. Even if you had only broken even on the original sale you would be ahead in profitability, because that buy enabled you to run a super-sale and gain all the extra traffic in your store.

Buying Directly from Manufacturers.

In some cases you can buy directly from the manufacturer or processor, even if you must import the goods yourself. (See Chapter 3 on purchasing for more ideas here.) You should, of course, get the full discount offered a distributor or wholesaler. The U.S. Government has a standard reference for ensuring that federal agencies are given the best prices possible; it's a contract clause that requires a supplier to certify that the prices quoted by the supplier are at least as low as those "offered to the most-favored customer." This is a standard you might well emulate in your purchasing activities.

54.

THE LOSS LEADER

Spinoff Profits Count, Too.

Actually, you may reap even more profit than postulated earlier in discussing the super sale if you have a general-merchandise retail operation, for the super-sale will bring a great deal of extra traffic into your place of business. That cannot help but produce additional sales and profits as a spinoff. This is something else to consider when you are offered unusually attractive discounts.

But you do not have to wait for special opportunities to offer special buys as a means of bringing customers to your place of business. The loss leader is a standard method for marketing, and you can create and advertise one any time. This is not necessarily an item you literally lose money on, although the definition of "losing money" in business is rather a variable one. That notwithstanding, we can say that the loss leader is not necessarily an item for which you paid more than the price for which you sell it. It may be an item that barely returns its direct cost. The point is simply that it brings customers to your place of business, and if you should literally lose money on it, you can console yourself that it is not a true loss but an investment in advertising—and quite possibly the cheapest kind of advertising available to you. It is certainly likely that most people coming in to buy the leader will buy something else while in your establishment.

55.

OPPORTUNITY BUYS

Purchasing Grand Slams.

Fred Klein, in the excellent book cited earlier, distinguishes between "replenishment buying" and "anticipation buying." The first is, of course, purchasing to maintain an inventory of those items carried regularly in stock. The other refers to buying seasonal merchandise or new items, items that are new to the marketplace in general or are new to your own business. In anticipation buying, you must estimate the market for these items, accepting the risks of being wrong in those estimates and suffering the consequences of being stuck with a large quantity of unsold merchandise—or of ordering too little to meet the demand and being unable to replenish your stock rapidly enough. The Nehru jacket is one classic example of a product that fizzled badly and stuck retailers everywhere with unsalable surpluses. The Hula Hoop was a classic example of a fad item that spurred demand of great proportions but lasted such a short time that there was not enough time for sellers to replenish their original stocks before the fad died. The price you pay in such cases ought to be related to the risk you take, and you must remember that these kinds of buys, anticipation buys are risky by definition.. Therefore, you should be aggressive in demanding maximum discounts in buying such items.

However, there is another type of buying that ought to be considered here; it has been referred to in Chapter 3. I would call it "opportunity buying." That term refers to the occasions when you can find a great deal of merchandise available at exceptionally low cost. For many venturesome entrepreneurs, such buys have been veritable grand slams of merchandising success. The late Joe Karbo, a true marketing/merchandising entrepreneur, made such a grand slam on more than one occasion, such as the time cited in Chapter 9 when he bought and marketed those "spy in a door" devices. Obviously, to do this you require certain special characteristics, one of which is imagination: the ability to conceive a way of disposing of the items profitably. The other characteristic is the courage to take substantial risks. In other words, you have to be something of a gambler, a high roller.

Assessing Opportunities.

Entrepreneurs, especially those with enough resolve to work long shots, necessarily fly by the seat of the pants a great deal of the time. They rely on instincts—gut feelings—as much as on judgment. Still, there must be some standard for assessing cost, sales potential, and risk. At the least, I suggest that you make a worst-case analysis: Assume, as a first step, that you will succeed in selling only one-half the lot. What price would you have to get to earn a reasonable profit? *Can* you get that price for the item? What price do you need to break even? What value would the remainder of the lot have—i.e., what would you do with it? Only after having examined such questions closely can you evaluate how promising the venture really is.

56.

GETTING MORE COMPETITIVE

Cutting Costs with Value Management (VM).

Value management is an increasingly popular way of becoming more competitive by cutting costs while increasing quality. It is a spinoff of value engineering (also known as value analysis), which in turn was a product of World War II improvisation at the General Electric Company. GE management found that substitutions of cheaper materials, forced by wartime shortages, often resulted in better quality at lower costs. It was pure serendipity, but subsequent studies showed that such benefits could be achieved deliberately and regularly—given methodical discipline on the part of management.

It soon became clear that the principles were not peculiar to engineering; they could be applied everywhere in the business with similar results. I am among the many who encourage the idea of calling this concept *value management* rather than *value engineering*, which intimidated many and inhibited non-engineers from becoming seriously interested in the idea.

The underlying principle is simple enough: a healthy skepticism and a desire to scrutinize perceived needs and values in order to identify true needs and values. Why, for example, should an automaker manufacture and include in the same car some bolts with a six-sided head for hexagon wrenches, some with a slotted head for blade screwdrivers, and some with a Phillips head for Phillips screwdrivers? Why not a single bolt designed with a head that will accommodate all three tools? It's easily done, and this simple idea reduces costs in tooling, manufacturing, parts inventory, hand tools, and maintenance. Author Lynn Tylczak documents such a case in *Get Competitive!*

On an even more basic level, why hire a secretary and pay a secretary's salary to someone whose duties consist of making coffee, occasionally filing papers, typing odd jobs, and answering the telephone? More to the point, why have a full-time secretary if you can't keep a secretary busy with proper secretarial functions full time? Robert Townsend (*Up the Organization*, Alfred A. Knopf, New York, 1970) answered that question by calling on someone from the typing pool when needed, instead of having a personal or full-time secretary.

Is Value Management Just Common Sense?

Value Management is today a formal discipline, with well defined methods and processes. Unfortunately, some managers reject the idea of formal value management programs, such as are today embraced by the Department of Defense and other government agencies, Ford Motor Company, B. F. Goodrich, Hughes Aircraft, Martin Marietta, Westinghouse, Western Electric, Amoco, General Electric, IBM, and many others. Some managers prefer to believe that what certified value specialists (the Society of American Value Engineers has a certification program) do as their specialty is merely the application of "common sense." If that were true, value specialists would never be able to work significant improvements—as they do every day.

The major fault with VM is that it is often applied too late, after the commitments to tooling and gearing up have been made, so that the costs of retooling or otherwise restarting the process are greater than the savings to be realized. The best time for VM is in the concept and design stages, before investments are made or committed.

But VM does more than cut costs. It also *increases value*. We will have a look at VM again in later pages.

57.

CUTTING OVERHEAD

Overhead can and should be defined differently for different businesses because it has different significance in different applications. The labor-intensive or service business tends to define overhead as a percentage of direct labor costs. That makes sense there as a way of determining what your true costs are and how you must price your services. In retailing, there is a tendency to define overhead as a percentage of total sales because that makes good sense in managing that kind of business, where determining what your markups must be is an overriding question. This brings us to a special opportunity to increase profitability across the board.

Suppose, for example, that your overhead proves to be 30 percent of sales. That is, your markups must include that 30 percent as part of the cost of the item being marked up. Only that part of the markup that is in excess of 30 percent is gross profit. Obviously, if you can reduce your overhead by, let us say, five percent, your profit will rise by five percent.

The interesting thing about overhead is that it in almost all cases is not linear. That is, doubling your sales does not in turn double your overhead. Your rent, insurance, heat, and light, for example, do not increase. You may need some extra help, but you probably don't have to double the sales force. Therefore, if you have a super-sale or offer a loss leader, you benefit by increasing the gross sales figure, thus simultaneously lowering the overhead rate—which makes your remaining sales that much more profitable.

PART THREE

Increasing Gross Sales

Obviously, your profitability is linked, both directly and indirectly, to your gross sales volume. The direct benefits of a great sales volume are obvious. However, in the previous chapter you saw how increasing total sales volume can be beneficial in a special and unexpected way: reducing your overhead by spreading fixed costs over a much larger sales base. This is effective, you saw, even when you are selling a loss leader or having a huge sale at breakeven prices. In this part of the book, we are going to look at sales and other ways to increase your gross sales figures.

CHAPTER 13

Increasing Your Marketing Success

Marketing success—the degree to which you persuade the buying public to buy what you sell—is not and cannot be a constant. It will vary as a result of many influences: seasonality of some kinds of products and services, general economic conditions, and other unpredictable circumstances and events. But you cannot afford to let chance determine the fate of your business. You must manage circumstances and events as much as humanly possible, while gaining and keeping control through aggressive marketing methods. These include sales, advertising, publicity, special promotions, and many other methods available to an imaginative and resourceful entrepreneur. Let's look at a few ideas for doing this.

58.

INCREASING ADVERTISING IMPACT

Copy That Sells.

If you are not convinced that copy makes a substantial difference in results, try out two small advertisements, as follows (or adapt the idea to your own product or service).

Advertisement number 1:

> NAME AND ADDRESS LABELS
> Distinctive & Different
> SPECIAL OFFER:
> $1 per 1,000 labels

Advertisement number 2:

> DISTINCTIVE AND DIFFERENT
> Here is CLASS with a capital C.
> Name and address labels. Park Avenue Script and gold borders.
> Only $1 per 1,000 labels
> SPECIAL OFFER

Which is the better advertisement? Both advertisements will produce orders. But which one will product the *greatest number* of orders? The second one will, of course. "Naturally," you say, "it's a bigger advertisement, so it must get more attention and produce more orders."

That may be true, but it is not relevant. What is relevant is that the first advertisement does not offer the reader anything special in the way of a benefit, whereas the second one does—it promises "class" and then explains what "class" is, in this case: It is that special Park Avenue Script and gold borders. What is "Park Avenue Script?" It is your invention, a descriptive name you devise to provide snob appeal. Name and address labels for one dollar is one thing, a bargain in itself. But class for one dollar—ah, that is different. Who else offers class for only a dollar?

If That Isn't Enough
You can make the appeal even stronger by calling your type "NEW Park Avenue Script." "New" is an appealing word in all advertising, as are FREE, NOW, SALE, and many other popular words that never wear out. Customers always want what is new, free, on sale, or special in some way.

Your Image.
Bloomingdale's of New York has a certain distinctive image. Lord & Taylor's has another, and I. Magnim still another. Even the customer who has never set foot in one of these establishments understands their image, because what the customer *does* see is advertising and/or sales literature. They *are* the business. They must be attractive. Not necessarily expensive, mind you; that's not the same thing. In fact, frequently the more expensive paper and ink are actually less expensive-*looking* than are the cheaper papers! Moreover, much of the extra money spent for typesetting, two-color printing, and slick paper is a complete waste. Good, clean typewriter or computer-printer composition is perfectly adequate, as long as the copy is well laid out, clean, and articulate. Remember the doctrine of perception in business: The truth

is what the customer perceives or can be persuaded to perceive as truth. Perhaps there are other truths, but they don't count in marketing.

Advertising Illustrations.

There are those who, for whatever reasons, worship at the shrine of illustrations in advertising. Illustrations help, of course, but don't be misled by this. Illustrations do not do the selling; what they do is help to attract attention and direct the reader's eyes to the words that do the selling. If they do anything else, they are not doing their job.

59.

COPY THAT SELLS

Don't Neglect the Headline.

The major part of the selling is done by the headline. Let me repeat that, because it is a vitally important point. The major part of the selling is done by the headline. Get yourself a good, selling headline and the body copy does not need to be inspired: all it has to be is competent to complete the selling job. But write a poor headline, and even inspired body copy won't do the selling job. Most readers, uninspired by the headline, won't bother to read the body copy!

People don't really buy products; they buy what products do. They prefer labels printed in "Park Avenue Script" with gold borders over labels printed in ordinary type because "Park Avenue" has a touch of class. Your words in that little advertisement "positioned" your product by making it a class product, one with a bit of snob appeal. It helps the buyer gain some enhanced self-image.

A man who is driving a perfectly serviceable automobile buys a new one. Why? Is it because he doesn't want to seem or feel to be less than his neighbor or brother-in-law, who is driving a new model? It's a good bet. He can't afford—emotionally or in terms of self-esteem—to appear less successful than others. Especially if, in his heart, he thinks he really is less successful!

Some people actually like the taste of beer or liquor; others like only what it does to them. And still others drink only "to be sociable"—to be able to relax with friends and feel equal to them. And some drink an expensive "name" brand products—even convince themselves that it tastes better—because it has snob appeal.

A homemaker doesn't want floor wax. What she wants is a shiny, waxed floor, and she wants it with the least amount of effort required to get it. And she really wants not even the waxed floor, but the approval of everyone who sees her beautiful kitchen floor. Don't sell her floor wax; sell her the swift, easy achievement of a waxed floor. But make that the secondary, follow-up argument: first sell her the unrestrained admiration of friends and neighbors who are astonished at the beauty of her kitchen floor and her skills as an expert homemaker. Then show her that a gleaming waxed floor will win her that admiration, and that your product will produce that waxed floor easily and painlessly. (Innumerable TV commercials can provide a model for this type of selling.)

Decide what your customer really wants—what the desired end result it. You may be sure that is some sort of emotional satisfaction. Write a headline that appeals directly to that desire, that promises to fulfill that dream. Then write the follow-up body copy to reinforce the promise made in the headline. Here are a few classic real life examples of successful headlines:

HOW TO FORM YOUR OWN CORPORATION WITHOUT A LAWYER FOR UNDER $50

THE LAZY MAN'S WAY TO RICHES

HOW TO PROSPER DURING THE COMING BAD YEARS

DO YOU MAKE THESE MISTAKES IN ENGLISH?

HOW TO WIN FRIENDS AND INFLUENCE PEOPLE

HOW A NEW DISCOVERY MADE A PLAIN GIRL BEAUTIFUL

FIVE ACRES AND INDEPENDENCE

HOW TO SUCCEED AS AN INDEPENDENT CONSULTANT

HOW I MADE A FORTUNE WITH A "FOOL IDEA"

What Should Be in the Headline.

The headline should attract the prospect's eye and arouse enough interest to induce him or her to read the body copy. The two cardinal sins of headline writing, punishable by immediate execution, are being clever and being cryptic.

You attract the reader's attention and arouse his or her interest by telling at least some of your story in the headline—enough to tell the reader *why* he or she ought to be interested in reading what you have to say, i.e., what benefit you are offering. Here is a brief example of how not to write a headline taken from one of those weekly tabloids sold in the supermarkets:

An Unforgettable Collection
for Sweethearts Everywhere!
The White Cliffs of Dover
42 Great Love Songs From World War II
* Original Hits!   * Original Stars!

What's wrong with this headline? Simply this: The wrong line is used for the main head. For many, even veterans of World War II, the headline is cryptic: Not everyone who served in that war knows what the white cliffs of Dover are. And even for those who do know, the headline carries no message of its own. Probably the best headline would have been "42 Great Love Songs From World War II." The subheads could have remained the same, although "For Sweethearts Everywhere!" would also have made a better headline that the one that was used.

Here are two headlines from the same source that are good in that they deliver a message and immediately explain the benefit offered:

A 90-SECOND FACE LIFT

A FIRMER STOMACH WITHOUT SITUPS

60.

SALES ARE FOREVER

Don't Be Bashful About Having Sales.

A chain store operation known as "Bill's Carpet Barn" in my area runs sales frequently as a regular method for doing business. (The firm once announced a sale every week without a break for over a year.) Many businesses have perpetual sales, and display a quite amazing ability to find "excuses" for having a new sale every few days: Every holiday is an occasion for a sale: It is necessary to celebrate Lincoln's and Washington's birthdays with sales, of course, as well as Veteran's Day, Labor Day, and all the rest. I shouldn't be much surprised to find some imaginative marketer running a special Groundhog's Day Sale. Here are a few other ideas for sales:

Manager's Sale
Founder's Day Sale
Closeout Sale
Remnants Sale
Inventory Sale
Clearance Sale
Shed a Tear Sale
Our Buyer's Mistakes Sale

Beat the Recession Sale
First Snow of the Year Sale

I think it is quite possible to come up with 365 good ideas for
sales, which would allow you to have one every day of the year!

61.

MERCHANDISING

Another Word for Selling.

In retail establishments such as department stores, managers often speak of "merchandising" as the key to effective and efficient selling of goods. All they mean by this fifty-cent word is "make the merchandise more attractive to the customer."

There are many ways to do this. In the typical retail setting, the customer inspects the merchandise before buying it. The merchandise must therefore be physically attractive—handsomely packaged, well displayed, brightly lit, etc. In mail order, however, the customer does not get to inspect the merchandise before buying it, so "merchandising" and "packaging" have other meanings here.

In short, the visual appeal in the retail, point-of-sale operation—the retail store—is the package and its setting. This is especially the case with luxury goods (jewelry and cosmetics, for example), which are a direct and unabashed appeal to vanity, love of luxury, desire to be attractive, yearning to be admired, and perhaps that slight bit of snobbery most of us have a secret longing to indulge. Clever merchandising in walk-in stores is designed to make just such appeals, and to help the prospect visualize himself or herself owning, wearing, and displaying such upscale items. When I advertised a proposal-writing seminar by calling it a "Graduate" seminar and explained that it was an advanced seminar for proposal-writing experts and not meant for neophytes, I was merchandising it. I gave it snob appeal, and the result was a sellout attendance—including many of those neophytes who wanted to know why they should be excluded from something so special!

To help the undecided or wavering prospect make the transition to happy buyer, other pressures are applied. Bonuses are commonly offered—perhaps two for the price of one, a discount, or some other special inducement. (The words "sale" and "discount" are in the category of those that seem to never wear out their appeal!) And then even more pressure is applied: "No cash needed. Buy now, own it, wear it, use it now, and pay later! All major credit cards accepted!" Often, such inducements are decisive.

It works in every business, including mail order. Special sales, tie-ins, credit, immediate delivery (shipment), bonuses, discounts, snob appeal, and gifts make it difficult for the prospect to refuse.

Retailers also play percentages, following probability logic. A great many sales result from impulse buying: the customer sees an item, likes it, and buys it—especially if it is easily available with "plastic money. Get enough people into your store—create enough "traffic" there—and sales will result, because a certain percentage of impulse buyers will buy something they did not plan to buy or know that they wanted. It follows, then, that the more traffic—people in the store—you have, the more sales you will garner. We see again why retailers run frequent loss-leader sales. It pays to lose a few cents on some popular item when doing so brings many people to the store. This approach is often cheaper than "real" advertising, and it often gets far better results as well.

The principle works in mail order as well. Here, "traffic" is created through mass advertising. Presumably, if your proposition is an appealing one, the percentages will work for you. The more people you reach, the more orders you will get.

But we are, in the end, talking about merchandising—making offers more attractive so as to increase sales. Given enough advertising and mailing, how do we raise that percentage of prospects who plunk down their plastic and give you the order? Remember, advertising is only a preliminary to merchandising.

62.

CHARGES AND CREDIT

There is a Time and Place for Credit Sales.

Customers do not need (or seek) a line of credit when they make $2 or $3 purchase. But if you are in mail order sales you will need to do better than $2 or $3 sales if you are to succeed. So, how to you arrange to give your customers a charge account?

It is not difficult today to set up arrangements to permit your customers to use their "bank cards"—VISA and MasterCard, for instance—to buy from you. Your own bank can probably arrange things for you. If not, call any bank in your area that issues these cards; one of them will be able to arrange setting you up to handle this. The bank will supply the forms and explain the system. You will have to allow the bank to make a few percentage points—discounting your paper—but there are compensations. You don't have to wait for checks to clear (and you do not have any bad-check problems); you deposit the slips as though they were cash and you have immediate access to your money.

There is at least one other expedient. If you sell expensive items, you may want to set up a direct credit system, wherein your local bank discounts your paper. Here is how that works: You sell, let us say, a $100 order, getting a $10 deposit and setting up time payments for the balance. (You add some kind of a financing charge, of course.) When you have several of these, perhaps five or ten, representing perhaps $1,000, you take this "paper"—the signed notes—to the bank and discount it there. That is, the bank buys the paper from you for perhaps $900, and collects the payments from the customers. (You may hear this referred to as "assigning" the account to the bank.) Your banker can help you in setting this up and explaining all the details.

Either way, you benefit; we all use "plastic money" today. Some businesses do nearly 100 percent of their business via credit cards and charge plates, but all who offer such credit options to consumers do a significant amount of business that way, probably at least 25 percent in most cases.

63.

TIE-INS AND FOLLOW-UP SALES

All the Eggs in One Basket?

It's difficult to build a successful business on just one product, although it has been done. It's certainly not efficient, though. It costs a great deal of money to capture each customer, and over the long haul, sales to established customers are far more profitable than initial sales to new customers. In fact, in some businesses it is almost impossible to turn a profit on the first sale to a customer. Only by making customers for repeat sales can you make such a business successful.

There are mail order "experts" who will assure you that you should never offer more than one item in a single mailing. That may be true in some kinds of ventures, but I found it to be sheer nonsense in my businesses. I started that way and nearly went broke immediately—with a low-priced item. I wasn't getting back my most basic costs. Later experience reinforced that lesson. Here are a few things I learned.

1. Many of my customers started by buying one of my lowest-priced items, but cam back later with large orders. (Were they testing me to see if my merchandise and performance were worthwhile?)

2. Other customers, even when buying for the first time, ordered almost everything in the line. (There have been many orders for $200 and more.) If I do not come up with new items, I can't sell to these customers again. (Mine are not consumable items that need to be replaced.)

3. Some customers have written to beg me to keep their names on my mailing lists.

4. Some ask for my suggestions as to what they ought to buy, and some even make suggestions as to what they would like to buy if I offered it.

64.

INCREASING THE
AVERAGE-SALE SIZE

Ready for a Surprise?

It costs you as much to offer $10 worth of items by mail as to offer
$200 worth. Well, almost as much. Your printing bill will be
slightly larger because you need more literature, but the postage
and handling costs are the same. If your average sale is only $10
you can easily take a loss, unless your response is very good and
your markup is very high. On the other hand, if your average sale
is $20, there is far, far less risk of loss because you have much bet-
ter margins to work with.

One way to raise that average-sale size is, as I have pointed
out, to offer a wide line. But another is through merchandising
techniques. Package deals are one excellent way. Take several related items and offer them all, as a package, at a special price.
Once, I offered a newsletter subscription and two related
manuals, listed at $142, for $99. My average order size went to
over $65, and I was highly profitable at a mere 1½% response
rate.

There are many variations on that approach, such as a discount on all orders over some fixed amount, or a free gift of some
sort with all orders over some amount.

Don't make the mistake of selling too cheaply. Yes, people do want bargains, but they lose their respect for anything that is too cheap. A friend who offered a booklet for $2 with good results decided that it ought to sell even better at $1. He found to his despair that at $1 sales fell off sharply! And I discovered that truth with a $50 set of books that sold reasonably well—profitably, in any case—but bombed out completely at $15.

Here are two truths I will vouch for out of my own experience:

1. There are $1, $2, and $3 customers. There are $10 and $20 customers. And there are $40, $50, and $100 customers. The $2 customer will never spend $10, but the $10 customer will spend $15 or $20 if he or she really wants what you are selling. Price, within a reasonable range, never stops someone who really wants the item. But cutting a $100 item to $60 will *never* draw sales from the $10 customer. In short, there are classes of customers, and it is extremely difficult—nearly impossible—to get one class to cross lines and join another class.

2. Many customers judge value by price. If it seems to be too cheap for what it is represented to be, they won't believe it. (Would you buy a $1 watch?) Sometimes sales increase when you raise prices.

What is more valuable, 10 customers at $15 each or 20 customers at $5 each?

There are no true formulas for pricing. You must use judgment, and you must test. Run your ads, try different ideas and different prices, keep records, and draw sensible conclusions from your experience and tests.

65.

WHEN PRICE COUNTS

The "Unbeatable Deal."

Strangely enough, and in spite of all I have just told you about prices and motivations, there are cases where savings or bargains are decisive in making the sale—in persuading a customer to say "yes."

A successful newsletter publisher told me an interesting story along these lines. When he was starting up and working capital was a problem, he issued a special offer to his readers. His annual subscription price was then $24. He offered his readers a two-year subscription at $25—an extra year for an extra dollar. It worked well. He had unusually brisk renewal activity, and many whose subscriptions had a long way yet to run took advantage of his limited-time special offer to add two years to their subscriptions.

That was the good news. The bad news was that he had saturated the market; the following year renewals were extremely low, because everyone had already renewed for two years. And when he tried to salvage the situation by offering a free book with each new subscription, it fell flat. Obviously, his subscribers wanted to save money more than they wanted a free book.

The reason the first offer went so well was that the $24 value was already accepted, and so it was a reference: the extra year for an extra dollar was an easily recognized value. Perhaps he would have done as well with a little less generous an offer—perhaps a half-price offer. It would have been worth trying, I believe.

If you offer discounts, be sure that the prospects can recognize them as true discounts, discounts from *established* prices.

CHAPTER 14

Diversify Your Direct-Sales Channels And Media

Direct marketing (or "direct sales") is the sole or principal means of marketing for many organizations, but it is also an ancillary marketing method for organizations with multiple marketing approaches (such as Sears and Montgomery Ward). Those firms were best known at first for their catalog sales operations, a popular direct marketing (DM) approach, but later opened retail outlets, some of them full department stores. On the other hand, some retailers, such as large department stores, have added catalogs and other DM tools to add to sales volume.

Direct marketing is a simple enough idea. It is based on the philosophy of selling directly to the consumer, rather than via retail establishments that wait for shoppers to drop by. It has, over the years, become most closely identified with direct mail, which has become an industry unto itself, accounting for many billions of dollars worth of sales annually. Still, there are other ways to go out aggressively in pursuit of customers instead of waiting for them to come to you. All merit inclusion as DM methods.

66.

DIRECT SALES CHANNELS

Reactive Versus Proactive Selling.

Reactive selling is what most retailers do. They wait for customers to approach, and do little else aggressively in marketing, other than to advertise sales and try to make their merchandise displays attractive. There are some marketers who do not have the patience for this, or even the conviction that this is the best way to do business. For them, marketing must take the opposite tack. It must go after the customer aggressively, knocking on doors, figuratively and literally, pressing the prospect hard to become a customer. The general term for this proactive approach to marketing is *direct marketing*, often known by the abbreviation "DM," which is in turn also used to refer to *direct mail*, one of the several forms of direct marketing, and almost surely the most prominent and most widely practiced. It dominates the field to such a degree that discussions of direct marketing are usually posed in terms of direct mail. Even casual reading of the direct marketing trade journal, *DM News*, reveals its almost total concentration on direct mail.

Direct sales offers several immediate advantages. Probably the most important is the economy of location. Some merchants operate both retail across-the-counter establishments and direct marketing programs. However, the costly retail location is totally unnecessary to direct marketing sales approaches because you are not looking for in-person visits from your customers. You can pursue the several direct-sales approaches from any location as your base of operations.

The Traveler.

One traditional direct sales channel (an ancient one) is the itinerant sales representative—the fabled "traveling salesman." This person calls directly on prospects in their own homes, work places, places of business, and wherever else one may meet consumers. The traveling salesman—termed salesperson or sales professional today—is not exactly a new idea: Merchants, especially those from the Middle East, traveled as itinerant salesmen throughout the Mediterranean basin in biblical times and probably even earlier. Direct sales channels can hardly get more basic or more direct than that. But these traditional methods, while still in use, are today supplemented by many newer developments: Businesses today make direct sales contacts with prospective customers in other ways, some of them using modern technology.

The Direct Mail Approach.

Direct-mail enthusiasts are fond of saying that anything can be sold by mail. It's a theoretical truth. As a practical matter it requires some qualification. A small-tag item—one of modest cost—can be sold directly by mail as a result of a single, initial solicitation. Big-tag items normally require follow-up sales effort, so that the initial solicitation is, in this case, a means for developing sales leads. However, there are no fixed definitions or size standards for such items. The definitions vary according to several factors. One is the nature of the respondent: An executive earning $150,000 a year views "small" and "big" differently than does a secretary earning $300 a week. Another is the nature of the item. Few people, no matter their income, will buy an automobile, house, or even a computer without inspecting it first, doing some comparison shopping, and even talking it over with spouse or friends. And still another factor is the identity of the seller: Most consumers will trust the large, prestigious company to back up their guarantees sooner than they will the unknown seller, and thus may buy relatively large items sight unseen if sold by a well-known, large company.

Direct mail works well, but you must be clear about your objective. Are you, and should you be, pursuing sales—or sales *leads*?

Telemarketing Is a Similar Approach.

Telemarketing once consisted principally of hiring housewives to spend a few hours a day calling people and trying to win orders or generate sales leads. In that, it was and is similar to direct mail marketing. The hard part was recruiting enough people to make the calls and training those people in sales techniques.

Those problems severely limited the applications. Modern technology, however, has led to a telemarketing rennaissance. Telemarketing no longer depends on recruiting callers. It is often automated, with recorded messages and computer-controlled automatic dialers to play messages and record responses. In overall scale, telemarketing does not even approach the multibillion-dollar direct mail industry, but it is nevertheless a serious marketing alternative you may wish to consider as a supplement to your other marketing initiatives.

67.

THE DAILY NEWSPAPER AS A DM RESOURCE

A First Principle.

Advertising isn't worth much if it isn't seen and read (or heard, in the case of aural copy). Getting attention is primary goal of all advertising. Some advertisers go to extremes to create copy that screams, "Look at me!" Even so, many neglect the first principle of getting the copy in the right place, the place where it is easiest to get that attention. Consider the daily newspaper, a valuable medium sadly overlooked by many advertisers who don't understand it, at least not in terms meaningful for advertising purposes.

Understanding What a Newspaper Is—As an Advertising Medium.

The daily newspaper is a valuable medium for all marketing, although what we see most in it are the large-store advertisements—those of department stores, supermarkets, major chain stores, and other full-page and multi-page spreads that seem to dominate the paper. The newspaper is especially neglected by most of those in direct marketing, and that is a mistake. It can mean more business for you even in direct marketing, but you must learn how to use it well.

Today's *Washington Post* (Friday) is not an especially heavy edition. It is often much thicker. Still, it offers readers 156 pages of reading matter, not counting advertising inserts. In the upper right corner on the front page it lists these sections:

A News/Editorials
B Sports
C Style/Television/Classified
D Metro/Obituaries
E Metro 2/Comics
F Business
Inside: Weekend

Weekend is a 68-page tabloid, a newspaper in itself, boasting lots of advertising. It supplements the rest of the newspaper—the six sections named above, which themselves number 88 pages. There are other tabloid inserts on other days, covering different subjects—such as food and health—and periodically there are special tabloids on careers or some other special subject.

I read the main news section (which is itself divided into general news and a subsection devoted to "world news") and the business section. I may or may not read other sections. My wife always reads the *Style* section, and may or may not look at any other pages of the daily newspaper.

This is typical. Hardly anyone reads the entire newspaper, all sections of it. Most people break the paper down into sections immediately and discard the ones that do not interest them. In short, the newspaper is not one publication, for advertising purposes; it is several. It is a daily news magazine, a health magazine, a society magazine, a business magazine, and perhaps a few others. On Sunday, when it includes a magazine and an even more subsections, it is even more diversified melange of periodicals.

Position is Everything.

It doesn't take an expert to conclude that if you are selling sporting goods, your advertising belongs in the sports section of the newspaper, or that advertising for a new kitchen gadget fits in the food section better than in the society pages. But those are only the rudiments of positioning. There are other important considerations of position within the section of the paper you select.

Above the Fold.

We have all learned to read from top to bottom, so our attention goes immediately to the top of the page, whether it is a 6- x 9-inch page in a book or a 14- x 24-inch newspaper page. The favored position for advertising that is less than a full page is therefore in the top half of the page—i.e., "above the fold."

Left or Right?

We—most of us—tend to favor the right-hand side. The right-hand page (the odd-numbered one) has most impact—except for the back page of a section.

Front or Back?

The front page of a section is the best one, because it gets the most (and the most immediate) attention. Front pages usually do not carry advertising, however, as a matter of editorial policy. The back page is second in favor only to the front page, and more often than not does carry advertising, usually a full-page display. It is a prized spot. (For one thing, even those who do not normally read that section of the paper are likely to see that back page.)

When You Can't Have the Back Page.

It's not easy to get the back page of a section. There are a limited number of back pages, and many others want them. Newspapers tend to favor full-page advertising for back pages. (Check your own newspaper and verify this.) The next best choice, then, is a right-hand page as far forward—i.e., as close to the front page—as possible.

The News Story Ploy.

Many readers rush on past anything that appears to be ad copy, especially when they are catching up with the news, as reported in a newspaper. And so some advertisers use an effective device of making their advertising look like a news story, complete with a headline, and sometimes even with a dateline, as though it were a hot press release. (Of course, you can't use line art or oversize headlines if you want the advertisement to appear to be a news story.) The copy must be identified as advertising; the publisher will insist on it. Usually, the copy is boxed and carries the word "ADVERTISEMENT" to identify it as such. The word is in small type, however, and hardly noticeable. By the time the reader is aware that this is advertising copy, he or she is well into it.

68.

CATALOGS AND DIRECT MAIL

Cataloging is Hot.

Catalog mailings are an increasingly popular way of pursuing business. Catalogs are used most frequently as direct-marketing sales literature. From the customer's viewpoint, the major appeal is convenience and selection. The customer can shop and order without leaving his or her chair. Another appeal is the wide selection a thick catalog offers. (Somehow, you can often find things in a catalog that you can't find on the shelves when you visit the store and wander through it!) Another benefit to you is that catalogs are easier for consumers to turn to—and use—than many other marketing methods.

There are at least 8,000 catalogs, large and small, in circulation today, and the number is growing steadily. Some companies rely on cataloging exclusively or primarily—Spiegel, L.L.Bean, Land, and Fingerhut, for example. Others are both across-the-counter retailers and catalogers—e.g., Sears and Montgomery Ward. But for every well-known, large cataloger, there are hundreds of smaller ones, some even operating catalog-sales businesses from their homes.

Preparing, printing, and mailing a catalog can be a costly business if you publish your own catalog and demand a thick slick-paper, process-color product, a la Spiegel and the other major players. But you don't have to go that route. Nothing in cataloging requires you to create an expensive mailer. Yesterday I found the catalog of the "Wholesale Supply Company" in my mail box. The wrapper/self-cover is a rough, brown-paper item that looks like a fugitive from a paper-bag assembly line. (It was almost surely selected for effect—to dramatize the firm's image as a no-frills, money-saving supply source—as much as for practical benefit.) The interior 55 pages are an inexpensive white sulfite paper, with simple line drawings and black-and-white printing. The whole piece is on 11- x 17-inch, folded to 8-½ x 11 inches and saddle stitched—i.e., folded with center staples. Inside are listed hundreds of items most businesses have need for, most of them at attractive prices. The sales strategy is quite obviously one of offering a no-frills service at the lowest possible prices. It is quite effective.

Catalogs Do Not Have To Be Thick and Slick.

I get my share of those thick catalogs of hundreds of smooth-paper pages in full color, but I also get even simpler catalogs than the one I just described. The very word *catalog* is quite flexible. Some of the sales literature I see in my morning mail would not be called catalogs by most consumers, who think of catalogs as thick and slick publications. Some of thes pieces I receive are mere folders, even single sheets. But they are catalogs technically because they describe the individual items, furnish prices for each, and include ordering information, usually with ordering forms of some sort.

It Doesn't Have To Be Your Own Catalog.

Many catalogs that arrive in your mailbox are not the creation of those who mailed it to you. A number of large companies provide their dealers and distributors with catalogs imprinted with the dealer's name. If you handle a complete line of a company of this type you can buy your catalogs from them, with your name on it, at wholesale prices. As you might imagine, the savings here can be substantial.

Easy to Create.

You may prefer to create your own catalog (your situation may mandate that you do). A simple catalog is easy enough to create and doesn't have to be expensive. Text may be composed or set by typewriter. But even the smallest offices today have desktop computers and printers, which can turn out high-quality text resembling formal typeset material. Illustrations can often be obtained free of charge from the manufacturers of the items. (For that matter, manufacturers often will furnish camera-ready materials you can incorporate in your catalog.)

69.

NEWSLETTERS AND DIRECT MAIL

Overcoming the Discard Factor.

Many businesses are turning to the newsletter as a modern direct marketing tool. One immediate advantage to this approach is that even those respondents weary of the daily morning flow of what they often refer to as "junk mail" are likely to take the time to look at any newsletter that pops out of the morning mail, if it is obvious that the piece is truly a newsletter. That is the first advantage, but certainly not the only one.

Soft Sell.

Most direct mail is hard sell. Typical of the DM package is a sales letter of several pages sprinkled with black, blue and red ink in the form of dashes, underlines, exclamation marks, circled words, and handwritten notes in a bold hand exhorting the reader to immediate action. The typical DM envelope is a cornucopia of brochures, cards, broadsides, and circulars, often with special gimmicks urging the addressee to sign on the dotted line. Not so the newsletter. The newsletter that looks like a salesletter defeats itself. This is not to say that you do not sell in your newsletter, but you cannot expect it to be 100-percent advertising and succeed. It has to be a newsletter, with selling a subordinate theme, skillfully executed without detracting from the usefulness of the piece as a newsletter.

You can sell both directly and indirectly with a newsletter. That is, you can devote a reasonable amount of space to un-abashed advertisements of what you sell, or you can mention the items and their prices in the editorial copy. You can also do both, of course. Software developer XyQuest®, for example, publishes a free quarterly newsletter for users of their XyWrite word processor software. Among the many features in the current issue is a question-and-answer column, a page devoted to "tech tips," and a story on dictionaries available for installation on a computer's disk. That story carries price information. An even softer sell, however, is offered in a story on new features being added to the product for a future release of an upgraded version.

On the other hand, consultant-trainer Howard Shenson publishes a bimonthly newsletter for which he charges an annual subscription fee. In it he includes an advertising center section, distinguished from the purely editorial matter by virtue of its being printed on a heavier colored paper stock.

Many newsletters begin life as free publications distributed entirely for their advertising/sales value, but later become self-supporting, and sometimes even highly profitable, through sub-scription fees. Whether you choose to set a subscription fee or not is up to you, but you will probably do well to remember that the purpose of the newsletter is to help increase sales, and it may be more profitable, in the end, to keep it a free item.

How Often Should You Publish?

Many publishers of free newsletters opt for quarterly production schedules to minimize costs and labor. The quarterly schedule means being burdened with production labor and printing costs only four times annually, having a time frame of three months to mail all copies of each edition, and benefiting from the economies of large-quantity printings. On the other hand, those benefits are often traded for the greater sales impact of more frequent reminders to customers and prospects. (Of course, you can mail the newsletter once every three months and mail other kinds of reminders between newsletter mailings.) Probably the best plan is to begin with a quarterly schedule and increase the frequency to bimonthly or even monthly if results warrant.

70.

DIRECT MAIL LITERATURE AND DIRECT MAIL

The Specialized Specialty.

Direct mail can be used to sell virtually anything. Even if you are selling swimming pools, farm tractors, or something else that seems inappropriate for direct mail, you can still use DM to generate good sales leads. It can be used to supplement any other marketing you do, and although it is sometimes costly, it is usually much cheaper than retailing by standard means.

In many ways, conventional direct mail marketing is more difficult than DM marketing with such special media devices as catalogs and newsletters. Direct mail is essentially hard-sell marketing that requires a good understanding of copywriting. But writing direct mail copy is an art unto itself. Writing good salesletters and brochures—even order forms—is much more specialized than writing newsletters, catalog copy, and even ordinary advertising and sales copy. If you hire someone to prepare your direct mail package and, especially, to write your copy, be sure of his/her credentials in this type of copywriting. (You should also be sure that you know whether you are after sales or leads, and that your copywriter has a clear understanding of those goals, too.)

The conventional DM package has a somewhat obligatory pattern in the array of elements considered by experts to be essential: a salesletter as the centerpiece, a brochure, an order form, and a response envelope, preferably prepaid—i.e., with the no-postage-necessary indicia. In practice, the response envelope is a superfluous and unnecessary expense if you mail to businesses; respondents from business offices almost invariably use company envelopes and postage. (If you mail to businesses, you might try using return envelopes in your early mailings, then monitor to see if the respondents use them; if they do not, eliminate the response envelopes and save your money for more profitable applications.)

Two Kinds of Waste Commonly Found in DM.

"The more you tell, the more you sell" is one of the more reliable bits of conventional wisdom. (I have verified this for myself by tests.) You are allowed one or two ounces of content for your basic postage (depending on the class of mail you use), and it is wasteful to use less than the allowance. You can mail five 8-1/2 by 11-inch sheets of ordinary paper (20# bond or 60# offset) or their equivalent for each ounce. In practical terms, that is about 10,000 words of sales arguments per ounce if you print on both sides, as you should.

It is equally wasteful to use anything in your package that is superfluous—anything that does not contribute to sales arguments. Even the order form can and should use selling words. If you write your own copy, go over your drafts again and again, and rephrase every statement for maximum sales impact. If you have someone else writing copy for you, review it to verify that all opportunities for selling have been utilized.

Tell the Customer What To Do.

A cardinal sin in all sales and advertising, and especially in DM, is stopping short after presenting a powerful sales argument—i.e., waiting for the reader to act spontaneously, and failing to *tell* the reader what to do next. Most of your readers will have an incredible lack of initiative. Customers must be provoked into responding, actually ordered or instructed to respond, whether you are seeking orders or leads. You must actually tell the reader to send in the order form, to write in a credit-card number, to use the free-postage response envelope, or to dial the fax number supplied. Providing explicit (imperative!) instructions definitely increases the response rate. Study advertisements you see in magazines and, especially, direct mail that you get; you will see many examples of this. Sales experts often call this "asking for the order," for that is what it is, but it must be done in a way that takes the prospect by the arm—figuratively, of course—and leads him or her to place the order. The usual theme of such imperatives is to emphasize how easy it is to order ("Just write your name and credit card number on the enclosed order form") or how necessary it is to act immediately ("Limited quantity available; order NOW if you want to be sure to get this remarkable bargain").

The Cumulative Effect.

All effective sales and advertising copy tends to work better with repetition. If you mail to the same list repeatedly, the response will probably grow steadily over at least the first three or four mailings, and often even beyond that, before it begins to level off to a more steady-state level of response. There are several reasons for this, but the most significant ones are that the prospect becomes more and more aware of you and what you offer, and his or her confidence in you tends to grow as you become a continuous and obviously stable presence. There is another, equally important factor: Many people are procrastinators. They mean to respond, but they put it off and forget about your offer. Successive mailings remind them and prompt their order.

This cumulative effect is vitally important. Given a choice between one mailing to a list of 100,000 names and addresses, and five successive mailings to a list of 20,000 names and addresses, I would opt without hesitation for the latter alternative.

The Mailing List.

Given a marketable product (that is, one with market acceptance) and a reasonably well executed DM package, the chief factor dictating success or the lack of it is the mailing list. Not many apartment dwellers buy snow blowers, and not many bank presidents buy surgical instruments. Of course, mismatches of mailing lists with services and products offered are usually more subtle than, this but even subtle mismatches can be deadly. In the retail store, you deal with the world at large and depend on the individuals who want your wares to seek you out. In direct mail, you must seek out the individuals who are likely to want what you have to sell.

There are many mailing-list brokers who can and will help you find the right lists. They will suggest which *of the lists they can supply* are, in their opinion, most suitable for your needs. Still, they are motivated by their own business interests, and they are not experts in your business. You must, therefore, look after your own interests. Think hard about what kinds of people you must mail to, and insist on finding the right list, seeking out the right broker. Brokers do have different lists and different sorting programs. However, it is entirely possible that no one has the right list for you, in which case you will have to build your own.

Building Your Own Lists.

Inquiry advertising is the most popular way to build mailing lists. Some large mail order companies run advertisements offering loss leaders (just as in retail store advertising) and even free items to attract inquiries. They then mail their catalogs, newsletters, and DM literature, along with the loss leader or free item, while accumulating the names for follow-up mailings. In many ways, such a list is far superior to any you can rent from a list broker, because it is a customer list—or at least a list of prospects who now know of your existence and have expressed enough interest in you to respond to your advertising.

Alternatives to this are compiling lists from other sources, such as membership directories and other published sources. (I compiled a highly successful mailing list for my own needs primarily from help-wanted advertising in newspapers.)

CHAPTER 15

Add Indirect Sales Channels

Attractive as direct marketing is, indirect marketing methods are not without their virtues. For one, such methods can generate what is, in effect, an army of marketers selling your products or services—without the problems of adding salespeople as your own employees, or opening numerous outlets of your own.

There are many ways to sell indirectly—i.e., to or through others' business establishments and sales efforts. There is the traditional dealer operating and selling via a retail store, DM, a vehicle, or perhaps other methods, direct or indirect. Regardless of how the dealer sells, for you it is an indirect marketing method, since you do not sell directly to the consumer, but through dealers, distributors, franchisees, or licensees. However, you do need to understand all the methods others may use in order to work with them to sell your own goods and services. You must also understand all the other methods, so that you may decide which is the best arrangement to make with others for your mutual benefit.

71.

TRADITIONAL INDIRECT SALES CHANNELS

Expanding the Old-Fashioned Way.

The classic method of selling indirectly—i.e., via others' business ventures and establishments—is through a simple network of dealerships or distributorships. This is the alternative to building your own network or chain of outlets.

Typically, in selling this way, you sell to dealers at some wholesale price, and they resell to the ultimate consumers at retail prices. Normally, they buy from you in wholesale lots only—by the case, by the dozen, by the gross, etc.—and they maintain an inventory of your merchandise for resale. However, for very large marketing networks, where there are too many dealers over too wide an area for the prime source to service directly and individually, there is another level, that of the distributor. The distributor buys in large quantities and services the dealers within his/her own area—e.g., the state, the tri-state area, or whatever area the distributor is assigned.

Such a system has its drawbacks. One is financial. As the prime source, you must usually finance enormous inventories. (Wholesaling means that you must carry a substantial number of accounts receivable.) Another is production control: It is essential to try to estimate demand, and that means an unending struggle against being overproduced/overstocked or being under-produced/understocked. (Normally, you look to your director of marketing to tell you what he or she anticipates in sales, and use this as a guideline to set your production and inventory levels. However, these estimates are not always accurate, and those over- and understock situations arise frequently.)

These are troublesome issues given today's inflationary pressures and current exorbitant interest rates that inhibit expansion via traditional methods. There are some newer ideas of selling via indirect channels of distribution, however, that manage to navigate around much of the financial burden of traditional business expansion.

Dealership Works for Services Too.

Deals in products such as storm windows, drapes, blinds, shower doors, and television sets must often provide installation service, and many customers look to the original dealer for maintenance service as well. Some dealers may have their own installation crews and service departments, but many do not, turning instead to contracted services. Those may be provided by service companies or by individuals who freelance. And even some large stores, such as Sears, with their own service departments, may contract out certain specialized tasks.

In some cases, the dealers earn nothing from the installation and service work, providing it at their cost as an accommodation to the customer; in other cases they earn income from such services by charging the customer a retail price and paying the service provider a wholesale price. You may be able to establish such an arrangement.

72.

THE FRANCHISING SALES CHANNEL

Not Every Business is Easily "Franchisable."

Franchising has become a popular way to expand a business through indirect sales channels. It offers certain benefits over expansion via adding dealers and distributors to the marketing network. In fact, franchising is a business in itself; some franchisers own none of their outlets. It is, however, practiced in many different ways, according to individual conditions and needs.

The franchise is a good fit for some businesses and a poor fit for others. McDonalds, the hamburger chain that launched a new kind of restaurant (indeed, a new industry) found an ideal fit: It achieved national prominence—a firm and well-established image and physical recognizability—and great marketability. It was "an original," far better known than its many rivals and imitators; its name became almost a generic term; the public embraced it enthusiastically. It was operated with a meticulously defined and detailed *modus operandi*: Founder Ray Kroc had firm ideas of the requirements for a McDonald's establishment and established specifications for everything imaginable. A McDonald's franchise was therefore valuable, its prescribed MO profitable, and its rules enforceable.

The viability of franchising your own business and selling your wares via your franchisees is dependent largely on the extent to which you and your business can measure up to this model. However, there is more to it. There is also the question of whether franchising is the way for you to go—whether it is suitable for your business situation.

Why Franchise?

One major reason for franchising is that it represents a way of expanding your business and diversifying your marketing without the severe and often intolerable financing burdens of expanding via opening new outlets (as chain-store operators do), or adding dealers and distributors (which carries with it the additional burden of rapidly growing accounts receivable). In franchising, you open many new outlets and branches, in name, but they are not yours and the burden of creating them is not yours. For some kinds of businesses and operators, this is far better than traditional expansion. In fact, instead of costing money, franchising can produce new money!

The Financial Benefits.

There are several direct financial benefits to franchising. One is the initial cash payment required of a new franchisee. Another is the cash flow and profit from the purchase of products and/or services that the franchisee must buy from you or from a subsidiary you have established for the purpose. And still another is the "tax" or royalty on each unit of sale made by the franchisee. These are payments for the use of your name, image, guidance, know-how, and support (e.g., national advertising, training, and other help in succeeding). There is at least on indirect benefit to franchising: To the extent that your franchisees succeed and promote good will, your image and reputation become more and more valuable, to your ultimate further enrichment. This is a real advantage.

The Inevitable Downside.

Franchising is not without risk. You undertake the burdens of support—advertising, training, and guidance—while you must also police your franchisees to ensure total compliance with your rules. You must also be sure that franchisees make an honest accounting to you, so that you get everything to which you are entitled. In addition, you are placing your own success partially in the hands of your franchisees: Poor performance by them can destroy your image and reputation.

There are alternatives to franchising that may be more desirable. One of them is licensing.

73.

LICENSING AS AN INDIRECT
SALES CHANNEL

Licensing is a way to sell certain, defined rights to property that is yours. Usually, your title is established through some legal protection such as a copyright, patent, or registered trademark. Licensing has a resemblance to franchising, but only a faint one. In fact, franchising generally includes licensing as one element of the franchise: that element that permits the franchisee to use the name, image, and in many cases, the product of the franchiser.

Licensing is a simple idea, compared to franchising. It lacks some of the financially rewarding potential of franchising, but it is also free of some of the burdens. Like franchising, however, licensing is not universally applicable. It is suited only to some businesses and situations.

Examples of licensing are found commonly in manufacturing industries. Manufacturers of radio and television receivers, for example, must buy licenses for many of the circuits used in these receivers. RCA, for example, developed and patented the most reliable horizontal synchronization control circuits, and the circuit was widely licensed to virtually all other manufacturers. Many copiers and laser printers today use the "Canon engine," a proprietary design, as the heart of their copying and printing functions. These are only two of many such examples.

Payment to the owners of such patents is usually on a royalty basis—so much for each use or each unit sold that uses the device or idea licensed. Book publishing is generally on the same basis, with royalties paid to authors. One difference here, however, is that the right or license in book publishing is generally exclusive to one publisher, whereas patented devices are most often widely licensed to many manufacturers.

There are two mandatory minimum conditions for licensing. First, the licensed item—design, device, publication, name, trademark, or idea—must be something to which you have a clear and enforceable title. Second, it must be something others want badly enough to buy from you under license, rather than trying to develop their own equivalent. In other words it must be *marketable*.

It is common knowledge that individuals whose names are well known are often paid large sums for their testimonials endorsing various products. That idea has now been carried considerably further. The names of prominent people are today licensed for commercial use—e.g., Roy Rogers' name is in widespread use to identify a fast-food chain once owned by the Marriott Corporation, since sold to Hardees. (The name Roy Rogers is still used by Hardees, however, to identify the fried chicken it sells by agreement with Marriott Corporation.) Prize fighter Jack Dempsey (among many other prominent sports figures) has been paid for the use of his names for a restaurant. Well known golfers such as Jack Nicklaus and Sam Snead are paid for the use of their names on golf clubs. In almost any popular sport you can find equipment offered that bears the name of some well-known figure of that sport. As we saw earlier, Elizabeth Taylor now has "her own" line of cosmetics, and the idea has caught on with other prominent actors and actresses whose names are now used to identify lines of cosmetics, jewelry, and clothing.

There are many other ways to adapt the basic idea of licensing to expand your business base and increase profitability. Suppose, for example, that you publish a successful newsletter as a marketing too, and it occurs to you that a great many businesspeople would like to distribute such a newsletter of their own. You know, however, that most do not know how to create one and would not wish to invest the necessary effort and money. Your newsletter is general enough to be applicable to a great many enterprises, except for a small area of information that is peculiar to your own company. You could conceivably license others to use your newsletter; you would supply a master copy each month, with blank space for the licensee to insert his/her own material and imprint his/her own company name and address. This is a viable idea and has proven successful for more than one entrepreneur.

You can modify this idea in various ways, such as handling the printing and distribution for the licensee (for suitable fees, of course). Or you can broaden the service by selling the licensee a master plan for producing and using the newsletter for maximum marketing benefits. (Note the increasing resemblance to franchising, as you add services to simple licensing.)

In short, anything you own and can protect as your own property, whether it is a physical device, a design, a copyright, a trademark, a name, or an image, can be the basis for licensing—if it offers something that is useful to others and more difficult or more expensive to obtain elsewhere or create independently.

74.

HOME OFFICE SMALL BUSINESS CHANNELS

The "Home Office" Has a New Meaning.

The "home office" used to mean the corporate headquarters of a multi-branch corporation, or the office to which field employees, such as traveling salespeople or field engineers, report on a regular basis. Times change. Today, "home office" is more likely to refer to one of the thousands of independent home-based businesses, most of them equipped with a computer, fax machine, and copier. Such businesses are smaller in scale but comparable in function to the large corporation.

These are the small dealers and cottage industries of this era, using the most modern tools and technology known. Many of them are engaged in service businesses where they are the prime sources, the creators—e.g., resume-writing, word processing, and desktop publishing services (the modern-day letter shop and public stenographer). Many others are dealers of one kind or another, often engaged in MLM (multi-level marketing) ventures. Home entrepreneurs may also be manufacturers' representatives, brokers, or professionals of any of a hundred other types.

For many businesses, the home office phenomenon represents a new opportunity to diversify and expand sales through indirect sales channels. The small, independent broker of only a few years ago was someone who trudged about all day calling on prospects in quest of business. Today's broker does much of his or her calling and order taking via the telephone, the modem-equipped computer, and the fax machine, also utilizing these kinds of facilities to call orders in to suppliers. If you run a printing business, for example, and imprint standard forms with customers' names and addresses, brokers based in home offices can submit copy and orders to you via fax and/or computer-to-computer hookups.

This approach works equally well for other kinds of ventures. With proper computer equipment at both ends of the connection, even the small, home-based entrepreneur can send in custom copy—e.g., resumes, reports, and proposals—spontaneously and have it printed out camera-ready at the print shop. But many other kinds of marketing can be decentralized via the home offices of the new breed of small, independent entrepreneurs. If you are a home-based entrepreneur, you can often provide faster service to your customers than the competition, and save your own time as well. If you are a supplier to a home-based business, you can derive many of the same benefits, namely orders you might otherwise never have gotten and a much more efficient delivery system.

75.

DROP-SHIPPING FOR DEALERS

Drop-Shipping Benefits Everybody.

Many small dealers, especially those operating from offices in their homes, lack space for inventory. Even if they had space for storing inventory, they lack space for shipping operations. Many depend, therefore, on drop-shipping support by their suppliers. If you are willing to drop-ship orders for small dealers, you can diversify your indirect sales channels in this manner.

The concept is simple enough. The dealer prepares a shipping label and sends it to you, along with the order payment. (Payment is generally included with the order.) You fill the order, using the dealer's label, so that the order appears to the customer to have come from the dealer.

The benefit to the dealer is obvious: He doesn't have to carry inventory or maintain shipping facilities to fill orders. The benefit to you is twofold. You get additional business you would not have had, and you earn a large profit because you offer a smaller discount on drop-shipped orders than on orders shipped by the dealer.

76.

MISCELLANEOUS INDIRECT SALES CHANNELS

Multi-Level Marketing.

"MLM," or multi-level marketing, has achieved popularity as an effective way to move merchandise via indirect channels. Amway, which sells household products through an extensive network of small dealers, is perhaps the best known and most successful of these firms, but there are others. The marketing organization is a pyramid, albeit a legal one, wherein each dealer in the distribution chain tries to build a "downline" of subordinate dealers. Each dealer is supplied by the dealer of whose downline he or she is a part, so that each dealer with a downline is both a retailer and a distributor. Of course, discounts, markups, and profits must be such as to permit several levels of distribution.

Party Sales.

Party sales, mentioned briefly in an earlier chapter, are big business, and serve as the marketing mainstay for some ventures. The "party" is a gathering of individuals in a private home, who are served refreshments—e.g., coffee and cake—and presented with a demonstration of a line of merchandise, such as pots and pans, lingerie, cosmetics, jewelry, or household products. The demonstration is usually by a representative of the company (not necessarily a direct employee, however), who takes orders from those present. The hostess earns a commission on the sales for hosting the gathering and for being the medium of delivery and collection: The merchandise is delivered to her, and she sees to getting it to the customer and collecting payment. (It is also customary to give some merchandise free of charge to the hostess for her service.) The presenter canvasses all of those present in the quest of new hostesses for future sales parties. There are companies who do all or nearly all of their marketing in this manner; others use this as one of several marketing approaches.

Itinerant Dealers.

The Fuller Brush Company built a large business by employing itinerant salespeople who went from house to house, knocking on doors. They were actually independent dealers, not employees. The company issued each dealer a sample case and financed the first week's orders, which were delivered to the dealer's home. The dealer was responsible to deliver the merchandise and to collect for it, paying the company when submitting the next week's orders. Many companies—Avon cosmetics, for example—sell a line of products in precisely this way, through independent dealers, as well as salespeople. These dealers work as true independents, buying the merchandise discount (wholesale) and selling at the suggested retail, rather than as commissioned employees.

Ancillary Products and Profits.

Many businesses take on added lines as supplementary products producing additional profits. Newsletter publishers, for example, often start mail order bookstores, generally specialized for their audience. For example, Jerry Buchanan, Vancouver, Washington publisher of the *Towers Club* newsletter for self-publishers and other writers, sells books of special interest to his readers. Jim Kennedy, who publishes *The Consultant News* in New

Hampshire, offers his readers a line of books connected with consulting and operating a professional practice. Stores selling computers and computer software usually carry a line of computer books and magazines. Supermarkets carry drug items; drugstores carry some food items. Drugstores also often carry prosthetic devices and sickroom supplies, as well as automobile parts and office supplies. Gasoline service stations, supermarkets, and neighborhood convenience stores often have coin-operated copiers and cigarette machines. Whichever end of the transaction you are on, the seller of copiers or the convenience-store owner, the transaction means extra profits for you.

Ancillary Services Also Bring Added Profits.

Such examples represent opportunities for distribution of your own products that you may not have considered. But the opportunity is not limited to products. The same approach may be applied to services. Sellers of office supplies may be set up as brokers for printing services, rubber stamp manufacturers, and providers of many other services that their customers are likely to need. Dealers in medical supplies will find it profitable to carry computers and the specialized software that many plastic surgeons and other physicians use today. Sellers of art supplies may find it useful to carry desktop publishing equipment and software useful to illustrators.

It Wasn't Here Only Yesterday.

That raises another point: Almost every day brings change, new and better ideas, and new and better products. The vast majority of businesses today are not doing and selling what they were doing and selling ten years ago—or even five years ago, in many cases. Many of these new developments mean new and better markets: Desktop copiers, computers, and fax machines, for example, are just three new products that brought with them new markets. The market for videocassette records did not exist only ten years ago, and the market for color TVs is not a great deal older.

In some cases, entrepreneurs set up special outlets to sell these popular new devices and related items, but in many other cases they established dealers in other lines simply add these new items. A dealer from whom I bought a typewriter 20 years ago today sells computers and computer printers, as well as typewriters. He probably could not stay in business today on the strength of his typewriter sales alone. The convenience store is a modern version of the one-time "Mom and Pop" store on almost every corner, but it was a new idea when the exodus to the suburbs was getting underway.

CHAPTER 16

Ways Of Getting Free Advertising And Promotion

There are many ways to promote sales, the most basic and least imaginative of which (next to knocking on doors) is paid advertising in the media—print and broadcast. Paid advertising is also among the most expensive options, and very likely *the* most expensive sales promotion you can think up.

Ironically, getting yourself and what you sell into the news is not only the cheapest general category of sales promotion, but it is usually the most effective when handled well. It is free, or nearly so, because you don't pay for the space, time, or coverage. What it costs you in terms of time, effort, and cash to get free coverage is a quite modest outlay—if you do it yourself.

There are, of course, many public relations (PR) firms, and you can call on them to mount campaigns for you. At that point, it is no longer free or nearly so; it begins to become quite expensive. However, it is not difficult to mount modest PR efforts without the help of the professionals.

For the large and prominent corporation, a great many duties and functions fall into the category of public relations. For example, the PR office in a large corporation may design the corporation's letterhead, recommend a change in the logo, run an in-house lecture bureau, sponsor a Little League baseball team, and write speeches for executives, among other duties concerned with the corporation's public image. But here we will pass over peripheral PR activities and focus instead on that activity of PR that aims directly at sales promotion.

77.

THE BASIC TOOL OF PROMOTION: THE RELEASE

The Basic Law of PR.

"PR" stands for public relations, but it really means *publicity*, and is far better known by those initials, PR, than by the words for which they stand. In fact, for the small and medium-sized business PR is a much different proposition than it is for a major corporation or government agency (where it is most likely to be called the Office of Public Information).

PR as Publicity and Promotion.

The fundamental idea of PR is a simple one: Do something to get yourself/your product/your business/your proposition in the news—in newspapers, tabloids, newsletters, magazines, trade journals, on radio and on TV—in a favorable light that will aid your marketing. PR represents free advertising for you, and it also represents something newsworthy for the publisher or journalist who provides the media exposure. It's a fair exchange: You furnish something the other wants (newsworthy material) and he or she furnishes what you want (media exposure).

Stunts Are for Hollywood.

In the movies, PR specialists often pull off fabulous stunts that get their clients' names splashed in major headlines across the world. In real life it rarely happens on that scale. In real life, PR is slow and steady, an everyday activity geared toward building a presence and an awareness of what you want to project. Professional PR people (those who work for PR companies and handle the PR work for client companies) write news releases—also called publicity releases, product releases, and simply releases—make up bulk mailings, plant items with columnists, dream up and run contests, buy baseball uniforms for the local high school team, arrange for and write speeches for clients, turn out newsletters, plan convention and trade show participation, prepare press kits, and do a potpourri of other chores that are calculated to win media attention. They spend lots of time on the telephone with friends in the media. (Many PR people are former journalists.) PR people aren't usually aiming for and rarely have any hope of winning their clients publicity on page one of *The New York Times*. They expect attention in the financial or business pages, the style or society section, or wherever in the print or broadcast media their message is most likely to reach the people who are the best prospects for whatever the client wants—donations, votes, or, as in our case, business press.

Thousands of press releases are written and mailed every day. The vast majority wind up deposited swiftly, with hardly more than a glance, in the "circular file," or wastebasket. That's not so much because of the many common deficiencies in style and format the releases contain, although they do not help, but more because so many releases violate the basic law of PR: They fail to be newsworthy.

What is "Newsworthy?"

Newsworthiness is a vague idea. The yardstick any editor applies to judge it when he or she glances swiftly through a release is simply, "Will my readers be interested in this?" Rule number one then, would read as follows: Know who the readers are and what interests them.

Where to Send Releases.

Many releases wind up in the wastebasket simply because they were sent to the wrong offices. If you send an item that belongs in the financial or business section to the city editor, it is unlikely that the busy city editor will bother to send it on to the business editor. A release announcing a new electric shaver for women should go to *Cosmopolitan*, but not to *Popular Mechanics*.

Publishers Weekly, to use another example, is a trade journal of the book publishing industry. The editors are not interested in news about the clothing industry; that is not newsworthy for *Publishers Weekly*. They *are* interested in news about book manufacturing, paper, personnel changes in the book publishing industry, audiocassette books, and whatever else happens in their industry. *The New York Times* is not a trade journal; it is intended for the general public, and the editors of the business pages are interested in news of any industry that has national impact or local (New York) impact. *Publishers Weekly* will probably print a release announcing the opening of a large new bookstore in Boise, Idaho; you would be hard pressed to find such an item running in the *Times*.

The Minor Sins.

Releases should be prepared to make it as easy as possible for editors to use them. A marginal release will almost surely land in the trash basket if it is single-spaced, is typed on both sides of the sheet, features no contact name and number, and is poorly written. It's tough enough to get a good release accepted; don't handicap your releases with minor sins.

A Few Simple Rules.

Always double-space the copy. Always use only one side of the sheet. Number the pages if there are two or more. Use "more" at the bottom of every page if there is another page following it. Otherwise, used END, - 30 -, or ### to signify that there is no more. Furnish a contact name and number, someone the editor can call for more information. And use a headline. Not everybody does or believes you should, but editors like being able to get the meat of the story in a quick glance. Use the headline to sum up the message, especially to furnish the reason for using it.

A Special Tip.

Editors of local media want items of local interest far more than they want items of national or statewide interest. The headline on the sample release that follows stresses the local angle in the headline for that reason. Even if your release has national significance, try for a local angle if you are sending it to local media.

The Product Release.

A special kind of release is used to announce and introduce a new product. Many magazines have a special section for new product information, and they often use photographs or drawings when these are appropriate. If the product you want to tell the world about is something that can be and should be illustrated, supply a black and white 4- x 5-inch print or line drawing with your release. Explain the product (its uses and how it works); furnish price information; let the reader know whether it is already in the stores or, if not, when it will be.

Special Help in Distribution.

If you want national (and even international) coverage in daily newspapers, try sending 400 printed copies of your release to the Washington News Service, 908 National Press Building, Washington, DC 20045. They will distribute the release to all the press offices in the building, which means virtually all the newspapers and press services in the United States, and they charge only $65 for this service. (That's less than the postage for mailing them yourself!) For more information, call 202-737-4434.

You may miss the small, local papers, especially the weeklies, so you will want to supplement even that "grand slam" distribution by doing some mailings to local papers, and perhaps to other targets such as periodicals and the news directors of local radio and

TV stations. But go to the trouble of mailing your pieces to the right people and offices; doing so makes a large difference in the results.

NEWS

HRH COMMUNICATIONS, INC.
P.O. Box 1731   Wheaton, MD 20915
301 649-2499   Fax 301 649-5745

Contact:
Herman Holtz
301 649-2499

PROPOSAL WRITING SERVICE FOR SMALL BUSINESS
TO BENEFIT SILVER SPRING AREA

Wheaton, MD, November 30, 1990 - HRH Communications, Inc. announced today the availability of proposal writing and bid-preparation services designed especially to aid small businesses in the Silver Spring area in winning and keeping government contracts in the area. The array of services offered includes writing, editing, illustrating, and consulting. The services can be performed on the client's premises or on the premises of HRH Communications, Inc.

HRH Communications, Inc. are veterans in government contracting, with a lengthy record of success in winning contracts. In supporting local companies we are ready to furnish a highly experienced proposal leader, if desired, and any or all of the team required to perform all or any part of the proposal preparation, subject to the client's technical input, review, and approval. Individual services will include guidance and/or direct help in requirements analysis, strategy formulation, writing, pricing, and production. (We can offer a full complement of desktop publishing facilities.)

The service will be available to clients in Montgomery County only.

Sample News Release

78.

PERSONAL APPEARANCES

Building an Image.

You've probably noticed that many successful entrepreneurs make frequent public appearances at a variety of events and thereby become quite well known. Or perhaps it is the other way around—perhaps being successful is partly due to one's becoming well known through public appearances. Whatever the case, making speeches, sitting on panels, cutting ribbons, being interviewed, being written about, and engaging in other such activities are important PR events.

The In-House Lecture Bureau.

There are several ways of going about getting yourself invited to speak frequently, and you may not have to do it alone or even participate directly if you work within an organization. Many organizations develop internal lecture bureaus, made up of the executives of the organization. You then supply speakers free of charge for meetings, seminars, conventions, panels, TV shows, and other events where the publicity pays off for your company. Be sure that your speakers are equipped with appropriate slides, posters, brochures, and other handout materials. Such meetings represent an opportunity for effective and inexpensive advertising.

You must, of course, make this service known. Write a release announcing the availability of this free service and send it out to those journals covering the area where you will provide the service. You can get a double payoff from this approach by sending out *another* release or article explaining the service to others in your industry as a suggested PR measure. You can also keep the PR fires burning by sending out subsequent releases to the trade journals of your field reporting the results of your program and what you have learned about running such an effective program.

Send notices and handouts detailing the availability of your speakers to local schools, associations, public agencies, and other organizations. Invite interviews by the press and the broadcasters, where you explain this great civic-minded program that benefits others as much as it benefits your own company.

Seminars and Night Courses.

Most urban areas today boast at least one community college, and such colleges usually run many seminars and brief night courses on a wide variety of subjects. They are always looking for presenters and instructors, because the pay is quite small. However, there is frequently an excellent bonus in publicity to be gained. At the least, such activity can be a link in the chain of PR events.

There is a fairly easy way to approach this. Get a copy of the college's announcements, usually a semi-annual tabloid listing the courses offered, and examine it carefully. Some of the courses are pretty standard fare; others are more specialized. But all are a reflection of what is available, and many are the result of individuals approaching the faculty with an offer to present a seminar or a course on some subject in which they are expert—e.g., consulting, computer programming, writing short stories, or advertising.

Look for gaps in the curriculum, subjects that *ought* to be covered there but are not, in areas in which you are yourself expert. It is likely that you can arouse interest and win a slot.

79.

APPEARING IN THE PRESS

Get Published.

Your name appearing on the byline of an article in the trade press carries a magic all its own. This is a sign that you have something to say and you are being taken seriously.

Write or have members of your staff write for appropriate trade journals. (Some organizations have programs in which employees are paid a bonus when they have an article published that identifies the company in some way.) Not only are such articles good PR on their own, but reprints of the pieces make excellent mailing pieces.

Use Your Newsletter for PR.

Your own company newsletter was suggested in an earlier chapter for use as a centerpiece for direct-mail marketing; it is also an excellent medium for your public relations efforts. In connection with that, here is a useful tip: Copyright your newsletter, but print a notice in it that anyone may quote freely from your newsletter as long as they make full attribution. That helps you gain additional publicity via others' newsletters. And to further that aim, be generous with complimentary subscriptions to other publishers.

Get Written About.

Appearing in the press as the subject of an article by someone else is also something of a PR coup. However, if you wait for it to happen, you can wait for a long, long time. But you *can* find ways to engineer this, although getting yourself interviewed and written about is a bit trickier than writing your own article. In one case I wrote to a freelancer who wrote frequently on business subjects for a local newspaper. I described the somewhat unusual nature of what I did (helping clients write proposals to win government contracts), suggesting that his editor might find it interesting. He queried the business editor, got a go-ahead to do the story, and came to my office with a photographer. A half-page story and photograph followed in a few days.

Every large newspaper runs a few columns by nationally syndicated writers. But there are many, many more columnists writing on any number of topics whose names you may come to know because they happen to appear in the newspaper you read. There are columnists whose work appears elsewhere in the paper (and in other periodicals) who deal with a huge variety of subjects—advice, health, automotive matters, hobbies, science, careers and jobs, business, investing, ecology, and on and on. Like the editors of the various departments of the newspaper, the columnists are always under pressure to present new and interesting ideas. Be sure that the ones whose interests are relevant to your own are on your distribution list for your releases and on your "comp" list for your newsletter. One mention in the column of a prominent columnist can be worth much, much more than a full-page advertisement in a major newspaper or magazine. (One such mention I received brought in over 3,000 inquiries from readers a few years ago.)

The Effect Snowballs.

The more you do along these lines, the more additional publicity comes your way—much of it generated spontaneously. As a result of my first appearance in one newspaper, another freelance writer approached me and interviewed me for a magazine article. Some time later I was visited by a staff writer from the newspaper who interviewed me for yet another story.

Press Kits Are a Must.

When you have a special announcement to make try to organize a press conference. But be prepared to hand over a press kit to every journalist who wishes to interview you, no matter the occasion. This is simply a folder full of your literature, with reprints of your articles, photographs, and any other material a journalist needs to learn about you and your business. A good press kit is a standard requirement for any PR program. It should include such boilerplate materials as those just mentioned and any material designed especially for the occasion, such as the script of a speech you are delivering.

80.

OTHER LAUNCH SITES FOR PR

Associations Are Good PR Seedbeds.

Be active in relevant associations—as many as you can handle. Be sure that you or some of your staff are members and are active in relevant trade organizations, especially at conventions, trade shows, symposia, and other major public events. There are several ways to stand out at conventions. You can rent a booth in the exhibit hall, set up a hospitality suite in the hotel or convention center, organize seminars, and/or have some kind of souvenir item or advertising novelty to give away. These are just a few of the possibilities open to you. (A tiny $25 booth at a trade fair launched Gary Dahl's million-dollar "Pet Rock" novelty when a *Time* magazine reporter who was intrigued by the idea wrote a small item about it for the next issue of the magazine. How's that for cost-effective PR!) No one knows when media lightning may strike; you must be alert and ready for it at all times.

Getting on Talk Shows.

There are many talk shows today on both radio and TV. If you watch them regularly, you soon notice certain familiar names and faces. These are individuals in demand—or at least highly welcome—on talk shows. In some cases, they happen to be well-known individuals of special talent or experience—e.g., a lawyer who has handled the divorce cases of prominent personalities, or someone who just happens to be an especially entertaining guest. Some of the guests have been sought out by the producer and/or his/her staff. But many are ordinary, unremarkable citizens who engineered their own appearances for whatever reason. It can be done.

To do this, call the producer (*not* the host or star of the show); the producer handles such details as selecting guests. You may and probably will have to do a selling job, and you will probably not succeed immediately in being invited. However, you can increase your chances immeasurably if you arouse the producer's interest by offering evidence that you are likely to prove an interesting guest who will cause no problems. Explain your interest— why you wish to appear—and tell the producer a little about yourself. If you have ever made such appearances before, mention them and cite time, place, and occasion. If you are experienced in appearing before the public, that reassures the producer that you won't freeze up on camera. Perhaps most important, be available to appear on very short notice. Many talk shows overbook—in other words, book three guests when they ordinarily do not have time for more than two—because they do get last-minute cancellations and have to fill the void on an emergency basis. That also means that you may be brought in on a low-priority basis and not get on at all that day. But if you are a good sport about such disappointments and show up reliably when called for, the producer will probably be at pains to get you on the next time. If you are an interesting guest and are reasonably tactful about how you plug your company or your product, you will be invited on to other shows. Here, too, there is a snowballing effect.

CHAPTER 17

Magnifying Sales
Opportunities

Many businesses "do okay," earning their owners a fair living. Other businesses do much better, making their owners quite wealthy and sometimes creating virtual dynasties. The difference is usually in the effectiveness with which the business sells, and that in turn is largely dependent on the vision of the entrepreneurs to perceive and take advantage of opportunities— or to create new opportunities. Here are a few examples of both.

81.

MAKING ONE-SHOT PROMOTIONS PAY OFF

Making Sales or Making Customers?

The late Joe Karbo (author of *The Lazy Man's Way to Riches*) was, as we have seen, essentially a promoter. So was Joe Cossman (author of *How I Made $1,000,000 in Mail Order*), who discovered and promoted such special items as ant farms, and Ken Hakuta, who made a fortune promoting the "wall walker" toy. Theirs is a business of making sales, not customers. It is based on finding an item that will "click" with the public so it can be sold in great volume through heavy promotion. The promotion goes on until sales begin to decline. Then it is abandoned and the promoter searches for the next item he or she hopes will be the next hula hoop, mood ring, Pet Rock, Rubik's Cube, or other great success.

The essential ingredient here is a high markup—a selling price that is several times cost—and intense promotion to get high volume and the economies of scale in marketing. It's a tough, high-risk business, where luck is a large factor. It costs a great deal of money to make a single sale from the cold start of this kind of venture. That is why the extraordinarily high markup is needed. It's also wasteful when no effort is made to sell the buyer something else, not even a follow-up or "bounceback sale."

(There is an upside to all of this, however. For one thing, you have no firm, permanent commitments. Between promotions you are free of obligations to maintain a warehouse and inventory, carry permanent advertising budgets, and other such permanent obligations. And when a promotion disappoints you, it is relatively easy to terminate the program and cut your losses.)

The Bounceback Sale.

Bounceback sales are the orders you get from buyers as a result of sales literature enclosed with the original order. That presumes you have something additional to sell. Most promoters of the kind referred to here do *not* have something else to sell. The only bounceback sales they can hope for are additional orders for the same item. In their view, that is enirely acceptable. They have kept their business totally uncomplicated and operated under the "take-the-money-and-run" philosophy. But bounceback sales reduce risk and add to the profits. They sometimes salvage a marginal promotion and make it profitable, and they can also make a profitable operation more profitable without increasing investment or risk to any substantial degree.

82.

YOUR CUSTOMER LIST IS WORTH MONEY

You Are Building an Income-Producing Asset.

Renting mailing lists usually for single use, is big business, a mainstay of the direct-mail industry. (These lists are rarely sold.) Lists are rented to mailers by the thousand names and addresses at rates that can range from as little as $20 per thousand to well over $100 per thousand. Lists of known buyers—customer lists—are more valuable than lists of inquirers, and lists of inquirers are more expensive than "cold" lists (compiled lists of people with no known buying or interest characteristics).

Lists are rented by list brokers. Most of the lists belong to someone else (although list brokers may have "house" lists that they own outright). The list broker markets the information on a commission basis. That's how you get access to a list of subscribers to *Popular Mechanics* or to a list of L.L.Bean's customers: You rent the lists from brokers who manage those lists for the owners.

Your own customer list is rentable as soon as it reaches a large enough size to interest a broker (probably a minimum of 5,000 names, but preferably much larger). The broker will rent it out over and over, producing recurring income for you. And the more new names you add to it, the more profitable the list becomes.

83.

PIGGYBACK MAIL PROFITS

If You Don't Have a Bounceback Item.

There are other ways to pick up some added profits in a one-shot promotion. One is to offer piggyback mailing to others, a rather simple idea that pays out well for many. You have probably seen it in operation, although you may not have understood the mechanics of the method. When you get your monthly credit-card bill, you probably also find in the envelope a handful of colored brochures advertising various items. That's a piggyback mailing. In its simplest manifestation, the credit-card company is paid something by every one of the sellers represented by those brochures. (Mailers call them "stuffers.") Both parties benefit. The sellers represented by the brochures are gaining in two ways: They are getting access to someone else's mailing list and they are saving postage. If you don't have a bounceback item of your own to sell, you can earn income by letting others offer *their* bounceback items via their circulars and other stuffers enclosed with every item you ship out to your customers.

It Works Both Ways.

You can be on the other end of this kind of promotion—i.e., you can arrange to piggyback your own offer with other people's mailings. This approach doesn't have to replace your own promotions; it can supplement them. In fact, it would be wise to key each mailing to compare costs and determine which are the most profitable ones. (See the earlier section on testing.)

Piggybacking Has Other Possibilities.

Piggyback mailers may be paid a fee for stuffing someone else's brochures into their regular mailing, but there are other ways to make the plan even more profitable to both parties. You can arrange a P.I. or P.O. deal here, as explained in an earlier chapter. If you are mailing the stuffers, you can have your address printed on the brochures, get the orders, extract your commissions, and send the orders on to the source to be drop-shipped. And this can work both ways: You can have others enclose your circulars and send *you* labels for drop shipping.

84.

PURCHASING CAN MAGNIFY
MARKET OPPORTUNITIES

Range of Choice Makes a Difference.

For many customers, the variety and range of merchandise available is a major factor in their choice of where and from whom to buy. Their preference is for the establishment that "has everything." In the advertising business they might refer to this image of having everything as *positioning*, which is the impression of your business you create in the customer's mind.

This "everything-in-one-place" concept has significance for you whether you are a wholesaler, manufacturer, or retailer. It is one reason for many customers choosing to patronize department stores and shop in malls, for example. But it is also a consideration for many distributors and retailers in choosing their own suppliers and the lines of merchandise they choose to sell. Their theory is that they maximize sales by offering the widest possible variety of goods and services.

Diversification applies to more than one parameter, depending on the nature of the goods or services. It may apply to types of goods, to sizes, to colors, to brand names, and even to a few other aspects. Diversification is equally applicable to service businesses. A service may be offered on a routine or emergency basis, and may be general or customized, as in the choice between the general automobile repair shop and the specialized one that handles only one make of automobile or only one type of repair work. A long-run printer, such as one who prints magazines with large circulations, cannot handle short-run printing efficiently with the same equipment and processes, as explained earlier, but one can diversify and have both a long-run and a short-run shop on the same premises.

This does not mean you should make a mindless effort to stock and offer everything; that would be impractical and would result in your carrying a great deal of slow-moving stock and carrying many loss items. Instead, consider *trying* a wide variety, perhaps even a complete spread, of sizes, colors, items, and so on, and keeping careful records to determine which choices your customers want. *Then* be careful to keep those items in stock. Guessing rarely works well. It is necessary to record and measure.

A Reputation for Having the Newest and Latest.

Perhaps even more important than diversifying and providing a wide range of choices is gaining a reputation for always being up-to-date—always having the latest, newest products and services. When your customers learn of new products and services, but are compelled to go to many sources other than your establishment to find them, you risk losing those customers. On the other hand, acquiring a reputation for always having the latest in products and services is a great aid in gaining new customers to increase your sales volume.

Being successful in this effort requires a purchasing program that is as aggressive as your marketing and sales program. It means reading the current trade literature, attending conventions and trade shows, being active in trade associations, and having an open door—i.e. being highly receptive—to salespeople calling on you.

It can be most important to be first or among the first to offer new items. (Again, this is part of the positioning idea.) A Rubik's Cube or any other item that has a period in which it is a popular fad pays out most handsomely to those who have it to offer first. No one knows how long a fad will last, and latecomers to the market miss the mainstream of profit opportunity. There is some risk in this stocking a new item immediately, before anything is known of its appeal, but the risk can be minimized by organizing your purchasing for spontaneity of action, just as marketing should be equally capable of rapid adjustment.

85.

SPECIALIZATION MAGNIFIES
SALES OPPORTUNITIES

A Narrow Focus Makes for Efficiency.

The other side of diversification is specialization. It has been a trend of recent years, manifested in many ways, in both retail sales and in service businesses. The fast-food industry is one notable example. The advantages are simple inventory and simplified operations generally, which means that inexpensive, unskilled help is suitable for most functions. Efficiency is usually high. (It should be!) That results—or ought to result—in competitive prices.

Automotive service is another good example, and a highly visible one. It probably started with the seat cover specialists and brake repair specialists, who were among the first, to specialize in only a few kinds of automobile service. Soon, however, we had muffler specialists, and then shops who did nothing but tune-ups, and most recently we have while-you-wait lubrication specialists.

Although the automobile repair industry has made extensive use of specialization, the concept was certainly not invented there; it started many years earlier. In the thirties, for example, there sprang up many specialized services. One common one was the while-you-wait shoe repair and dry cleaning shop. (In those days of the Depression, many men had only one "good suit" and one good pair of shoes.) These shops usually offered hat blocking and cleaning also. (Of course, men wore hats much more commonly in those days than they do today.) In shopping malls today you can find the modern versions of such specialized establishments: tobacconists, silversmiths, coffee shops, appetizer stores, cutlery artisans, computer software sellers, tea and coffee vendors, and many others who carry a specialized line of goods or perform a narrow range of services.

A major advantage of such an orientation is its marketing appeal. The customer may have more faith in the specialist than in the generalist, on the premise that the specialist is better supplied, better equipped, and better trained in his or her specialty. (This is, again, positioning and to some extent this image is true.) But there are other advantages as well. One is that in many cases employees need to be less highly qualified and—ironically—less specialized or highly trained in knowledge or craftsmanship. The tune-up shop, for example, is equipped with special machines and routine procedures that make it possible for employees with relatively little knowledge of automotive repair procedures to learn to do tune-ups. In such establishments it is common practice to train junior employees in many of the tasks, enabling substantial cuts in payroll costs. The same principle applies to lubrication specialists, muffler-repair shops, and other such establishments, of course.

Despite the advantages of specialization, even specialty shops look to diversification to expand their operations, once they are well established. A muffler shop often adds brake repair and shock absorber replacement, for example. Overall, the philosophy of such ventures is to follow trends and offer the service most commonly needed by people. Every automobile, for instance, eventually needs to have brakes repaired and its engine tuned up. Specialized services can be organized into a set routine requiring a narrow range of skills. Perhaps this is especially true in our current age of automation, where computer-controlled machines replace human judgment and experience in so many things, such as automotive trouble diagnosis and tune-ups. Such specialization thus tends often to result in an efficiency in advertising, in purchasing, in inventory, in personnel, and in many other facets of business, maximizing profitability.

86.

FINDING PROFITABLE MARKET SEGMENTS

Market Segments are Customers.

Advertising and marketing specialists speak of market segments, referring to groups and subgroups within a defined and identifiable general market. But remember that a "market" is made up of people—customers—grouped in some way. If your business is a neighborhood retail store, your market is the local one: the people who live in the neighborhood. Most likely, they belong to the same economic class, and they may even be a more or less uniform group ethnically, but there are still differences. No group of people is absolutely homogeneous; there are bound to be subgroups.

Every market has segments, but they are not always obvious. It may require some ingenuity to identify and appeal to market segments in many cases. You may assume that you "know your customers" and thus know exactly what they will and will not buy. The fact that Mrs. Greene buys ground beef and chuck roast almost every time she comes in does not mean that she will never buy porterhouse steaks, and the alert butcher never tires of suggesting the steaks and other cuts. You may assume, if you are doing a brisk business in cheap watches, that your customers would not be interested in more expensive ones. Suppose you are only partly right. Perhaps 80 percent of your trade are customers for only cheap watches. But suppose two out of ten of your customers *would* buy expensive watches if you had them? You could miss a great deal of profitable business by trying to decide what your customers do and do not want without asking them. You can, in fact, lose an entire business this way. It happens often enough; this is the reason underlying far too many small business failures.

Don't be misled by what your competitors are doing or selling. You don't know that their judgment or information is more accurate than your own; they may be dead wrong.

Don't be deceived by what was true last year, either. Times and tastes change, almost continuously in fact. Business was once considered to be inevitably slow in the hot summer months, and many businesspeople planned their operations based on that premise. But that was before nearly universal air conditioning, which changed many people's habits in hot weather.

Begin with the assumption that you do not know everything there is to know about your market—your customers. Take it for granted that you are missing sales you could have had. It's almost certainly true. Probe constantly to see what else your customers would buy: related items, more expensive varieties, less expensive varieties, totally different items, related services. Finding a profitable segment is, in essence, finding a new market.

How about your business hours? Are they planned to meet customers' desires, your own convenience, or the standards of others in your inudstry? The 7-11 stores long ago gave up the 7:00 a.m. to 11:00 p.m. idea, and most are open all night now because they do enough business in those late hours to make it worth while. Many supermarkets also find it profitable to be open all night. Banks long ago added drive-in banking to extend their hours, and there are some banks that provide *all-night* drive-in banking.

87.

SEGMENTS MAY BECOME MAIN MARKETS

Growth is Not Always Planned.

Erol, a poor immigrant from Turkey, came here about 25 years ago and opened a TV repair shop. Slowly, Erol built his little business and began to sell TV receivers in his shop. When videocassette recorders came along and the Hollywood movie moguls discovered that there was a growing market for movies on videotapes, he started a little sideline of renting videotapes. Videotape rentals took off—and took over his business—and he built one the largest chains of videotape rental "clubs" on the east coast. He has since given up selling TV and videocassette recorders, although he still handles service and repair. Videotape rental became his main business, and a very big business at that.

It is not unusual for one small segment or sideline of a business to grow and dominate the business, as in Erol's case. A Washington lawyer started publishing newsletters, tried his hand at presenting seminars, and soon found the seminar business to have much more potential for growth and profits. Seminars became his main business, and publications a sideline. A New York engineer started out writing technical manuals, but found the provision of technical temporaries a route to rapid growth; later, he started a fledgling typesetting service that soon became the dominant sector of the company. A Virginia housewife started an editing service as a part-time venture in her recreation room, but soon found that her occasional provision of editorial service on the client's premises was a dominant growth factor. Today that little business has become a substantial firm providing technical temporaries for editorial work of various kinds.

88.

THE WINDS OF CHANGE

Change is Inevitable and Often Profitable.

Most businesses that have survived over many years, even major corporations, are not what they started out to be. IBM did not start out as a dominant force in computers; computers didn't even exist at the time of IBM's founding, and when they were being developed later, founder Thomas J. Watson thought so little of their commercial potential that he was reported as saying in 1943, "I think there is a world market for about five computers." (IBM had begun life as CTR—Computing-Tabulating-Recording—Company, makers of scales, time clocks, and tabulating machines.) U.S. Industries, today a conglomerate of companies selling consumer goods, began life as the U.S. Pressed Steel Car Company, founded by "Diamond Jim" Brady in the heyday of railroads. It was forced to change or perish as railroads went into decline.

There are many causes of change, and ours are times of especially rapid change. What you do or sell today is likely to be obsolescent in a few years. You cannot be absolutely sure where you are headed or where you will land when you launch a new venture today. What you start out to do as a business may be overtaken by unexpected events that propel you into a different venture; one of the market segments you undertake to serve may grow and prove to be a far greater market than that one you originally planned to serve. The important thing is to recognize the winds of change and take advantage of the opportunities change almost always offers to the imaginative and resourceful among us.

Obsolescence Equals a Need for Change.

Wise entrepreneurs recognize both need and opportunity for change and act accordingly. (Those who do not usually perish.) The W. H. Hoover Company produced saddlery and other leather goods for the then fledgling automobile industry, but the father and son Hoovers running the business saw the handwriting on the wall for their saddlery business. It was that foresight that impelled them to begin the manufacture of vacuum cleaners that bears their name today. Fingerhut, a prominent cataloger today, originally offered do-it-yourself seat covers by mail: Every buyer of a new automobile could be reasonably sure of getting a packet of literature from Fingerhut before the durable new material, vinyl, became the almost universal material used by automobile manufacturers for upholstering seats, putting the seat-cover business to death rather rapidly. Fingerhut was quick to read the handwriting on the wall and quickly switched to the sale of other products, ultimately going to cataloging.

Opportunity Inspires Change.

Wise entrepreneurs do not always wait for change to be forced on them, but they perceive opportunity and change to accommodate it. The Simmons Company was manufacturing wooden insulators and cheese boxes in 1870 when the owner decided to add the newly invented wire bedspring to the items he manufactured. He soon recognized the great potential in this item, if it were improved and made less expensive to manufacture, and soon the company made nothing but mattresses.

Economic Necessity Brings Change.

Cream of Wheat is a well-established product today, but its marketing was an act of desperation by a failing company. A small North Dakota flour mill was facing bankruptcy in the Panic of 1893. The head miller himself had been using a part of the wheat as a "porridge" of which he was fond. He persuaded the partners who owned the mill to package that part of the wheat and try it on the market. Fortunately, it was an immediate success and has remained a popular breakfast food to this day.

PART FOUR

Reducing Tax And Insurance Burdens

Taxes and insurance are steadily increasing burdens of business. Governments demand more and more of all of us, and create ever more complex tax codes for all of us to cope with. Insurance is also a growing financial burden in an increasingly litigious society, where most of us need the support of insurance companies to defend ourselves against lawsuits. Unfortunately, tax codes change so often and so drastically that even the specialists have difficulty keeping up with changes, legal opinions, and tax court decisions. But here are some tips that will help you minimize the share of your profits consumed by taxes and insurance premiums.

CHAPTER 18

Minimizing
Insurance Costs

To most of us, the subject of insurance is a mysterious one, straddling the specialized knowledge and jargon of the legal profession and the accounting profession, with heavy overtones of probability statistics and other arcane arts associated with underwriting risks. Insurance is frightening enough in its complexity to intimidate many of us, and so we tend to surrender decision making power to the greater knowledge of experts, usually the sellers of insurance, often to our great cost.

89.

THE OBJECTIVE IS TO REDUCE RISK

Buying Only What You Need.

Many of us are over-insured, victims of persuasive sales presentations by insurance professionals and fear of the consequences of being underinsured. (Insurance is almost invariably sold via fear motivation.) So we play it safe, or so we think, paying heavily for our "caution." Paying for $100,000 coverage of $50,000 worth of assets, for example, is not an uncommon extravagance, and is one example of sheer waste: The underwriter will not compensate you for more than you have lost; it is enough of a struggle to get full compensation for your real losses.

Paying extra for insurance when renting an automobile is usually waste also. Most of us are covered by clauses in the insurance on our own automobiles. Insuring rental property, such as rented offices or equipment, may be duplication of insurance already held by the property owner. Check on all such possibilities before buying insurance that you may very well not need at all. Most important, ask plenty of questions before you sign up.

One of the basic problems is that the harried business executive either thinks that insurance policies are too complicated to be understood by ordinary humans or is too busy to spend the time to study the policies. "Just sign me up for what I need," are words uttered too often, an invitation for someone to put their hands in your pocket and help themselves. The truth is that if the seller cannot answer all your questions in such a way that you fully understand what you are buying, you ought to hold off buying until you do fully understand what you are getting.

Insurance Basics.

You buy some of your insurance for protection of the business against disasters. That is (or should) be the consequence of organized risk assessment. Aside from the group plan to be offered to employees as a fringe benefit—life and health insurance—you need first to identify all the kinds or sources of risks—e.g., theft, accident, strikes, ill health, fire, flood, lawsuit, survivor, or other—against which you need protection. That varies with the nature of your business, of course.

You must also estimate for each kind of risk the amount of risk (in dollars) and the probability of loss. Businesses typically use several kinds of insurance: property, automobile, casualty, life, and health. You must then look at the cost of the insurance needed to protect you against each loss and the alternatives available to you in insurance plans. You will want to weigh, for example, the cost of insurance at various levels of deductibles and judge which is the best plan for you.

In short, you need an insurance *program*, one that covers all the bases—all the risks you might reasonably expect to encounter in the type of business in which you are engaged, but *only* those risks, and not a dollar's worth more.

If customers and others visit your premises regularly, you may need liability insurance guarding against the risk of someone being injured on your property. If no one normally visits your premises, such insurance is a waste of money. If you have no showrooms or retail fronts, it is unlikely that you need glass insurance. If yours is a strictly cash and carry business, you do not need credit insurance.

You can ascertain these facts for yourself, but other insurance matters are more specialized and require guidance from insurance experts.

Experience Keeps a Dear School.

You must learn to ask questions. Advance knowledge is always cheaper than that which comes out of experience. Many policies, for example, compensate for property losses at "current value" only, which is a depreciated value, almost always far less than the original acquisition cost or the real cost of replacement. It comes as a shock to learn that your settlement covered only a part of what it will cost you to replace the property. It is possible to get "replacement value" coverage, but you must usually specify that that is the coverage you want.

Where Will You Get Advice?

No matter how many questions you ask, there will always be questions you should have asked but did not because you didn't know that you should have asked them. You need professional guidance. Where will you get it? From an insurance direct writer? The direct writer works for his company, the underwriter, not for you. It is in his or her interest to sell you as much insurance as you are willing to pay for, and he or she is locked into that single underwriter (although there is a possible advantage in having all or most of your insurance with one underwriter and possibly getting a slightly lower rate). A broker or agent? He or she usually represents more than one underwriter, and can offer greater flexibility. But the broker also has an interest in selling you as much insurance as possible, although the broker can cast about for the best deal on each kind of insurance, and is a great asset in helping you when you must make a claim. (Experience with that benefit alone prejudices me in favor of brokers.) So there are pros and cons to the use of both direct writers and brokers as guides in what you need. What is most important is arranging to get guidance that is based on expert knowledge and is not biased against your own interests. Whichever you choose, get more than one estimate or assessment of your needs and compare one with another. In addition, let the brokers or agents know that you are shopping for the best deals so that no one thinks he or she has you locked up. But most important, as in dealing with any outside expert who purports to advise you, insist on getting explanations— in English—complete enough and clear enough so that you can fully understand the rationale of any recommendations made.

You Must Be the Final Judge.

Unfortunately, insurance people, like lawyers, appear to have a complete prejudice against the use of everyday English when discussing their professional specialty; they use all sorts of complicated terms that often do not mean, what you think they mean or simply leave you completely baffled. Evidently the word *payment* is a forbidden term. In the world of insurance policies, payments are *premiums* for some incomprehensible reason.

Your complete understanding of pros and cons and the rationale of all recommendations is most important. Don't be afraid to admit that you don't understand some term or some explanation offered: That reluctance to ask questions can cost you dearly. Do not accede to or accept anything you do not fully understand or with which you do not fully agree. If you feel the need for an outside opinion, consult your attorney or a special risk management consultant before agreeing, but even then ask for a detailed explanation of the rationale behind every recommendation. It's your risk, your money, and your decision; you are certainly entitled to ask questions and get understandable answers.

Service Contracts.

You pay for insurance before you use it, and you may never use it. (You hope never to use it, in fact.) But even that can take special forms. Buy a major appliance from Sears or other merchants, and it is quite likely that you will be invited to buy a service contract. That is a specialized form of insurance, and even small appliance-service companies find it a profitable idea, as well as a boon to the cash flow of the business.

90.

ONE SOURCE OR MANY?

Having Your Cake and Eating It Too.

Like the supermarket owner who doesn't want his money "in bricks," you don't need to spend hours becoming your own insurance expert and manager, spending all your time searching out the best insurer for each of your needs. You also don't need to spend hours keeping track of a welter of insurance policies, each placed separately. Those are unnecessary distractions, wasting time you can spend far more profitably in looking after your own business.

Consider working through an insurance broker who can help you plan your program and place your coverage with many underwriters. Such a broker can also keep track of your overall insurance program. The experienced broker is certainly in a better position than you are to know which underwriter is best for you for each kind of insurance. And if you place all your insurance with or through that broker, he or she will be motivated to advise and represent you honestly—in your own best interests, if not always in his or her best interest. As in every worthwhile deal, each party gets what he or she wants: The broker gets your entire insurance package, and you get the freedom to devote your time to your own business.

How to Minimize the Premiums.

Every business has its own risk category, and the rates quoted you for coverage are based on the risk category the underwriter thinks is the right one for you. If the underwriter has any doubt about your risk category, you can bet that you will be assigned the risk category with the highest premiums. It is important, therefore, that the broker and underwriter have an unequivocally clear understanding of your business. Be sure to ask how you are classified as to business description and risk category, and verify that your business classification is accurate. Better yet, if a substantial amount of insurance is involved, go with your broker to a meeting with the underwriter and see to it that not only is your business accurately defined, but that you present explanations of how you have minimized the risk with safety procedures and risk-minimization measures.

Choosing the Right Deductible.

The size of the deductible, that portion of a loss you must pay in case of a claim, has a great influence on the cost of the insurance, for obvious reasons: The greater the deductible, the smaller the premiums. You must decide for yourself which deductible amount you will choose. There are several considerations. How much can you afford to pay out of pocket if and when you encounter a loss? How much will the difference in premiums be if you opt for a higher or lower deductible? What is the probability of encountering a loss? Finally, which is the deductible likely to cost you the least in the end?

Underwriters usually have favorite brokers, and brokers usually have underwriters with whom they enjoy special relationships—great influence or clout, that is. Ask your broker where he or she has the greatest influence and suggest that underwriter as a first choice, provided the price is right. (The broker knows more about insurance than you do, but there is no harm in making suggestions.)

91.

RATES AND TERMS ARE OFTEN NEGOTIABLE

Tips On Reducing Costs Through Negotiation.

Underwriters are not immune to offers to negotiate rates. For example, on health and hospital coverage, you might ask the underwriter for a ten percent discount on premium rates in exchange for your guarantee to pay the difference, up to the amount of the discount, if the underwriter suffers a net loss for the year on your policy.

Services at Real Cost.

Another arrangement sometimes made by those with very large policies is to have the underwriter provide services at the real cost of the services plus a fixed charge for overhead and profit.

Limited Self-Insurance.

Still another way some organizations save money on health, disability, and life insurance is to set up an in-house program covering some large portion of anticipated claims—up to perhaps 90 percent—the underwriter paying only the excess over that.

Extending the Grace Period.

The usual grace period for payment of premiums is 30 days. In some cases you can negotiate a longer grace period, 60 or even 90 days. This is, of course, helpful for your cash flow.

92.

THE SPECIAL CASE OF
LIABILITY INSURANCE

The Catch-22 of Liability Coverage.

Liability represents a high risk for manufacturers and other businesses in these litigious times. Insurance against liability claims and lawsuits is a high risk for underwriters, and is therefore expensive. (One perceived cause of the surge in such lawsuits has been the growing indifference to and cavalier treatment of customers and their complaints. Better handling of customer complaints is an effective defensive measure in itself, and will reduce the likelihood of litigation.) In fact, aside from prohibitive premium costs, smaller firms often have difficulty getting such coverage, although underwriters tend to insist that this is true only in isolated cases. No one knows where the best crossover is between disastrously high deductibles and impossibly high premiums. For all firms, then, "going bare" (without coverage) and trying to absorb prohibitively high insurance premiums or deductibles is a problem almost without solution. Among the solutions or partial solutions employed by various organizations are these:

- A "disappearing deductible," in which a deductible applies only to small claims, but not to larger claims.

- Some form of self-insurance, whole or partial.

- Stepped up quality-control, safety, and customer-relations (complaint handling) programs and a program to educate and persuade underwriters that liability risk is minimized.

It will probably put dollars in your pocket to discuss these kinds of possibilities with your broker.

93.

CLAIM STRATEGIES AND TIPS

Substantiating Losses.

Many claimants lose money in settling claims with their insurers because they cannot substantiate their loss claims. This problem is often due to a lack of detailed record keeping. For example, if you claim a loss of any kind—inventory, cash, or other valuables—you will have to produce records to prove the loss. You can take a physical inventory of what is on hand, but if your latest record of inventory immediately before the loss is many weeks old, you will probably have a problem proving your loss. (In fact, you don't really *know* what the actual loss is if you don't have a reliable and accurate pre-loss inventory.)

Regardless of the nature of the loss—burglary, holdup, fire, flood, or other disaster—from the insurance viewpoint you must begin as quickly as possible to develop a realistic assessment, and not an estimate of the loss. Estimates, especially initial ones, are made under stress and often in shock. They thus tend to be grossly inflated. An experienced insurance adjuster will operate on that premise, but in any case will want more evidence than an early estimate, which he or she will almost surely regard as a rough guess and discount heavily, waiting for a more thorough investigation.

Be cautious in making initial estimates. There is an understandable impulse to make a high first estimate, but too high an estimate casts doubts on your credibility, and perhaps even on your integrity; too low an estimate prejudices your case if you must later raise it. Unless you are reasonably sure that your estimate is within 20 percent of actual loss, refuse to make it until you have checked a bit.

Writing Repair Estimates.

Many claimants leave it to the insurer's contractor to write repair specifications and estimates. It will probably pay you to have a contractor of your choice review those estimates and specifications, and possibly even make independent estimates and specifications before you sign off. You are entitled to have your losses repaired and replaced in like kind and quality. It makes sense to have someone who represents your interest and is expert enough to effect that replacement have a voice in an assessment.

The Public Adjuster.

In some cases, especially where the loss and claim are substantial and perhaps beyond the abilities of yourself and your broker to assess realistically, it may be in your interest to hire a public adjuster. This is an individual who will charge you a fee based on the amount of your collection from the underwriter (probably in the range 5-10 percent), but who is usually well worth the cost. But be sure that any public adjuster you select is well qualified. Your own insurance broker or lawyer can probably recommend someone to you if the need arises.

94.

HIGH-LOW CLAIMS
SETTLEMENTS

Avoiding Costly Trials.

Occasional disputes between underwriters and claimants are inevitable. Unfortunately, these disputes sometimes reach such irreconcilable extremes that the two parties wind up in a long drawn out, wearisome court battle that can be unbelievably expensive for both parties.

Both would probably agree that arbitration is cheaper and faster and usually more satisfactory than lawsuits and court trials. But how does one get an arbitration process started? A special method for breaking deadlocks and settling claims by arbitration was worked out not too long ago by an insurance company, and the approach has gained a good bit of popularity.

The idea is simple. It consists of a meeting designed solely to reach agreement on two extremes, the highest and lowest acceptable settlement figures. For example, on the one hand is a claimant who insists on demanding $150,000 as a settlement. The insurer offers $50,000 and insists that it is the maximum settlement merited by the claim. Neither side is willing to yield. Negotiations are at a standstill, and the issue is headed for court.

Now the high-low procedure comes into play. A special meeting is held to try to identify the lowest figure the claimant would accept and the highest figure the insurer would pay. That is the high-low bargain. For example, suppose the insurer agrees to pay a minimum of $75,000, regardless of how a court trial turns out, and the claimant agrees to settle for a maximum of $110,000, regardless of a jury's decision. No matter what happens in court, it is agreed, the case will be settled for a figure within those bounds. Once that is agreed to and accepted, the need for a trial appears less pressing. The whole idea of a trial is suddenly almost irrelevant, since *some* agreement has been reached. Arbitration becomes much more feasible and settlement out of court usually follows.

CHAPTER 19

Tax Avoidance

It has been pointed out more than once that there is a vast and important difference between tax evasion and tax avoidance. Tax evasion is a criminal offense. It is the failure to pay taxes one rightfully owes by whatever means taken to evade the taxes due. Tax avoidance, on the other hand, is entirely legal and one's right to pursue. It is arranging one's affairs so as to gain maximum tax benefits, and taking advantage of every legal loophole and escape mechanism that permits one to avoid taxes.

Most of us, business owners and individuals alike, fail to take advantage of all the methods and measures available to us to minimize our tax obligations. Here we will look at some, but not all, of the measures we may take to do so.

95.

TAX ADVANTAGES IN INCORPORATION

Are You In Business or Self-Employed?

It may seem to make little difference, in practical terms, whether you call yourself self-employed or "in business," even if you are a one-person business. With regard to tax liabilities, however, it may make a great deal of difference if you incorporate your self-employment—i.e., establish a corporation, with yourself as both officer and employee of the corporation. (It is possible to have a corporation in which you hold all the offices yourself.) You may pay yourself and other employees salaries, commissions, bonuses, dividends, or combinations of these, and provide normal fringe benefits as well. You may have other officers or employees; you may wish to make your spouse or other family members officers and possibly employees of the corporation, for instance.

Kinds of Corporations.

There are various classes of corporations, but the most important difference lies in whether the corporation is public or private, with the private variety usually called a "close" corporation. The public corporation offers to sell shares to the public and usually sets the raising of funds through such sales as a primary objective. The close corporation is one in which all shares are privately held, often by a single individual (i.e., yourself). For the self-employed individual and for any business in which complete control and business advantage, not investor financing, is the purpose, the close corporation is the appropriate one. It is the one we refer to here.

Self-Employed Authors and Artists.

Formerly, self-employed authors and artists were permitted to write off expenses only by amortizing them over the period in which income was received from the work to which the expenses were attributed. Now, self-employed authors and artists may deduct expenses as they are incurred. If the business is incorporated as a personal services corporation, and all or nearly all of the stock is owned by the author or artist or his orher family, the same write-off provision now applies. However, as in the case of home-based businesses generally, the IRS may be suspicious, and may resist your writing off expenses in excess of income. (See the discussion of home office deductions below.)

Keeping Your Personal Taxable Income Down.

Incorporation does entail some additional paperwork and expense, including the necessity of filling out corporate tax returns in addition to your personal tax returns. However, it also acts as a legal vehicle for health insurance plans and other benefits, reducing the amount of salary you must draw from your venture—i.e, reducing your taxable income and taxes, both withholding and Social Security or self-employment taxes. This is a major benefit, but there are other benefits possible, depending on individual circumstances and needs.

Opting for Two Taxable Years.

If you are an unincorporated, self-employed individual, you are permitted only one taxable year: Your tax year and fiscal year must coincide, and you must report both business and non-business income in the same tax return. In fact, you must get permission from the IRS to report on a fiscal (noncalendar) year basis. When you incorporate, however, you are an employee, and you file your personal return on a calendar-year basis; you are then free to use the calendar year for business purposes or choose a fiscal year as the corporation's taxable year. (October 1 to September 30 is a popular choice of many corporations for the fiscal year.)

Gaining a Special, Short Tax "Year."

As a corporation, you define your fiscal year, which becomes your tax year. However, you can change your fiscal year. At the same time, you cannot have a taxable year in excess of 12 months, so if you change your fiscal year, you will have to make a special tax return of some period less than one year to get back on an annual basis for tax returns. Changing your fiscal year would be a rare occurrence, but business conditions might be such that you can enjoy a tax benefit from the change, or from having a short tax year.

96.

THE UNTAXED CORPORATION

The S Corporation.

For some self-employed individuals, the subchapter S corporation offers tax advantages. In this arrangement, the corporation is not itself subject to taxation. Instead, profits flow directly through the corporation to the stockholders, to be taxed as individual income. Forming a subchapter S corporation is thus a money-saving move when your personal tax rate is no higher than the corporate tax rate, and when you cannot draw enough money from the corporation to avoid the double taxation. (Double taxation is the process of taxing corporate profits as corporate income and then taxing that money again as personal income to stockholders when it is paid out.) However, there are some important special rules that apply to S corporations; one is that an S corporation must be on the cash method of accounting, with expenses deducted only when paid out.

Family Corporations.

A family corporation is a close corporation owned by members of a family (spouses, parents, children, ancestors, or trusts for any of these). An advantage of any family corporation is that salaries, dividends, and/or other payments may be distributed in such manner as to minimize tax obligations. However, in the case of an S corporation that is also a family corporation, the IRS is empowered to judge whether the compensation to any member of the family is proportionate to that member's activity and contribution. This power carries with it the authority to reallocate payments to individuals from the corporation. In other words, if the IRS judges that you received an unrealistically small amount of compensation for your contribution (and thus that you paid far less personal income tax than you should have, using the S corporation as a tax dodge), they may choose to correct this by redistributing income as salaries, dividends, or both.

97.

WRITING OFF CAPITAL ITEMS

Useful Life and Depreciation Schedules.

All property has a useful life. Paper, ink, staples, and thousands of other items referred to as "supplies" have short useful lives; in most cases their useful life ends when they are first used. At the opposite extreme are such items as art—for instance, paintings by masters. They tend to have indefinite useful life, and in many cases their value even accelerates over time. Between these extremes are properties more temporal in nature. They become used up, obsolescent, or otherwise of greatly reduced value—and, eventually, no value—over a few years.

The tax codes recognize these differences of scale in the useful life of business property. They thus allow you to treat the costs of supplies as a straight expense item, recognizing that such items have little or no useful life beyond their first use. That places them in the same category as office rent and shipping costs. The codes, however, take a different position for writing off or recovering the costs of durable property, such as real estate, machines, and furniture. The IRS determines a useful life for such property, and requires you to write the cost of the property off over a period of years. For example, you can deduct 20 percent of the cost each year of five-year property. There is an exception to this, however, which we will discuss a little later

Qualifying for Depreciation Write-Off.

The tax codes recognize that the business owner is entitled to recover all business expenses. Although there are exceptions, most property qualifies for recovery of its cost through depreciation if it is used more than 50 percent for business. That portion used for business is deductible (e.g., you can deduct 75 percent of the cost of an automobile used 75 percent of the time for business and 25 percent of the time for personal non-business use).

Depreciation Versus Expensing Options.

As we have seen, it is quite legitimate and respectable to minimize your tax liability under the provisions of the law. For example, the current tax code permits you to "expense" up to $10,000 of your purchases of business equipment, despite its status as capital equipment. That is, you may choose to put all business equipment on a depreciation schedule if you wish to, but you have an option: You may *either* deduct the full cost *or* the first $10,000 of the cost of the equipment in the year of purchase, rather than depreciating it over several years. If you (or your accountants) decide that it is to your advantage to take the latter option, by all means do so. This applies to personal property bought for business use, not to real property and not to a personal asset converted to business use, such as your personal automobile. There are certain other exceptions as well. If you have an excess over $10,000 and you elect to expense the first $10,000, you may depreciate the remaining dollars under the MACRS (modified accelerated cost recovery system), recovering the costs over a five-year depreciation schedule.

There is one limiting consideration on the $10,000 expensing option: If your total purchase of business equipment is over $200,000 for the year, the $10,000 expensing allowance is reduced by the amount over $200,000—so that if the total is $210,000 or more you cannot take advantage of the $10,000 expensing provision at all.

98.

JUDICIOUS TIMING CAN SAVE
YOU MONEY

The Importance of Choosing Your Time.

"Arranging your affairs" to your own benefit gives you the option of choosing when to buy certain items. If you a) have already acquired enough business equipment to be at or near the $10,000 limit for an expensing deduction, b) prefer to expense capital items, and c) are contemplating the purchase of more equipment, you can delay the purchase until your tax year ends. That puts the new purchase into a new tax year in which you can take the $10,000 expensing deduction again. Or the reverse may be the case: It may be in your interest to have the deduction this year and you may opt to make the purchase earlier than you originally planned. Tax considerations are often a guide to the most beneficial timing of purchases. (If you are on a cash system and have made a purchase this year—but payment is not due until the new year—you may still want to pay it this year for tax reasons.)

Sometimes You Can Influence and Benefit from the Timing of Income.

Depending on the accounting system you use (accrual or cash), payments by customers either become income when bills are rendered or are not income until payment is received. If you are near the end of a tax year and you find that it is in your interest tax-wise to delay receiving income until a new tax year, you may be able to influence the timing of some of your income due at about that time. That is, you may encourage customers (on a one-time-only basis, of course!) to take a little extra time to pay their current invoices, or you may decide to be a bit slow in sending out invoices at that time.

99.

HOME OFFICE DEDUCTIONS

The General Rule.

In general, an office or other business space in your home qualifies for tax purposes if the space is dedicated to business purposes, and all necessary expenses—rent, heat, light, taxes, etc.—may be allocated or prorated accordingly. However, using your kitchen table to fill orders or to write letters does not qualify your kitchen for tax deductions. Setting aside a room or a distinct portion of a room for *business use only* on a regular basis does qualify that space. It is that simple—in basis. But there are complicating situations and conditions, some of which offer good news, some bad news.

Principal Use of the Office.

The office must be your principal place of business. That means you must conduct most of your business activity there and spend most of your business—income-producing—time there. However, in at least one case, the proprietor of a small business (a laundromat) located separately had his office at home; his business location had no space for an office, and he could prove that he spent most of his business time in his office at home. If you use a portion of some room for business only, it helps to partition it off, if only by room dividers, to demonstrate the exclusivity of its use for business. There have been other recent and relevant Tax Court rulings, at least one posing an exception to the principle of spending most of your work time in the home office, but the IRS opposes this and warns that it may not be used as a precedent to justify such use to them. In other words, expect the IRS to disallow and contest such a deduction.

The Sideline Business.

You may be employed or have a primary business at point A, but run a sideline business from point B (your home office) and qualify for relevant tax deductions. The same rules apply. Note however, that you may claim costs for a home office up to (but not beyond) the total of income—gross receipts—from the operation of the home office. That is, you may not use losses there to reduce your tax obligations from a full-time job or other, separate business.

Business vs. Hobby.

Income from a hobby is taxable, and expenses deductible only to the limit of any declared income from the hobby. Losses resulting from a hobby are not deductible; they are treated as non-deductible personal losses. In some cases, the question of whether your venture is a business or a hobby may arise when you show losses. Normally, the IRS will not object to your showing losses in a business for the first three years of its existence; more than a few businesses require that much time to get well enough established to show a profit. Beyond that, if you continue to show a net operating loss, the IRS is strongly inclined to view your venture as a hobby, rather than as a business, especially if it is home-based and a part-time or sideline venture. You may be compelled to demonstrate that profit is the objective of the activity and that it is otherwise a serious venture undertaken for profit. (Formal bookkeeping records, bank accounts, business forms, and dedicated space are evidence of such intent.)

100.

OPERATING LOSSES AND TAX REFUNDS

Taking Advantage of Operating Losses.

For the self-employed individual, a net operating loss for the year—an operating loss that is greater than income for the year—may be carried back or forward (for example, a 1990 loss may be carried back to 1987 and/or forward to 2005, until it is used up). It reduces income for any year in which it is applied, and if it is a carryback to an earlier year, it reduces your tax for that year and qualifies you for a refund. (You can, if you prefer, opt for the 15-year carryforward, reducing your income for future years until the loss is balanced out. But once you select that option, you cannot change your mind.)

The losses you may claim are those resulting from casualty, theft, normal business deductible expenses, your share of an operating loss in a partnership or S corporation, and certain other losses in connection with stock ownership.

101.

DEDUCTIBLE BUSINESS
START-UP EXPENSES

Write-Offs and Capital Losses in Start-Ups.

Certain expenses incurred in starting a new business may be written off as normal business expense. These do not include expenses incurred in the general search for and investigation of business opportunities, other than market research for an established business; those are not deductible. However, expenses incurred in the initial phases of actually acquiring, taking over, and/or starting a business are deductible, if it is to be an "active" business, as defined by the IRS, and if the expenses are amortized over 60 months or longer. Typical of such amortized and deductible expenses are legal fees, costs of incorporation, market research, consulting fees, organization of distribution, research into supply sources, and travel expenses, among others. The amortization period begins when you begin efforts to acquire or start up the new venture. However, if, having incurred expenses to acquire and take over a business, the deal falls through, you may deduct the expenses incurred as a capital loss.

In one case a CPA deducted expenses he incurred in visiting clients to ask if they would retain him as an independent, self-employed accountant, should he decide to start his own private practice. The IRS treated his expenses as a capital loss suffered in setting up a new business, but the Tax Court reversed the IRS, finding it irrelevant that he was investigating the possibility of starting a new business because he was seeking the same kind of employment that he would if he were seeking to be employed by a firm.

102.

USE OF COMPANY CAR

When Is Use of a Company Car an Allowable Deductible?

The use of a company car on company business is nominally a deductible expense. A problem often arises, however, when the user of the car also uses it for personal travel, such as between his/her home and office. The IRS treats that portion of the usage as personal use and regards it as a dividend, if the user is a stockholder, or as compensation, if the user is a non-stockholding employee.

In one case, because the user of the car (the company president) did not own a personal car, the IRS assumed that the full value of the car was a taxable dividend to the president. When the president then declared that the use of the car should be regarded as part of his compensation, the IRS examined the corporate minutes and found no indication that this had been the intention in assigning the car to the president's use, whereupon they assumed that it was a dividend, exercising their clear privilege to do so. Moral: When in doubt, put it in the minutes or write a corporate resolution for the record.

Having Your Cake and Eating It.

A sole proprietor can drive a company car until it is fully depreciated and then switch it to personal ownership without tax liability until it is sold. At that point, there will be a taxable gain on the sale price of the car in excess of its depreciated value. (That is, if the depreciation was total, the sale price is taxable as a capital gain.)

103.

INVESTMENT TAX CREDITS

Often Overlooked Items that May Mean More Tax Savings.

Tangible personal and certain other property with a useful life of three or more years normally qualifies you to an investment tax credit, which can save you up to 11 percent of the price of the property. This category of property includes office equipment, furniture, machinery, fixtures, air conditioning, carpeting, signs, partitions, bookcases, and other tangible property. But tangible property includes property often overlooked. It excludes buildings and their components, but includes items used as integral parts of manufacturing, processing, production, extraction, transportation, and communication. It also includes components related to processing electrical energy, gas, water, and sewage disposal, among many others. Many structures are not, for this purpose, "buildings and their components." Structures that house gas or sewer equipment and facilities, for instance, which may be expected to be replaced when the equipment and facilities are replaced, are considered tangible property. Other facilities would include such items as steam boilers, air handlers, air and vacuum lines, refrigeration equipment, and numerous other items which may have independent housings.

104.

KEEPING CORPORATE TAXES
DOWN WHEN BUSINESS GROWS

How to Expand Most Economically (for Tax Purposes).

Most corporations add departments or divisions as business grows to facilitate efficient management. (Efficiency and such considerations as overhead are linked to the size of the organization.) But as corporate income and profits grow, tax rates grow with them. You can, for instance, expect the tax rate on $250,000 annually to be greater than it was at $100,000 annually. It is perfectly legitimate to form a new corporation, instead of a new division, to handle the expansion of some phase of your business. The original stockholders might retain all the stock of the original corporation, but transfer more than 20 percent of the stock of the new corporation to some key executive or outside investor. Then each corporation is taxed individually on its own profit base, for a net savings overall.

105.

CHILDREN AS EMPLOYEES

Hiring Your Small Children.

Hiring (and paying) one's children, to take advantage of the usual tax breaks for kids and deductions for employers, is a widely practiced stratagem. It does result in getting useful and necessary work done. Proof of that, plus proof that the children actually did the work, is all that is usually necessary to justify the expenses.

106.

COVERING SPOUSE'S EXPENSES ON BUSINESS TRIP

Covering All or Part of Spouse's Costs.

Taking your spouse along on a business trip is at your own expense—unless you can prove that the spouse's presence was necessary to the purpose of the trip (other than to perform minor, incidental services). Examples of necessary presence: Your spouse knows the language and customs of a foreign country, while you do not. Your spouse knows, from former business relationships, those with whom you must do business, while you do not. Your spouse has technical business knowledge that you do not. Your customer/prospect has specifically asked you to bring your spouse.

Of course, you must be able to document any such scenarios but remember that these documents become qualifying evidence of legitimate business expense and deductions.

Even when you cannot justify the cost of a spouse accompanying you as a fully deductible business expense, you can recover part of the cost. For example, the room rate for two is considerably less than twice the room rate for one. Determine the single rate and deduct *only the difference* from your expense account. Apply the same principle to all other expenses. To stay out of trouble with the IRS, establish and keep accurate records. Better to have them and not need them than the reverse!

107.

RECORDKEEPING FOR TAX PURPOSES

It's A Paper World.

It is too late to create records for the IRS after claims are challenged or disallowed. Nor is the IRS especially receptive to belated explanations of records proving that the expenditures were made, but not documenting their nature as allowable deductions. For example, your credit card receipt for luncheon or rooms is not enough in and of itself. On the other hand, an abundance of relevant records lubricates the process quite effectively. Record the names of luncheon guests and make useful notations about purpose, organizations, and other items that indicate the business purpose of the expense. Keep a diary or log that shows when, where, and why you paid for a dinner, hotel room, airline ticket, car rental, or other such expense. Have canceled checks, receipted invoices, bank statements, and other records readily available.

PART FIVE

Coping In Hard Times

Making It Through.

As this is written we are in an economic recession—hard times. (The White House prefers to refer to it as a "lull.") The point at which a recession begins depends on which of the many economists we quote and choose to believe; typically, they do not agree with each other, nor are they crystal clear or unequivocal in their declarations. (U.S. President Harry Truman was quoted as having said that if you laid all the economists end to end they still wouldn't reach a conclusion.) However, we are now witnessing a continuous and growing wave of cutbacks, layoffs, undesired growths of inventory, and other tangible signs of economic downturn. Among the latest signs of recession is a wave of price cuts by several of the leading fast food restaurant chains, including McDonald's and Burger King.

The reality is that have had and will continue to have recessions from time to time, apparently about every 10 years or thereabouts. (It seems to be an erratic pattern, despite the efforts of some economists to find and define economic cycles.) Recessions are times of layoffs and scarcity of jobs. The working class suffers. But businesses small and large suffer too when people are out of work and have little money to spend. Hard times are hard for businesses too.

This recession is a general one (even if it is unevenly distributed throughout the country); that, in fact, is the only type that tends to make national news. But even in the most prosperous of times there are many mini-recessions; often these are highly localized and selective business slowdowns in certain businesses or in certain seasons. Automobile sales may slump when every other business is doing well, for example, or some industries and businesses may have a poor summer when summer is usually a good season for them. Every business has such periods from time to time; probably none is immune to it. Business slowdowns, whether general or isolated cases, are a fact of life.

The majority of the solid, established businesses in this country survive periods when the economy bottoms out; a great many businesses do not. Many will find parallels in this economy with the conditions of the thirties. But things are not the same, and we will learn many new lessons in this period. How can you improve your own survivability index? Let's have a look at a few ideas and experiences to see what ideas can be borrowed and adapted.

CHAPTER 20

Businesses And
Ideas For Hard Times

No one welcomes recessions; we all suffer from them in many ways. The National Federation of Small Business, whose members are generally *very* small businesses (84 percent have annual sales of less than $1 million), found in a recent survey that 43 percent of its members plan to cut back on hiring and capital spending for now. Despite such ominous signs, certain businesses are inherently better suited to lean times than are others. Some even do better in recessionary times than they do in prosperous times. In many cases it is obvious why this is the case; these businesses are by nature well suited to the needs of the public in such times. Their services or products plainly aid the customer in saving money, earning extra income, or otherwise overcoming some consequence of the recessionary economy. In other cases the reasons for greater success under recessionary conditions are not at all obvious, although the success is so plainly evident that we feel we must work at rationalizing an explanation. We can, however, learn from such examples how many other businesses can condition themselves to hard times—that is, improve their survivability by adaptation to the circumstances of the times. So let's look first at those businesses that seem almost to have been deliberately designed for lean times.

108.

REPAIR SERVICES ARE
BUSINESSES FOR HARD TIMES

New Shoes Cost Money.

Many of those who grew up since WW II have never had a pair of shoes resoled or otherwise repaired. Then the neighborhood shoe repair shop all but vanished, and it took a real search to find a place to have shoes repaired or obtain soles, heels, or other shoe-salvage service. In the heart of the Depression, many had only one pair of serviceable shoes, and so patronized the while-you-wait shoe repair shops that had sprung up in many downtown urban areas.

Some of us remember the neighborhood cobbler and know what "half-soles" are (having shoes repaired with half-soles was cheaper than having shoes repaired with full soles). But even we have pretty much given up having shoes repaired in recent decades. Many of us simply took it for granted that when shoes wore out, buying a new pair of shoes was the right response.

Expensive as shoe repair is today, it is less expensive than new shoes, in most cases. In fact, even today more than a few individuals have only one pair of shoes or, at least, only one pair of "good" shoes. And so the shoe repair shop has recently begun to make a comeback. One shoe repair shop in Washington, DC, with branches in outlying Virginia and Maryland shopping malls, reports that its business is up 30 and 60 percent, respectively, at their two mall branches.

The neighborhood cobbler is not going to return since the nature of retailing has changed dramatically. Conditions favor large stores, national chains, suburban malls, and shopping centers. Most shoe repair will be done at large establishments who "wholesale" their services to dry cleaning stores and others who act as "middlemen" or brokers, taking in shoes for repair.

One method for coping with a tightening economy, then, is to solicit such repair work, but not only for shoes. The philosophy is equally valid for other kinds of repair and maintenance of clothing, appliances, automobiles, and other property. In short, we are likely to see a resurgence of repair and maintenance as the sale of some new products declines. In fact, we are already getting reports of an increase in repairs and a decrease in sales of durable goods.

Other repair businesses—e.g., clothing alterations and TV repairs—report similar increases in volume, as more and more people strive to make a garment or an appliance last a bit longer in order to postpone buying a new one. Dry cleaning stores are well-situated to add such services, even if they must send such work out to be done for them. In fact, one consequence of leaner times is that people have clothes dry cleaned and pressed less frequently, and the dry cleaning shop often needs the extra revenue of increased alteration work to take up the slack.

Two Kinds of Business Opportunity.

The situation offers growth opportunities to many businesses. You can develop an in-house repair service, or farm the work out to repair shops at a discount, which represents your own gross profit. Repair shops may add growth to their operations by soliciting such business from sellers of the products, doing a greater volume of work at discounted or wholesale rates. But there is still another option, a way of doing the repair work on your premises at minimal risk and expense, without adding any full-time employees at all. You can get tailors, seamstresses, mechanics, and/or technicians to come in and do necessary work on your premises on a part-time or subcontract basis.

109.

"DOWNSIZING" SPECIALISTS ARE BUSIER

Opportunities for Management Consultants.

Many corporations today feel a responsibility to employees they must let go, and thus try to ease the shock of layoff. Many are employing the euphemism "downsizing," instead of the harsher "layoff," to describe policies. Some firms are also sensitive to the possible legal consequences of laying off employees in these highly litigious times, and are mindful of the influence of today's greatly expanded labor laws and equal opportunity laws. For either or both of these reasons, an increasing number of corporations are therefore retaining management consultants to help make layoffs a bit less hurtful to the employees and to their own images. Some of these management consulting firms (sometimes referred to as "outplacement" specialists) provide the special service of counseling, retraining, and otherwise working with employees about to be laid off to help them make the transition and find other employment. The need for such services is likely to grow, and any management consulting firm can add such services.

Downsizing Provides Business Opportunities for Some Law Firms, Too.

Because of the possible legal consequences of layoffs, many firms compelled to reduce forces consult law firms who specialize in labor relations. For such firms today it is probably wise to make their specialty well known to the industrial and commercial communities, especially among the larger employers in their service areas. Perhaps a law firm feeling the pinch of the recession might benefit from adding such counseling services.

Awards vs. Raises.

Still another beneficiary of the downturn in business has been the management consultant who specializes in employee-award programs. Many employers today are interested in the idea of instituting bonus and award programs for employees instead of raises. Although there are many firms who specialize in designing and administering such programs, this is a service that any management consulting firm can add to an existing line of specialties. It is a particularly appropriate activity for those management consulting firms who specialize in employee benefit programs.

110.

DISCOUNT SALES

Cutting Expenses is an Almost Automatic Response to Hard Times.

There is nothing new in the discount store (or in the idea of discounting), but the discount store is today attracting many new customers who would have once scorned the very idea of discount shopping. This is particularly true for discount stores selling products that meet daily needs, but only to a slightly lesser extent for those selling clothing and other less frequent needs. The head of one grocery discount chain, Shoppers Food Warehouse, reports a decrease in sales of the more costly or "luxury" food items, with a corresponding increase in less costly foods. A large fabrics retailer reports sales of materials for home decorating are increasing, but in the area of the less expensive fabrics. It is clear that the trend to making dollars stretch further is well underway already, and customers will respond to opportunities you offer them to do more in this regard.

Medical care is one area most agree they cannot afford to skimp on, but there are many health-care alternatives, and some are less expensive than others. Health care maintenance (HMO) memberships and plans are more and more attractive, and some are less costly than others. Ideally, an HMO offers a variety of plans, with corresponding ranges and degrees of benefits, to permit the   individual to select that which he or she can best afford. Those HMOs offering the lowest rates are reporting sharp increases in sales. The message for other health care providers: Find ways to eliminate or minimize less important services and offer lower overall rates—or devise alternate plans with lower rates.

111.

DO-IT-YOURSELF SUPPLIERS PROSPERING

Hardware Stores and Others Are Naturals.

There are many for whom doing it yourself is a hobby, pastime, or source of great pride, and who would do it themselves in good times or bad. For them, the local hardware store and lumber yard is a natural attraction. But another predictable beneficiary of the slumping economy is the business specializing in do-it-yourself supplies and instruction. A Maryland supermarket-sized retailer of craft supplies is crowded every day with people buying supplies to make their own Christmas wreaths, greeting cards, doilies, dolls, signs, jewelry, posters, toys, and sundry other items; smaller vendors of do-it-yourself materials report similar increases in business.

The trend toward more do-it-yourself activity leads directly to needs for equipment, supplies, information, and instructions (patterns, instruction books, and classes, for example). This is a clear signal to retailers whose businesses lend themselves to the addition of such items and/or services in the do-it-yourself field.

Publications.
One need not be directly in a do-it-yourself business. With an increase in do-it-yourself activity, the market for instruction expands. The bookstore and newsstand may take note here and add do-it-yourself instruction books and magazines, which will themselves increase in number.

112.

SMALL BUSINESSES WILL INCREASE

A Modern Paradox: Hardship Creates More Business Starts.

Recession makes small business survival more difficult, as published figures on business bankruptcies demonstrate. But increased unemployment also accompanies recession, and that leads to an increase in small business starts by many who are unable to find jobs—or, at least, jobs that will support them and their families. The great increase in starts of what some have termed "mini-small business" is a development worth monitoring. These one- and two-person business enterprises are often home-based: mail order, editorial services, stenographic services, small-scale catering, referral agencies (for babysitters, practical nurses, housekeepers, and other such services), clipping services, news stands, route deliveries, consulting, crafts, manufacturing, teaching, and many other fields. But in today's world there are many new ideas that can be utilized from a home-office base properly equipped with the modern business tools available to even the self-employed individual, tools we have discussed in earlier pages. What is true about furnishing equipment, supplies, services, training, and information to support do-it-yourself activities is equally true for those who wish to cultivate the nouveau mini-small entrepreneur as a customer.

113.

MOVERS AND VEHICLE RENTERS BENEFITING

On the Move.

Painful although it may be to acknowledge, business is usually on the increase in hard times for firms specializing in implementing evictions—actually physically moving people's possessions out of the building and placing them on the lawn or sidewalk in front of the residence. Specialists in this field are already reporting not only increases in business—the number of eviction orders assigned them to carry out is now on the rise—but also an increase in number of middle-class houses in "better" neighborhoods requiring such services. It is not only the traditionally underprivileged of our society who feel the pinch of inflated rents and mortgages they can't afford.

For the same reason, movers are noting an increase in business from many seeking less expensive domiciles, and from owners of expensive homes who sell them because they cannot maintain them under current conditions. However, there is also an increasing number of people who are moving, for whatever reason, and find it necessary to avoid the high cost of professional moving services. They therefore choose to use the do-it-yourself method of moving their household goods. This has resulted in an increased demand for rental trucks and trailers, which represents opportunity for local service stations and others in a position to offer such services.

114.

CHANGES IN THE WAY YOU DO BUSINESS

Revolutionary Change.

Many businesses lack the inherent advantages to help them get through slowdowns and recessions of the businesses we have just examined. Some can adapt, but many are not in a good position to do so without undertaking a special risk. For example, an emporium or restaurant of any kind, catering to a discriminating and moneyed class—a "carriage trade"—risks losing its regular patrons if it creates anything resembling a bargain-counter, runs spectacular sales, markets too ostentatiously, or appears in any way to be willing to compromise quality standards to solicit a different kind of trade. Perhaps such a business is based on snob appeal, but that appeal is a true business asset, in that case, regardless of what anyone thinks. In addition, many retailers who cater to relatively affluent customers—Neiman Marcus is one—believe that their "average" patrons, with incomes of at least $65,000 per year, are far less affected by recession than are those lower on the income scale— and so are likely to make little if any change in their buying habits, regardless of the recession.

Calculate the Risk.

In general, there is always some risk in changing one's established image as a business. Recession-fighting methods must be in keeping with your basic image—unless you are willing to change your business posture. That is itself not unprecedented, however. Many businesses have done this successfully. Willard Marriott Sr. started with what was little more than a root beer stand, became well known and prosperous as a restaurateur (operator of the *Hot Shoppe* chain, which were "family" or "coffee shop" restaurants), best known today as the operator of the many Marriott hotels, although still operating a large number of coffee shops. The original McDonald's restaurants were primarily carryouts, hardly more than hamburger stands, but today are doing much more business as self-service, sit-down establishments than as carryouts. They once served little more than hamburgers; today they do a large breakfast business. So drastic change—complete makeovers—need not be ruled out, but once initiated they are normally irreversible and cannot be undone. Consider, then, the advantages and disadvantages of making a serious change in how you do business.

Mental Set—the Positive Attitude—Helps.

Monroe Milstein made just such a serious change in going from wholesaling coats and suits to retailing them. He did so, against the counsel of his father and partner, Abe Milstein, by buying out a coat factory outlet store in Burlington, New Jersey. Today Burlington Coat Factory sells through 156 stores. It helps to be a positive thinker, as Milstein is. He says that if you believe in a recession and *plan* to do less business, you will somehow manage to carry out your plan and you will indeed do less business. It doesn't hurt either that Milstein practices his own brand of opportunism by utilizing whatever fixtures and carpets are already available in the former supermarkets, bowling alleys, and who knows what other kinds of former establishments he rents to open as new outlets. He is a definite believer in minimizing overhead, while his retailing philosophy is to mark up his goods more modestly than do his competitors and do a high-volume business.

Less Serious Changes.

Changing your business posture is not a sink-or-swim proposition; there are innumerable degrees of change possible. Even if the change contemplated is revolutionary it may be carried out slowly, by degrees. This eases the shock, so there is not an abrupt transition likely to confuse and confound regular customers. Perhaps more important, changing by degree affords you the opportunity to weigh the result of the move and halt it if the result appears to be unsatisfactory, or accelerate it if it is helping you.

115.

ADVERTISING AND PROMOTION

Cut, But Not Your Own Throat.

There is a natural tendency to retrench—cut expenses—in a recession, sometimes even before sales show any sign of decline. For many people, advertising and other sales promotion budgets are the most visible and tempting targets for cutbacks, on the assumption that the advertising/promotion are not producing enough new sales to justify their expense. Often, the assumption is a correct one; many advertising and promotion budgets are largely waste, and the programs do not pay their way. However, it is not logical to discontinue sales promotion entirely—that is taking a poison pill. The objective should be to replace promotions that do not work with promotions that do work.

Doing this—determining which promotions work—probably will require a good bit of experimentation, with continual testing to see what works best—produces the greatest amount of business per dollar invested. If you did not test all your advertising and other sales promotion before, start doing so now.

116.

THE FAMILIAR SHIBBOLETH: CUT OVERHEAD

As in the case of testing your advertising and sales promotions, you should always try to minimize overhead, even in the most prosperous of times; if you never cut your overhead before, by all means do so now. Cutting overhead is a first line of defense against recession because most overhead makes no direct contribution to success, and minimizing it does not hamper success from happening. Here are a few general guidelines that are appropriate:

Discriminate Between One-Time and On-Going Overhead Costs.

Paying $50 too much for a filing cabinet or computer printer has no significant impact on your profit. Paying 10 cents an hour more than you must for daily cleaning services for your 48 stores does. The second example of waste is thus far more important than the first. Obvious? Yes, but too often overlooked as a basic truth by those who will spend $100 worth of time and effort to save $10.

Don't Fix What Isn't Broken.

Monroe Milstein of Burlington Coat Factory doesn't tear up the existing carpeting in a building he rents for one of his stores, even if it is a bit shabby, nor does he install carpeting if it isn't there to begin with. The arithmetic is simple: New carpeting does not contribute to his bottom line, and the lack of it does not reduce profits.

Don't Pay for Quality Where Quality Doesn't Count.

It is probably worthwhile to be sure that you have the latest and best in cash registers and related items. It is usually a waste to pay more than you have to for "top of the line" thumbtacks, rubber bands, and paper clips.

PART SIX

Reducing the High Cost of Labor

Labor is a Highest-Cost Item.

The high cost of labor in general today is indisputable: Everyone is aware of high labor costs today and everyone experiences it in some form. (Have you had your automobile serviced recently? Or called for service on your TV, VCR, dishwasher, or furnace?) For many kinds of business, especially but not confined to service businesses, labor is the highest of all the costs that must be recovered in setting selling prices.

The high costs of labor stem from more than one cause. They begin with those high costs incurred in recruiting—finding and hiring competent people. This is itself no small problem even in today's market, but the roots of labor costs go well beyond that of hiring skilled people: For many kinds of products and services, labor is the major ongoing production cost, embedded in the heart of the product or service and much higher than the cost of materials. And even that is not a complete analysis of how and why the cost of labor hikes business costs in general: Labor cost is a major contributor to or cause of much of the overhead pool because it is a source for and cause of many collateral costs: the paid-time-off element of overhead, group insurance, numerous other fringe benefits, and the idle time you must pay for as an employer. Idle time, for example, is a special problem: Do you continue paying salaries to people for whom you do not have productive (i.e., income-earning) work to do at the moment? Or do you "furlough" them, pay heavy severance costs, and hope that they will be willing, ready, and able to return to work unhesitatingly when "things pick up?" That is, will you be faced with an expensive recruiting problem later, succeeding the expensive termination costs? These are not problems without answers, although the answers may not be obvious ones. Let's look at just a few of the answers you may be able to use profitably.

CHAPTER 21

Recruiting And Its Costs

Don't be deceived by statistics. Government statistics lately have reflected a rising degree of unemployment. However, those figures refer primarily to unskilled or semi-skilled workers. Despite those and a few other disquieting economic rumbles, we are still in a seller's market for skilled labor today: It is still expensive to hire people, even people with minimal skills. Moreover, people with even minimal skills have been taught to consider only "fee paid" (i.e., you, the employer, pay the placement fee) jobs, in a total reversal of history. (There was a time when the applicant was grateful to be even considered for a job for which he or she would pay a fee to an employment agency.) In spite of all, skilled workers are not breaking down your doors in an effort to go to work for you, and recruiting help is still a costly proposition.

A great many firms maintain a large personnel office and try to be their own "employment agencies." Doing this may or may not save you money; there is less and less reason to view it as a money-saving measure. There are many costs involved in all the alternative recruiting methods you are compelled to use in trying to be your own employment agency. There are the many associated and necessary measures and costs of advertising, participating in or conducting your own job fairs, sending your personnel people on the road to conduct interviews, transporting candidates from out of town to your facility for interviews, and/or hiring headhunters (executive recruiters) as an alternative to using the services of employment agencies. But to a large degree these are all the cost of convenience, the convenient methods for finding and hiring the help we need. However, we can eliminate most of that cost if we are willing to go to a bit of trouble. For one thing, there are various organizations who can be of help to us. Following are descriptions of some of the alternatives.

117.

ALTERNATIVES TO PAYING
PLACEMENT FEES

The "40-Plus" Club.

A great many urban areas today boast a "40-Plus Club." These are mutual support peer groups, made up of individuals at or past age 40 and unemployed. The rise of such clubs are an outgrowth of the myth that men past the age of 40 have special difficulty in finding jobs because employers think that men of that age are well past their prime. Men and women of 40 and beyond, therefore, have banded together to form these groups or "clubs," where they may have a few appurtenances deemed necessary to a job-hunting endeavor: A mailing address, a telephone number where someone will take a message, a place where there is a desk and chair to write and work to organize job-hunting efforts, and a community of job-hunting fellows who may be able to help each other with ideas and job tips.

Helpful as this is to those seeking jobs, there is a flip side in the helpfulness of this to employers who recognize the value of experience and wisdom in experienced executives and professionals who happen to be past 40 and unemployed for reasons having no relationship to their competence and worth. The 40-Plus Club is potentially a source of great talent at modest costs.

Calling up the nearest "40-Plus" club and listing your requirements with them is in itself a smart move.

State Employment/Unemployment Service.

Not enough use is made of the local "unemployment offices," which can list your requirements at no cost to you. Most unemployed people do register with these offices for their unemployment benefits. Like the 40-Plus clubs, the state's unemployment service can supply names and basic qualifications of candidates, as well as list your requirements, and no fee is required of either applicant or employer to hire any qualified and acceptable candidate who applies to you as a result.

Schools and Colleges as Sources.

Universities, colleges, and trade or vocational schools usually offer students help in finding jobs by acting as employment agencies. (This is especially the case for their graduates and graduate students.) Even the smallest college or school will post help-wanted notices on bulletin boards or list them in the school periodical. List your wants with local colleges, universities, and other schools, if recent grads or students will serve your needs.

"Networking" Is Another Method that Works Both Ways.

Many professionals and executives in quest of jobs today rely on "networking" as a means of winning jobs. This means, in principle, making new "contacts" at and through a variety of business organizations. These are associations of various kinds—trade groups, professional societies, and others. (Joining a 40-Plus club is in itself a limited form of networking, in fact.) The idea, for the networker, is to maximize the number of "contacts" he or she makes, and to make sure that all know what he or she normally does (i.e., his or her career specialty). The objective is to increase your range of "contacts," seeking tips, referrals, and any other lead possible. The networker hands out an adequate number of business cards, brochures, resumes, or whatever else he or she uses to document and support the quest. Thus, the individual hopes, he or she will be led to good job prospects.

The idea for the networker is to seek out both organizations and occasions—e.g., conventions, meetings, and other conclaves—where he or she can move about and meet others who can help them in their quests. The desired contact is not necessarily an employer, however, for it is, as in the case of the 40-Plus club, a case of peers helping each other by passing tips and leads to each other. In fact, the effective networker also maintains direct personal contacts with many others, further enriching the exchange of useful information.

However, this is a two-way street, as other approaches to job hunting have been, offering you opportunities to reduce your recruiting costs. As an employer, you can make your own "contacts" in these groups and let your own wants become known, encouraging networkers to pass the word of your openings about among their fellows so that qualified individuals will seek you out individually and apply for the openings in your own organization.

CHAPTER 22

Alternatives To Conventional Recruiting

Not all "Temps" are "Kelly Girls."

It is certainly no secret that today you can solve a transient work-overload problem with an office temporary— secretary, typist, file clerk—by simply making a routine telephone call to any of the many agencies who supply such individuals and their services for as long or as short a time as needed. It is probably not as well known that you can hire an accountant, lawyer, physician, engineer, writer, artist, architect, nurse, statistician, or other technical/professional specialist almost as easily as you can hire general office help on a short-term, hourly basis.

Until relatively recent times, temporary help beyond that of the most basic office help was available primarily in only engineering and related government projects. The burgeoning demand for technological specialists to staff the multitude of federal defense, space, and related high-tech projects had created a severe shortage of labor qualified in the relevant high-tech areas. The result was not only a basic difficulty in finding and recruiting specialists to man the many projects, but also problems of delays and lost time: In conventional employment, even after suitable candidates were found and recruited, weeks and even months expired before new hires actually reported aboard, ready for work. This and numerous other problems led to a streamlined method of hiring high-tech specialists on a temporary basis, much as office help had been hired: The specialists worked for a firm that might call itself a firm of consultants or a special-services firm, and who supplied the temporaries to work on the client's premises, under the client's orders and direction. The client paid the service supplier an hourly rate for each individual, and the individual was in turn paid an hourly rate by the service supplier, often called a "job shop." (Such temporaries were and often are called "job shoppers," sometimes as somewhat derisive term.)

The practice soon spread to business and commerce in general and encompassed a wider variety of skilled people, so that almost all kinds of specialists are now available on a temporary basis from a large number of firms who supply such services. Here are some of the types of temporaries offered:

- Accountants, all levels—junior, senior, CPAs, tax specialists, financial analysts, comptrollers, and others.

- Banking personnel—loan processors, financial specialists, loan officers, loan secretaries, bookkeepers, proof operators, appraisers, auditors, and marketers

- Escrow/mortgage specialists—escrow officers, loan underwriters, closers

- Computer specialists—systems analysts, programmers, management consultants, documentation specialists, computer operators, project leaders, software engineers, telecommunications specialists, database designers, MIS managers, technical writers, and engineers.

- Engineering specialists—engineers, electronic, mechanical, missile, rocket, chemical, civil, technicians, and designers, all classes.

- Draftspeople and illustrators, all classes

- Lawyers—attorneys, paralegals, legal secretaries, expert witnesses, law clerks, researchers, and others.

- Executives—senior corporate specialists, comptrollers, management executives, production executives.

- Editorial specialists—writers, PR specialists, artists, editors, proofreaders, indexers, researchers, proposal writers and managers.

- Sales and marketing professionals—closeout specialists, discounters, marketing consultants, others.

- Medical workers—physicians, dentists, technicians, nurses, therapists, and assistants.

- Insurance people—claims examiners and adjusters, underwriters, safety engineers, sales specialists, and others.

There are certain advantages to everyone involved in the system. From your own viewpoint as an employer you will pay a bit more per hour for such temporary employees (who are not really your employees, but the employees of a contractor), but you have no ongoing or collateral obligations, legal or moral: You have no fringe benefits or taxes, no recruitment costs, no severance costs, and no idle time to pay for in connection with these people. You can sever them with little or no notice when your situation calls for that—e.g., the individual is not satisfactory to you or there is a hiatus in the work—and you can "rehire" temporaries when you need them again. And in many cases you can contract directly with the individuals as temporaries—contractors—and save the middleman profits of hiring them via a service provider firm. (Beware of tax complications here, however; make sure that the temporary is a legitimate service contractor—i.e., does such contracting of his or her services on a regular basis, so that the IRS is not justified in suspecting that the temporary is really an employee using a subterfuge.)

The list offered here is a partial list, but there is already considerable overlap, so sorting and classification is necessarily limited. Check your own yellow pages directory, where you will almost surely find temporary services organizations. However, a starter list is provided in the appendix.

Telecommuting, a Relatively New Idea.

The advent of computers, fax machines, copiers, answering machines, and other high tech equipment in small and inexpensive versions has made possible and inspired a modern phenomenon known as the "home office." (Probably it is the desktop computer that was the main motivating force in this.) It is reminiscent of the cottage industries of an earlier century, and it was thus not surprising that Alvin Toffler in his book, *Future Shock*, made reference to the "electronic cottage."

There are two significant outgrowths of this that are pertinent to our discussions here, one of which is a new idea that has come to be called *telecommuting*. In essence, this consists of an employee working in an office in his or her own home, linked to the employer by telephone, fax, and computer equipped with a modem (a device for communicating with other computers via a telephone line).

Obviously, not every situation is suitable for this working arrangement. The work requirement must lend itself to telecommuting, and the worker must be one who can be relied upon to be diligent, and who can work well in a remote location without direct supervision. However, where these conditions are met satisfactorily there are benefits: You need not provide office facilities for the worker, for one. You can expand your staff without incurring additional costs for added physical facilities. You also gain access to certain labor not easily available otherwise, in the form of women who have small children to look after and need the general flexibility that affords them the opportunity to do so.

118.

OTHER SPECIAL
ARRANGEMENTS

Part-Time Labor.

There are often needs for part-time workers to do jobs that must be done but do not justify full-time employment nor the diversion of any full-time employee. Using part-time labor can be a double-edged sword, however, with potential drawbacks, as well as potential advantages. There are hazards in using part-time workers who are "moonlighting"—holding down a full-time job elsewhere and working part-time only in their "leisure" hours. They are not dependent on the part-time work, and they often tend to get weary of working two jobs. The result is too often a lack of dependability. It is wiser to use as part-time workers only those who have no other job, choose to work only part-time, and are available for work during normal business hours.

The advantages, on the other hand, are several: Part-time employees, especially if they work less than three-fourths the normal work week, do not qualify for fringe benefits. In general, you have a limited commitment to part-time employees because they are not normally career employees in any sense of the word. As in the case of telecommuting, using part-time workers may give you access to labor otherwise not available. In fact, telecommuters may be especially interested in part-time work, and telecommuting lends itself especially well to part-time commitment.

Contracting Out.

One way to reduce labor costs is to contract with others to do some of your work on their premises—i.e., instead of contracting for labor, you contract the work itself. If you wish to make a mass mailing, for example, and your mail room is already working at capacity, it may be much more practical and less costly to contract with a mailing house to handle what is essentially an overload for you. For that matter, even if you plan to send out mass mailings on a regular basis it is not necessarily good business or more economical to create an in-house capability to do the work; it may be far less costly and efficient to contract the work out regularly. In making an analysis to consider the alternatives, take into account the commitment you must make to doing work in-house versus contracting it out. Will you have to buy new equipment? Provide more space? Add new employees? Create collateral capabilities? (One employer decided to buy a small press when he found his printing bills mounting, but soon changed his mind when he discovered that he would also need a plate-maker, a bindery, ink and paper inventories, and a full-time operator.)

Surplus Opportunities and Sources

Surplus Spectacular.

Among the many ways to reduce or avoid costs is to buy surplus items. Surplus items are not necessarily used items. They may be well used and not in good condition at all, they may be well used but in good condition, and they may even be new or nearly new. Often, new items sold as surplus are offered as "closeouts," a more general term. Although the basic idea advanced in earlier chapters for considering surplus sales was to reduce the costs of furniture, fixtures, and equipment, buying and selling surplus and closeouts is a major business in itself, and you may wish to consider dealing in such merchandise. Information is offered here to support that aim also.

America is a land of plenty. We have enormous surpluses of many things, especially manufactured goods. When a new product appears—a transistor radio, a pocket calculator, a videocassette recorder—it is often an immediate sellout at high prices. (Small transistor calculators sold for $300 and more when they first appeared, and many people paid up to $2,000 for the first videocassette recorders.) Mass production and subsequent market saturation, plus competition from cheaper models (somebody will *always* find a way to make it cheaper) drives the prices down, and suddenly manufacturers and dealers are holding huge, slow-moving inventories. Or perhaps style changes, bankruptcies, miscalculations, "dumping" by foreign manufacturers, or other misfortunes and chance occurrences result in great surpluses of inventory. Whatever the cause, the result is usually the same: The goods become *closeouts*, items offered far below their normal prices, often even below their actual cost.

These are all opportunities for dealers, brokers, agents, finders (who don't even have to buy and sell or even see the merchandise to make thousands of dollars as a special kind of middleperson or broker) and other alert and astute individuals.

Some of these entrepreneurs buy the items for resale—in bulk, individually, at wholesale, at retail, by mail, to foreign countries, and perhaps even in other places and by other means. Sometimes these entrepreneurs buy closeout and surplus goods for their scrap or salvage value. (Some products contain valuable metals, such as copper, iron, and gold, for example.)

Some finders work entirely in closeouts, tracking down both buyers with needs for sources and sellers with needs for buyers, matching them up and collecting a finder's fee from one party or the other. Or, as a variant of this, the finder may act as the agent or broker, buying up only what he knows he can resell immediately—usually with a buyer already lined up and waiting to consummate the deal—earning more than the finder's fee he might have otherwise collected.

Closeouts can be in virtually anything—clothing, canned goods, machinery, tools, jewelry, raw materials, farm products, or anything else sold in the marketplace. Even the federal government has many closeout sales to get rid of government surplus, some of it used and not in the best of shape, some nearly new, and some new and never used—even in original packing. Some of those who deal in closeouts specialize in certain kinds of goods or certain kinds of sources, while others wheel and deal freely, ranging widely.

There are many reasons for selling perfectly good, new merchandise as closeouts or surplus. These include changes of style, slow-moving inventory and storage space needed, salvage from disasters of various kinds, bankruptcies and other going-out-of-business situations with stock to be disposed of, urgent need for cash, and oversupplies, among others.

Government Surplus

The federal government spends over $200 billion every year for just about every kind of product and service you can name. It is thus no great surprise that the thousands of government offices have a great many surplus items to get rid of almost continually. Often the government includes brand new items that are declared to be surplus for any of the many possible reasons we have just examined.

Most government surplus is disposed of—sold or given away—by the General Services Administration and the Department of Defense. There are a few exceptions and some special provisions. Timber is sold by the U. S. Forest Service (an agency of the Department of Agriculture) and the Bureau of Land Management (an agency of the Department of the Interior). And the Small Business Administration, although it does not sell excess property, sometimes orders excess property set aside to be bid on by small business only, to assure that small business gets a fair share of useful property.

Any adult may normally bid for surplus property, although there are a few cases where some government employees may be restricted from bidding. The usual process involves these steps: 1) the government agency announces the sale; 2) interested people request copies of the "bid set" and, following instructions contained therein, either submit a sealed bid or attend an auction.

(Both methods are common.) When a sealed bid is called for, the bidder may be required to post a bond the ensure that he or she is bidding in earnest, but that is returned if the bid is not the winning one.

How To Find Out About Surplus Sales

Sales of surplus goods are advertised in a number of ways. One is through the pages of the *Commerce Business Daily*, a Department of Commerce publication in which government needs are announced every day. (It is available by subscription from the Commerce Department or the Government Printing Office.) However, you can also register with the agencies and get on their mailing lists. Write to the General Services Administration and/or the Department of Defense (addresses are given below) and request an application form. The form will be sent to you with instructions. The General Services Administration has 10 regional offices in the United States, and each handles surplus sales and free donations in its own region. You must apply to each regional office in whose sales you are interested. Select the region(s) of your interest and address your request to:

> General Services Administration
> Federal Supply Service
> Personal Property Division
> (add correct address from list below)

You will then get an application form to fill out and return, and your name will go on the list of people to receive announcements of surplus sales.

To apply to the Department of Defense, request an application form from the following address:

> DoD Surplus Sales
> P.O. Box 1370
> Battle Creek, MI 49016

What Kinds Of Property You May Ask To Be Listed For

The government sells "real property"—land and buildings—and many other kinds of goods, referred to as "personal property." There is a third classification covering strategic materials—e.g., ores, metals, minerals, and others—that are stockpiled. For information on this type of purchase write to:

> Minerals and Ores Branch
> Office of Stockpile Disposal
> General Services Administration
> 18th and F Streets, NW
> Washington, DC 20405

Other Sources Of Government Surplus

The Government Printing Office occasionally sells surplus printing and binding equipment. The U.S. Forest Service and Bureau of Land Management sell timber, as already noted, but are not the only agencies that may sell timber. Some timber sales are made by the Defense Department, the Atomic Energy Commission, and the Tennessee Valley Authority. Addresses of these agencies follows:

Division of Reservoir Properties	Savannah River Operations Office
Tennessee Valley Authority	U.S. Atomic Energy Commission
Knoxville, TN 37950	P.O. Box A, Aiken, SC 29801

For Bureau of Land Management timber sales, write the Bureau as follows:

Federal Bldg, Room 4017	729 Northeast Oregon Street
650 Capital Avenue	P.O. Box 2965
Sacramento, CA 95814	Portland, OR 97208

Federal Bldg, Room 3022
Phoenix, AZ 85025

Federal Bldg, Room 334
P.O. Box 2237
Boise, ID 83702

Federal Bldg, Room 3008
300 Booth Street
Reno, NV 89502

8217 Federal Bldg
P.O. Box 11505
Salt Lake City, UT 84111

700 Colorado State Bank Bldg
1600 Broadway
Denver, CO 80202

Federal Bldg & U.S. Courthouse
316 N. 26th Street
Billings, MT 59101

U.S. Post Office & Federal Bldg
South Federal Place
P.O. Box 1449
Santa Fe, NM 87501

U.S. Post Office
   and Courthouse Bldg
2120 Capital Avenue
P.O. Box 1828
Cheyenne, WY 82001

Department Of Defense Sales Offices

Defense Property
   Disposal Region
P.O. Box 13110
Columbus, OH 43213

Defense Property Disposal Ships
   Sales Office
P.O. Box 100
Portsmouth, RI 02871

Defense Property
   Disposal Region
P.O. Box 14716
Memphis, TN 38114

Defense Property
   Disposal Region
P.O. Box 58
Defense Depot Ogden Station
Ogden, UT 84401

Defense Property Disposal Region
Sales Office Hawaii
DPDR-Pacific, Box 211
Pearl City, HI 96782

General Services Administration Regional Offices

Post Office and Courthouse
Boston, MA 02109

1500 E. Bannister Road
Kansas City, MO 64131

26 Federal Plaza
New York, NY 10007

819 Taylor Street
Fort Worth, TX 76102

7th & D Streets, SW
Washington, DC 20407

Denver Federal Center, Bldg 41
Denver, CO 80225

1776 Peachtree Street, NW
Atlanta, GA 30309

525 Market Street
San Francisco, CA 94105

230 S. Dearborn Street
Chicago, IL 60604

Federal Bldg
300 Ala Moana Blvd
Honolulu, HI 96850

GSA Center
Auburn, WA 98002

Alaskan Area
P.O. Box 1632
Anchorage, AK 99510

Closeouts And Surplus From Commercial Sources

You can buy closeouts and surplus directly from their owners at warehouse sales, auctions, and other events. But such items are also available from the many companies that deal in this area. One man I know, for example, was offered a large, ill-assorted lot of stationer's merchandise, salvages from a warehouse fire, for $200. He bought it and resold it to an office supplies emporium many hundreds of miles away for approximately $3,000, which was itself a bargain for the buyer.

Among the sources, in addition to the federal government, are local governments, auctions, bankruptcy sales, appraisers and adjusters, common carriers, and almost any retailer or wholesaler who holds special sales to dispose of unwanted and surplus goods. There are many businesses devoted exclusively to trading in surplus. To keep up with current markets, you must read all information you can find. There are also some general sources of information that often prove helpful:

- *The Business Opportunities Digest*, 301 Plymouth Drive, NE, Dalton, GA 30721, a particularly rich source of information. Publisher J. F. (Jim) Straw also offers a large number of reports and books of interest.

- The back pages of the financial section of *The New York Times* Sunday edition usually lists many closeouts and surplus sales.

- Newspaper classified advertisements. These often list bankruptcy sales, estate states, sales for unpaid taxes, and closeout.

- The financial or business pages of newspapers, especially *The New York Times* and the *Wall Street Journal*. These sources often furnish tips on where to find closeouts; those who take the time to inquire directly will often be invited to make an offer. Of course, you must negotiate and buy the merchandise at the right price. But if you are a good negotiator, you can often make an advantageous deal.

How To Estimate What To Pay

It's easy to get selling prices. You know what the goods cost you, what your related costs are, and what your profit margin ought to be. It's not so easy to know the maximum you ought to pay. You have to make an accurate estimate of how much you can get for the goods in resale. But there are some basic guidelines you can follow.

First, you must know the wholesale value. Often, a call to a regular jobber/distributor/manufacturer of the goods will get you that figure. If this doesn't work, calculate the retail price less 40% to get a rought maximum wholesale price. Of course, that is far too much for you to pay. You probably have to get the goods for not more than one-half that wholesale figure, and you probably should start by offering about one-quarter of that figure, no matter what the seller quotes initially. If you pay anywhere close to wholesale prices, you will probably be stuck with goods you can't get your money out of, let alone take a profit. So don't hesitate to offer, as your opening price, $1 or $2 for items that sell for $10 or $12; you'll be surprised at how often you will get the lot at that price!

Following is a small, starter list of closeout dealers, organizations, and publications. An effort is made to indicate the kinds of merchandise offered and other definitive information, but these comments are necessarily quite general, probably incomplete, and may change. Things change generally in the business world, as they do elsewhere, so it will pay to check out and verify any listing of interest.

Closeout Dealers

AAA Electronics, 1201 Broadway, New York, NY 10001. General electronics goods.

Adar Miami, Inc., 2878 NW 72nd Avenue, Miami, FL 33122. Closeouts of telephones, videotapes, boom boxes, stereos, other.

Aljac Enterprises, 1333 S. Hill Street, Los Angeles, CA 90015. General merchandise and closeouts.

Anthony Sales, 1300 Taylors Lane, Cinnaminson, NJ 08076. Closeouts and promotions.

Arsi Recovery, 1589 Reed Road, Trenton, NJ 08628. Bankruptcy and insurance company recovery and general closeouts.

Bargain Outlet Center, 5525 Hemlock Street, Sacramento, CA 95841. General closeouts.

Bay Liquidators, 8301 Torresdale Avenue, Philadelphia, PA 19136. General merchandise, school supplies, stationery.

Bay State Job Lot, 67 Commercial Street, Everett, MA 02149. Hardware, paints, housewares.

Braxton Jeans Corp., 1419 Essex Street, Los Angeles, CA 90021. Closeouts of jeans and jackets.

Closeouts International, 195 Northfield Road, Northfield, IL 60093. General merchandise.

Cutters, P.O. Box 4359, Clearwater, FL 33518. Novelty, china, glass, stationery items; brochures available.

D&J Import Co., 1206 Zaragoza Street, Laredo, TX 78040. Hand and power tool closeouts.

Famous Brands of Dallas, 1440 S. Buckner Blvd, Dallas, TX 75217. General merchandise.

Galan Enterprises, 6851 N. 21st Avenue, Phoenix, AZ 85015. Gift and novelty closeouts.

Galaxy Electronics, 5300 21st Avenue, Brooklyn, NY 11204. Closeouts of watches, calculators, automobile stereos, telephones, other.

George Wernick & Associates, 7011 Brittmore #A, Houston, TX 77041. Medical clothing and military surplus.

Ginsberg, Frank Enterprises, 901 N. 3rd Street, Minneapolis, MN 55401. General merchandise.

Good & Lucky Promotions, 645 Pueblo Blvd., Henderson, NV 89015. Closeouts, general merchandise.

Harvard Ties of Florida, 4835 University Drive, Miami, FL 33146. Men's neckwear at bargain prices.

International Liquidators, 6327 Brittmore, Houston, TX 77041. Closeouts, wide selection.

Inventory Adjusters, 720 S. 23rd Avenue, Phoenix, AZ 85009. Wide selection of closeouts.

Liss Brothers, 8901 Torresdale Avenue, Philadelphia, PA 19136 Hardware, glassware, kitchen items.

Lund & Company, Inc., 445 Bush Street, 4th floor, San Francisco, CA 94108. Gifts and housewares closeouts.

Mascorro Leather Co., 1238 Goodrich Blvd., City of Commerce, CA 90040. Wallets, all kinds. Free catalog.

Merchandise USA, Inc., 1741 N. Pulaski, Chicago, IL 60639. Closeouts, general.

Midwest Mdse Liquidators, 1935 Washington Avenue, St. Louis, MO 63103. General closeouts.

National Travelware, Inc., 10154 Culebra Road, San Antonio, TX 78251. Closeouts of luggage.

Plymouth Wallpaper, 720 Frederick Road, Baltimore, MD 21228. Wall coverings and paints.

Railroad Salvage, 1131 Campbell Avenue, West Haven, CT 06516. Closeouts, apparel, luggage, other.

R.M.J. Enterprises, Inc., 15161 S. Figueroa Street, Gardena, CA 90248. General merchandise.

Shelley Inventories, Inc., 1 East Superior, Ste. 304, Chicago, IL 60611. Surplus inventory closeouts.

U.S. Closeout Co., 200 5th Avenue, New York, NY 10010. General consumer merchandise.

Variety Hosiery. P.O. Box 923, Wake Forest, NC 27587. Many brands of hosiery.

Worldwide Tools, 429-433 Breckenridge Street, Owensboro, KY 42301. Closeouts of clocks.

Closeout Shows, Organizations, Publications

Administrative Brokers, 3463 Crowell, Riverside, CA 92504.

Army-Navy Store & Outdoor Merchandiser Magazine, 225 W. 34th Street, New York, NY 10001.

Associated Surplus Dealers, 1209 E. 8th Street, Los Angeles, CA 90021.

The Auction Block, Box 2412, Chicago, IL 60690.

Business Opportunities Digest, 301 Plymouth Drive, NE, Dalton, GA 30721.

Closeout Merchandise, Forum Publishing Co., 383 East Main Street, Centerport, NY 11721.

Closeout Report, 15 W, 38th Street, New York, NY 10018.

Institute of Surplus Dealers, 520 Broadway, New York, NY 10012.

Marketer's Forum Magazine, Forum Publishing Co., 383 East Main Street, Centerport, NY 11721.

National Closeout Show, 900 Bay Drive, Miami Beach, FL 33141.

National Merchandise Shows, Thalheim Corp., 98 Cutter Mill Road, Great Neck, NY 10021.

Trade Show Directory, Forum Publishing Co., 383 East Main Street, Centerport, NY 11721.

Transworld Closeout Exhibit, 466 Central Avenue, Northfield, IL 60093.

Other Publications Of Interest

Following are several publications of general interest in connection with matters discussed between these covers:

National Directory of Catalogs, The, Oxbridge Communications, Inc., New York, NY 10011 (an annual).

How to Get Publicity and Make the Most of It Once You've Got It, William Parkhurst, Times Books, New York, 1985.

The Telecommuter's Handbook: How to Work for a Salary without Ever Leaving the House, Brad Schepp, Pharos Books, New York, 1990.

Get Competitive! Cut Costs and Improve Quality, Lynn Tylczak, Liberty Hall Press, TAB Books, Blue Ridge Summit, 1990.

Wholesale-by-Mail Catalog, The, The Print Project, Perennial Library, Harper & Row, New York, 1990 (an annual).

Computer Shopper, Coastal Associates Publishing, One Park Avenue, New York, N.Y. 10016 (monthly magazine of mail order opportunities for variety of high-tech office equipment).

DM News, Mill Hollow Corp., 19 West 21st Street, New York, NY 10010 (biweekly tabloid).

Target Marketing, North American Publishing Co., 401 N. Broaa Street, Philadelphia, PA 19108 (monthly magazine).

Temporary Services
Organizations

The following is a partial list of organizations that supply temporaries of various professions and skills. The listing is alphabetical, with no attempt to sort or classify the entries. A complex cross-indexing system would be necessary to do so effectively because some of the organizations supply a variety of specialists, while others concentrate in some field, such as accounting, computers, legal services, medical services, or other. (In many cases, however, the name of the organization reveals such specialization.)

There is another important variable to be noted here: Some of the names and addresses given are those of a headquarters office of an agency with many field offices or even a nationwide chain of offices and scope of activities. (Day & Zimmerman, Consultants & Designers, and Volt Technical Corporation are examples of such organizations.) Others are addresses of field offices, which may be temporary, or of small, independent organizations.

In some cases two or more addresses and telephone numbers are listed under the name of an organization. In other cases, more than one name is listed for a given address. (Some organizations use different names to supply different kinds of temporaries, although operating at one address only.) Such lists are highly perishable because many of the offices are field offices, temporary and surviving only long enough to satisfy a given demand—e.g., to help staff a single project and therefore in existence only as long as the project is in existence.

One further note: The location of the office listed is not necessarily an indication of where available people are located. Any temporary-services organization may have resumes and rosters of available specialists all over the United States, and even outside the United States. Therefore, it is appropriate to inquire of any of these firms, whether the office is near you or not.

Aames Bureau of Employment Agency
9570 Wilshire Blvd
Beverly Hills, CA 90212, 213-271-6164.

Accountancy by CPA
489 5th Avenue
New York, NY 10017, 212-687-8605.

Accountants Exchange
5455 Wilshire Blvd
Los Angeles, CA 90036, 213-933-7411.

Accountants Express
3111 Camino del Rio
San Diego, CA 92108, 619-284-1804.

Accountants, Inc.
555 Montgomery Street
San Francisco, CA 94111, 415-434-1411.

Accountants on Call
1800 N. Kent Street
Rosslyn, VA 22209, 703-525-6100.

Accountants One
24133 Northwestern Hwy
Southfield, MI 46075, 313-354-2410.

Accountants On Call
95 Rt 17 S.
Paramus, NJ 07652, 201-843-0006.

Accountants Professional Staff, Inc.
316 N. Michigan Blvd
Chicago, IL 60601, 312-263-3278.

Accounting Force, Inc.
Plaza 600 Bldg., 600 Stewart Street
Seattle, WA 98101, 206-443-8840.

Accounting Personnel Consultants
210 Baronne
New Orleans, LA 70112, 504-581-7800.

Acro Service Corp.
17177 N. Laurel Park Drive
Livonia, MI 48152, 313-591-1100.

Adtec (Administrative and Technical Services, Inc.)
6290 N. Port Washington Road
Glendale, WI 53217, 414-332-4800.

Advance Personnel Associates, Inc.
50 Mall Road
Burlington, MA 01803, 617-273-4250.

Advance Technical Services
2425 Franklin Avenue E.
Minneapolis, MN 55406, 612-338-3770.

Aero-Detroit, Inc.
1100 E. Mandoline
Madison Heights, MI 48071, 313-583-4900.

Allied Technical Service, Inc.
2012 Bay City Road
Midland, MI 48640, 313-496-3010.

All Temporaries
2110 Nicollet Avenue
Minneapolis, MN 55404, 612-871-1439.

Ameritech
1100 17th Street
Washington, DC 20036, 202-822-8299.

Ampro Services, Inc.
2690 Crooks Road
Troy, MI 48084, 313-244-9500.

Andcor Temporaries, Inc.
575 Interchange Tower, 600 S. County Road 18
St. Louis Park, MN 55426, 612-546-0966.

Argus Technical Services
2835 N. Mayfair Road
Milwaukee, WI 53222, 414-774-5996.

Assets Temporary Services, Inc.
Pillsbury Center
Minneapolis, MN 55402, 612-340-9881.

Associated Paralegal Consultants, Inc.
Butler Square Bldg, 100 N. 6th Street
Minneapolis, MN 55403, 612-339-7663.

ATS Technical Services, Inc
ATS Medical Division, 3850 Beach Blvd.
Jacksonville, FL 32207, 904-396-4100.

Bank Temporaries, Inc.
5323 Spring Valley Road
Dallas, TX 75240, 214-243-8484.

Banner Temporary Service, Inc.
122 S. Michigan Avenue
Chicago, IL 60603, 312-580-2500.

Barry Services
813 West Street, P.O. Box 1751
Wilmington, DE 19899, 302-571-8000.

B & M Associates, Inc.
9535 Forest Lane
Dallas, TX 75243, 214-437-3188.

BECO, Inc.
8751 Warren
Plymouth, MI 48170, 313-451-0143.

Beverly Hills Bar Association Personnel Service
300 S. Beverly Drive
Beverly Hills, CA 90212, 213-553-6644.

Brandon Consulting Group
1775 Broadway
New York, NY 10019, 212-977-4400.

Brannon and Tully, Inc.
3169 Holcomb Bridge Road
Norcross, GA 30071, 404-447-8773.

B Windsor
4725 Excelsior Blvd
St. Louis Park, MN 55426, 612-922-1002.

BZ Engineering, Inc.
7207 W. Greenfield Avenue
West Allis, WI 53214, 414-257-3674.

Barrett Business Services, Inc.
Fourth and Vine Bldg., 2615 Fourth
Avenue
Seattle, WA 98121, 206-448-8410.

Butler Service Group, Inc.
990 N. Corporate Drive
Jefferson, LA 70123, 504-736-0056.

Cardan Legal Personnel
1 Park Plaza
Irvine, CA 92714, 714-474-3933.

Carlyle Consulting Services, Inc.
3 Park Avenue
New York, NY 10016, 212-213-0600.

CATS, Inc. (Computer Aided Technical Services)
P.O. Box 9355
Washington, DC 20005, 202-232-5266.

Certified Flexstaff
111 New Montgomery Street
San Francisco, CA 94105, 415-543-1700.

Certified Legal Assistant Support Services
625 Market Street
San Francisco, CA 94105, 415-495-5360.

Certified Techstaff
625 Market Street
San Francisco, CA 94105, 415-495-5360.

Chemists Group, The
P.O. Box 3365, Ridgeway Station
Stamford, CT 06905, 203-322-9210.

Claim Net, Inc.
4330 Barranca Pkwy
Irvine, CA 92714, 714-857-1232.

Claim Services Resources Group
13800 Montfort Drive
Dallas, TX 75240, 214-701-0606.

CompHealth
5901 Peachtree-Dunwoody Road
Atlanta, GA 30328, 404-391-9876.

155 S. 300 West
Salt Lake City, UT 84101, 801-532-1200, 800-453-3030.

Compu-Temp
10300 N. Central Expressway
Dallas, TX 75231, 214-739-3822.

Computer Advisory Group
14 S. Duke Street
Lancaster, PA 17602, 717-299-6653.

Computer Consulting Group, Inc.
1 Bellevue Center, 411 108th Avenue,
NE
Seattle, WA 98009, 206-455-3100.

Computer Resources Group Agency, Inc.
303 Sacramento Street
San Francisco, CA 94111, 415-398-3535.

Computer Temps, Inc. and Computer Professionals, Inc.
1252 W. Peachtree Street, NW
Atlanta, GA 30309, 404-888-0900.

Consolidated Technical Services
1001 Howard Avenue
New Orleans, LA 70113, 504-566-0044.

Consortium, The
1 Times Square
New York, NY 10036, 212-221-1544.

Consultants & Designers, Inc.
360 W. 31st Street
New York, NY 10001, 212-563-8400.

Consulting Lab Services, Inc.
334 N. 71st Street
Milwaukee, WI 53213, 414-453-2842.

Contract Employee Services, Inc.
3330 W. Esplanade Avenue
Metairie, LA 70002, 504-837-6069.

Contract Engineering Services
P.O. Box 801001
Dallas, TX 75380, 214-681-8436.

Contract Medical Staffing, Inc.
5200 Monticello Avenue
Dallas, TX 75206, 214-823-3381.

Contractor's Network Corporation
45 Charles Street East
Toronto, Ontario, Canada M4Y 1S2,
416-962-9262.

Contract Professionals, Inc.
5601 Highland Road
Waterford Township, MI 48095, 313-673-3800.

Contract Service Company
833 108th, NE
Bellevue, WA 98004, 206-451-3855.

Control Data Temps
3601 W. 77th Street
Bloomington, MN 55435, 612-921-4550.

Corporate Staff, The
120 Montgomery Street
San Francisco, CA 94104, 415-956-1202.

Data Communications Services, Inc.
1666 N. Firman Drive
Richardson, TX 75081, 214-437-0646.

Davis-Smith Medical-Dental Employment Service, Inc.
24725 W. 12 Mile Road
Southfield, MI 48034, 313-354-4100.

Day & Zimmerman, Inc.
1818 Market Street
Philadelphia, PA 19103, 215-299-8000, 800-523-0766.

Design Personnel Resources, Inc.
3583 Lexington Avenue N.
Arden Hills, MN 55126, 612-482-0075.

Delta Temporary Services, Inc.
111 Veterans Memorial Blvd
Metairie, LA 70053, 504-833-5200.

Dental Auxiliary Service
P.O. Box 25223
Dallas, TX 75225, 214-522-2008.

Dental Employment Services
12827 SE 40th Place
Bellevue, WA 98006, 206-747-8095.

Dental Fill-Ins
2277 Van Ness Avenue
San Francisco, CA 94109, 415-771-2426.

Dental Power, Medical Power
5530 Wisconsin Avenue
Chevy Chase, MD 20815, 301-654-4805.

Dental Professionals
6071 50th Avenue, SW
Seattle, WA 98136, 206-938-4258.

Dental Team Temporaries
7521 Acts Court
N. Richland Hills, TX 76180, 214-577-0434.

Design Temps, Inc.
3901 Roswell Road, NE
Marietta, GA 30062, 404-565-1116.

Doctor's Corner Personnel Services
3855 Pacific Coast Hwy
Torrance, CA 90505, 213-378-9349.

2825 Santa Monica Blvd
Santa Monica, CA 90404, 213-453-8990.

Doctors on Call
7104 Fort Hamilton Pkwy
Brooklyn, NY 11228, 718-748-1200.

Don Richards Associates
1717 K Streisand, NW
Washington, DC 20006, 202-463-7210.

8180 Greensboro Drive
McLean, VA 22101, 703-827-5990.

Dynamic Dental Services, Inc. (DDS, Inc.)
863 Holcomb Bridge Road
Roswell, GA 30076, 404-998-7779.

Editorial Experts Employment Service
66 Canal Center Plaza
Alexandria, VA 22312, 703-683-0683.

Entech Services, Ltd., Medical Division
777 Chicago Road
Troy, MI 48083, 313-588-5610.

EDP/Temps
100 Oak Street
Newton Upper Falls, MA 02111, 617-969-3100.

Electronic Office Personnel
5455 Wilshire Blvd
Los Angeles, CA 90036, 213-934-8211.

Employer's Overload
8040 Cedar Avenue
Bloomington, MN 55420, 612-845-5000.

Entech Services, Ltd.
777 Chicago Road
Troy, MI 48083, 313-588-5610.

Escrow & Mortgage Temporary Specialists
710 N. Euclid Street
Anaheim, CA 92801, 714-533-1521.

18520 Burbank Blvd
Tarzana, CA 91356, 818-708-8388.

Exec-Aids
P.O. Box 10651
Charleston, SC 29411, 803-554-1663.

Executive Corner
111 Pine Street
San Francisco, CA 94111, 415-362-4253.

Executive Staff Leasing, Inc.
19855 W. Outer Drive
Dearborn, MI 48124, 313-562-0970.

Experts, The
1 Washington Street
Wellesley, MA 02181, 617-237-1777.

Financial Professionals Unlimited
4100 Spring Valley Road
Dallas, TX 75244, 214-241-2368.

Freelance Advantage, Inc.
127 E. 59th Street
New York, NY 10022, 212-593-2965.

Freelance and Careers, Ltd.
60 E. 42nd Street
New York, NY 10165, 212-687-3210.

Freelancers Legal
310 Madison Avenue
New York, NY 10017, 212-370-4500.

Future Force
30805 John R.
Madison Heights, MI 48071, 313-588-3700.

Future Technical Services
914 Main Street
Hopkins, MN 55343, 612-936-9183.

General Devices, Inc.
3300 W. Mockingbird Lane
Dallas, TX 75247, 214-358-3548.

Global Group, Inc.
4901 N. Beach Street
Fort Worth, TX 76111, 817-489-7518.

**Greater Milwaukee Temporary
Services (GMTS)**
231 W. Wisconsin Avenue
Milwaukee, WI 53203, 414-276-3939.

**Holder-Hall, Inc., Holder-Hall
Health Care**
601 California Street
San Francisco, CA 94108, 415-956-5051.

Hollowell Engineering
16030 Michigan Avenue
Dearborn, MI 48126, 313-584-5560.

Insurance Overload
2500 Wilshire Blvd
Los Angeles, CA 90057, 213-380-2161.

Insurance Temporaries, Inc.
3703 NE 162nd Street
Seattle, WA 98155, 206-362-6460.

InsurTemps
6060 N. Central
Dallas, TX 75206, 214-361-9341.

**Interim Management Co.
(IMCOR)**
470 Park Avenue
New York, NY 10016, 212-213-3600.

International Technical Services
2701 Avenue E East
Arlington, TX 76011, 817-640-7698.

I.P.R. Medical
7207 W. Greenfield Avenue
Milwaukee, WI 53214, 414-257-3959,
800-545-4141, Ext 257.

**IPPS (Information Processing
Personnel Service)**
2001 Gateway Pl
San Jose, CA 95110, 408-286-7560.

Joseph Raniere and Associates, Inc.
61 Broadway
New York, NY 10006, 212-766-4055.

Judicate, Inc.
1608 Walnut Street
Philadelphia, PA 19103, 800-631-9900.

3435 Wilshire Blvd, Plaza Level
Los Angeles, CA 90010, 213-363-2100.

Key Accounting Temporaries
1901 N. Moore Street
Rosslyn, VA 22209, 703-243-3600.

1625 K. Street, NW
Washington, DC 20006, 202-463-0900.

4600 East-West Hwy
Bethesda, MD 20814, 301-656-8833.

Klivans, Becker & Smith, Inc.
3091 Mayfield Road
Cleveland Heights, OH 44118, 216-932-7119.

KRON Medical Corporation
The Kron Bldg
Chapel Hill, NC 27514, 800-968-4881.

Law Clerk Temporaries, Inc.
815 Connecticut Avenue, NW
Washington, DC 20006, 202-296-8882.

1360 Beverly Road
McLean, VA 22101, 703-821-9119.

Law Resources, Inc.
1747 Pennsylvania Avenue, NW
Washington, DC 20006, 202-371-1270.

Lawsmiths, The
2443 Filmore Street
San Francisco, CA 94115

Lawstaff, Inc.
92 Luckie Street, NW
Atlanta, GA 30303, 404-522-1095.

L.A.W. Temps
466 Central Avenue
Northfield, IL 60093, 312-441-8822.

Lawyer to Lawyer, Inc.
2603 Oak Lawn Avenue
Dallas, TX 75219, 214-528-7090.

Lawyer's Lawyer, Inc.
1725 K Street, NW
Washington, DC 20006, 202-362-3333.

Legal Assistance
8300 Douglas Drive
Dallas, TX 75225, 214-361-7283.

Legal Eagles Network
6012 Goliad Avenue
Dallas, TX 75206, 214-828-1110.

Legal Personnel Pool
1821 Walden Office Square
Schaumberg, IL 60173, 312-427-6588.

Legal Placement Services, Inc.
Plankinton Bldg., 161 W. Wisconsin Avenue
Milwaukee, WI 53203, 414-276-6689.

Legal Resources
150 5th Avenue
New York, NY 10011, 212-654-6626.

16 California Avenue
San Francisco, CA 94111, 415-982-7770.

Locum Tenens, Inc.
400 Perimeter Center Terrace
Atlanta, GA 30346, 404-393-1210.

Marathon Engineering Services, Inc.
4686 Jackson
Trenton, MI 48183, 313-671-0545.

MDA (Medical Doctor Associates)
11285 Elkins Road, Bldg F-4
Roswell, GA 30076, 404-442-1201.

Media Temps, Writer's Warehouse
3590 Shiloh Road, Executive Plaza
Kennesaw, GA 30144, 404-423-9049.

Medical Center Agency, The
870 Market Street
San Francisco, CA 94102, 415-397-9440.

Medical Relief Services, Inc., X-Ray Temporaries, Inc.
3004 Meandering Way
Bedford, TX 76021, 817-267-1472.

Medical Society Personnel Service
1707 L. Street, NW
Washington, DC 20036, 202-466-1875.

Medical Temps
70 Whitlock Place,
Marietta, GA 30064, 404-426-1600.

MediTemps, Inc.
28 W. 44th Street
New York, NY 10036, 212-354-0129.

Med-Plus, Inc.
P.O. Box 32263
Washington, DC 20007, 301-652-5837.

Medstat, Inc.
2828 Croasdaile Drive, P.O. Box 15538
Durham, NC 27704, 919-383-4075, 800-672-5770.

Metro Detroit Professional Service, Inc.
8401 Woodward Avenue
Detroit, MI 48226, 313-872-2212.

Metuchen Associates, Inc,
29 Broadway
New York, NY 10006, 212-943-6790.

Michigan Medical Nursing
25180 Van Born Road
Dearborn Heights, MI 48125, 313-392-5831.

Micro Might, Ltd.
450 Seventh Avenue
New York, NY 10123, 212-629-3500.

Micro Temps
109 Oak Street
Newton Upper Falls, MA 02111, 617-969-3100.

Milam Design Services, Inc.
8701 Bedford-Euless Road
Fort Worth, TX 76180, 817-267-3350.

Mini-Systems Associates
18631 Alderwood Mall Blvd
Lynnwood, WA 98037, 206-774-6374.

MMS Systems
7215 York Road
Baltimore, MD 21204, 301-583-8445.

Mortgage and Banking Temporary Service
9363 Wilshire Blvd
Beverly Hills, CA 90210, 213-271-8394.

MRA Associates, Inc.
1760 The Exchange
Atlanta, GA 30339, 404-953-2656, 800-523-1351.

MRI Temps, Medical Register, Inc.
396 Commonwealth Avenue
Boston, MA 12205, 617-262-4900.

Multi-Media Communications Co.
11473 Sobieski
Hamtramck, MI 48212, 313-892-7155.

Nationwide Medical Staffing
421 Frenchman Street
New Orleans, LA 70433, 504-947-9053.

Nelson Coulson & Associates, Inc.
9725 SE 36th
Mercer Island, WA 98040, 206-232-7131.

New England Engineers & Designers
400 Washington Street
Westwood, MA 02090, 617-769-4390.

Nexco, Inc.
1530 Rochster Road
Royal Oak, MI 48067, 313-543-9920.

North American Contract Employees Services
14335 NE 24th Street
Bellevue, WA 98007, 206-643-9020.

North American Contract Service
Group
2777 Finley Road
Downers Grove, IL 60515, 312-953-
9133.

Nursefinders
1400 N. Cooper Street
Arlington, TX 76011, 817-469-1058.

Nurse Providers
345 F. Gellerd Blvd
Daly City, CA 94015, 415-992-
4150/8559.

Olsten Legal Support Services,
Olsten Professional Accounting
Services, Olsten Health Care
Services
1 Merrick Avenue
Westbury, NY 11590, 516-832-8200.

Omega Technical Corporation
330 S Executive drive
Brookfield, WI 53005, 414-784-7410.

On-Call Medical Services
18353 W. McNichols
Detroit, MI 48219, 313-534-4185.

Paralegal Connection, The
8300 Douglas Avenue
Dallas, TX 75225, 214-890-4441.

PC Pros Temporary Personnel
11022 Santa Monica Blvd
Santa Monica, CA 90025, 213-470-
6600.

Personnel Pool/Law Services
303 SE 17th Street
Fort Lauderdale, FL 33316, 305-764-
2200.

PDS Technical Services
151 Kalmus Drive Bldg C-203
Costa Mesa, CA 92626, 714-540-7900.

Peak Technical, Inc.
400 W. Maple Road
Birmingham, MI 48011, 313-644-
6644.

Peopleware
4055 Wilshire Blvd
Los Angeles, CA 90010, 213-487-
0130.

Personnel Pool of America, Inc.
303 SE 17th Street
Fort Lauderdale, FL 33316, 305-764-
2200.

Personnel Services Group
Garrison Pl. W., 19855 EW. Outer
Drive
Dearborn, MI 48124, 313-562-0970.

Physical Therapy Registry, Inc.
5199 E. Pacific Coast Hwy
Long Beach, CA 90804, 213-628-
1781.

Physicians Relief Network, Ltd.
(PRN)
1000 N. Walnut
New Braunfels, TX 78130, 800-531-
1122.

Pioneer Engineering &
Manufacturing Company
2500 E. 9 Mile Road
Warren, MI 48091, 313-755-4400.

Professional Medical Record
Services, Inc.
188 W. Randolph Street
Chicago, IL 60601, 312-332-5148.

Platinum Temporaries, Inc.
545 Fifth Avenue
New York, NY 10017, 212-661-8355.

Pollak & Skan, Inc.
2401 Randolph Mill Road
Arlington, TX 75011, 817-640-5135.

Possis Technical Services
750 Pennsylvania Avenue S.
Minneapolis, MN 55426, 612-545-1471.

Pratt Personnel
703 Market Street
San Francisco, CA 94103, 415-777-9722, 800-643-3600.

Prime Design
16030 Michigan
Dearborn, MI 48126, 313-584-1485.

Prime Timers
5501 LBJ Freeway
Dallas, TX 75240, 214-386-8040.

Professional Assignments
31 E. 32nd Street
New York, NY 10016, 212-481-8100.

Programming Alternatives, Inc.
3105 Medlock Bridge Road
Norcross, GA 30071, 404-447-0609.

6750 France Avenue
Medina, MN 55435, 612-922-1103.

Quality Accounting Services, Inc.
21700 Greenfield Oak Park
Detroit, MI 48237, 313-967-4150.

Rent-a-Consultant
2409 18th Street, NW
Washington, DC 20009, 202-223-9175.

Respiratory Temporary Services
13666 S. Hawthorne Blvd
Hawthorne, CA 90250, 213-772-3792.

Respiratory Therapy Unlimited, Inc.
2017 Canal Street
New Orleans, LA 70112, 504-525-2323.

Romac
1 Harbor Place
Tampa, FL 33602, 813-229-5575.

Royalpar Industries
40 South Street
West Hartford, CT 06110, 203-249-6315.

SAC Technical Services, Inc.
18000 Pacific Hwy S.
Seattle, WA 98188, 206-246-9732.

Salem Technical Services
1000 Jorie Blvd
Oak Brook, IL 60125, 312-932-9200.

Science Temps
111 North Avenue
Cranford, NJ 07016, 201-272-1997.

Special Counsel, Inc.
200 Park Avenue
New York, NY 10166, 212-222-1208.

Specialized Technical Resources
1851 Central Drive
Bedford, TX 76021, 817-267-9865.

Spectrum Temporary Services, Inc.
4324 W. Bradley Road
Brown Deer, WI 53223, 414-355-5449.

Staff, Inc.
2121 Cloverfield Blvd
Santa Monica, CA 90404, 213-829-5447.

Stat Nursing Services, Inc.
1545 Broadway
San Francisco, CA 94109, 415-673-9791.

Streetwide, Inc.
11 Broadway
New York, NY 10004, 212-514-9700.

Swing Shift Artemps, Swing Shift Business Temps
1 Horatio Street
New York, NY 10014, 212-206-1222.

Systemp
1775 Broadway
New York, NY 10019, 212-977-4400.

TAD Temporaries, TAD Technical Services
639 Massachusetts Avenue
Boston, MA 02139, 617-868-1650.

Tech/Aid Corp, TAC Medical
109 Oak Street
Newton Upper Falls, MA 02111, 617-969-3100.

Techlancers, Inc.
19 E. 40th Street
New York, NY 10017, 212-370-1960.

Technical Complement, Inc.
2179 Northlake Pkwy
Tucker, GA 30084, 404-934-2557.

Technical Consultants
608 W. I-30
Garland, TX 75043, 214-226-4409.

Technical People Leasing
20017 James Couzens Fwy
Detroit, MI 48235, 313-861-4800.

Technical Services Clerical
1948 Buhl Bldg
Detroit, MI 48226, 313-963-5026.

Techniforce
2901 Metro Drive
Bloomington, MN 55420, 612-854-5955.

Technipower, Inc.
11800 W. Greenfield Avenue
Milwaukee, WI 53214, 414-475-1500.

Tech Specialists
470 Totten Pond Road
Waltham, MA 02154, 617-890-2727.

Techstaff, Inc.
11270 W. Park Place
Milwaukee, WI 53224, 414-359-4444.

Templaw
2023 Summer Street, P.O. Box 3485
Stamford, CT 06905, 203-327-0065.

Templeton & Associates
915 Lumber Exchange Bldg
Minneapolis, MN 54023, 612-332-8079.

Temporary Accounting Personnel
5354 Cedar Lake Road
Minneapolis, MN 55405, 612-544-1083.

Temporary Insurance Personnel, Inc.
880 Johnson Ferry Road
Atlanta, GA 30342, 404-257-9685.

Temporary Professionals, Inc.
24100 Southfield Road
Southfield, MI 48075, 313-443-5590.

Temporary Services International, Inc.
1 Naperville Plaza
Naperville, IL 60540, 312-369-6612.

Temporary Specialists, Inc.
2877 W. Maple road
Troy, MI 48084, 313-280-9711.

Temporary Techs
P.O.Box 401066
Garland, TX 75046, 214-352-5179.

Temtec Corp.
3927 S. Howell Avenue
Milwaukee, WI 53207, 414-769-6393.

Time Savers
2001 Gateway Pl. #5510
San Jose, CA 95110, 408-286-7560.

Travel Temps
25947 Cathedral
Redford, MI 48329, 313-937-8181.

Trinity Resource Corporation
8484 W. Brown Deer Road
Milwaukee, WI 53224, 414-355-8866.

Trojan Engineering Company
17300 W. 10 Mile Road
Southfield, MI 48075, 313-577-3700.

Troy Design Services
2653 Industrial Row
Troy, MI 48084, 313-280-0500.

Universal Personnel Service
7520 Hayne Blvd
New Orleans, LA 70126, 504-241-1724.

Upjohn Healthcare Services
2605 E. Kilgore Road
Kalamazoo, MI 49002, 800-342-7133.

Versapro, Inc.
P.O. Box 370
Mountain View, CA 94042, 415-960-3463.

Volt Technical Corp.
101 Park Avenue
New York, NY 10178, 212-309-0200, 800-367-8658.

Western Physicians Registry
710 Van Ness Avenue
San Francisco, CA 94102, 415-554-4375.

Western Practitioners Resources
1660 Central Avenue
McKinleysville, CA 95521, 800-345-5859.

Western Technical Services,
Western Medical Services
301 Lennon Lane
Walnut Creek, CA 94598, 415-946-0900.

Workload, Inc.
225 Baronne
New Orleans, LA 70112, 504-522-7171.

861 Camp Street
New Orleans, LA 70130, 504-523-2275.

XX Cal, Inc.
11500 W. Olympic Blvd
Los Angeles, CA 90064, 213-477-2902.